IRELAND from colony to nation state

ATLANTIC
OCEAN

North Channel

ULSTER

DONEGAL
Lifford
Strabane
(London-
Derry derry)
LONDONDERRY
ANTRIM
Belfast
TYRONE
Lough
Neagh
FERMANAGH
MONAGHAN
ARMAGH
DOWN
Donegal
Bay

Sligo
SLIGO
LEITRIM
Carrick
CAVAN
Dundalk
LOUTH

MAYO
ROSCOMMON
LONGFORD
MEATH
Drogheda
Irish
Sea

Westport
CONNAUGHT
WESTMEATH
DUBLIN

GALWAY
Galway
OFFALY
KILDARE
Dublin

ARAN IS.
Shannon
LEINSTER
WICKLOW
Wicklow

CLARE
TIPPERARY
LAOIGHIS
CARLOW

Shannon
KILKENNY
Kilkenny
WEXFORD

Limerick
LIMERICK
Tipperary
KILKENNY

Tralee
WATERFORD
Wexford

KERRY
Killarney
MUNSTER
WATERFORD
Youghal

Dingle Bay
CORK
Cork
Cobh

Bantry Bay

St. George's Channel

IRELAND

0   25   50   75   100
          MILES

—— NORTHERN IRELAND (U.K.)
········ REPUBLIC OF IRELAND

SCOTLAND

IRELAND
ENGLAND
WALES

FRANCE

IRELAND
from colony
to nation state

LAWRENCE J. McCAFFREY
Loyola University of Chicago

PRENTICE-HALL, INC., ENGLEWOOD CLIFFS, N.J. 07632

Library of Congress Cataloging in Publication Data

McCaffrey, Lawrence John (date).
    Ireland, from colony to nation-state.

    Bibliography: p.
    Includes index.
    1. Ireland—History—1691-   2. Nationalism—
Ireland—History. I. Title.
DA947.M18   941.508   78-6852
ISBN 0-13-506196-2
ISBN 0-13-506188-1 pbk.

Printed in the United States of America

10   9   8   7   6   5   4   3   2   1

PRENTICE-HALL INTERNATIONAL, INC., *London*
PRENTICE-HALL OF AUSTRALIA PTY. LIMITED, *Sydney*
PRENTICE-HALL OF CANADA, LTD., *Toronto*
PRENTICE-HALL OF INDIA PRIVATE LIMITED, *New Delhi*
PRENTICE-HALL OF JAPAN, INC., *Tokyo*
PRENTICE-HALL OF SOUTHEAST ASIA PTE. LTD., *Singapore*
WHITEHALL BOOKS LIMITED, *Wellington, New Zealand*

To JOAN

contents

preface

I want to express my appreciation to the scholars who over the past twenty years or so have contributed to a dynamic and rich Irish historiography. Without their efforts, people like me could not attempt books like this. I am particularly grateful to my many friends in Irish studies, particularly Thomas N. Brown, Gilbert A. Cahill, Joseph M. Curran, James S. Donnelly, Jr., Thomas Hachey, Maurice Harmon, Hugh Kearney, John Kelleher, Emmet Larkin, Ailfrid MacLochlainn, John and Betty Messenger, John Murphy, Maureen Murphy, Maurice R. O'Connell, Harold Orel, and Alan J. Ward. Their writings and conversation have taught me a great deal about Irish history and culture. I am especially indebted to Maurice R. O'Connell and Emmet Larkin, who read my original manuscript and offered valuable criticism and suggestions for improvement. The American Committee for Irish Studies has provided me with an opportunity to discuss and evaluate Irish culture within an interdisciplinary context. Loyola University of Chicago was kind enough to give me a semester's leave of absence to finish writing this book. I also thank Brian Walker, History Editor at Prentice Hall, for his interest in and encouragement of my work. My wife Joan, my son, Kevin, and my daughters, Sheila and Pat, have sustained and consoled me through difficult periods of the writing process. Portions of essays I have previously published under the titles "Irish Nationalism and Irish Catholicism: A Study in Cultural Identity," *Church History*, December, 1973; and "The Catholic

Minority in Northern Ireland," *Divided Ireland* (Rockford: Rockford College Press, 1971), Francis O'Brien, editor, appear in this book. "The Roots of the Irish Troubles," *America,* January 31, 1976, comprises a substantial portion of my Conclusion. I want to thank the Director of the Rockford College Press and the Editors of *America* and *Church History* for giving me permission to publish sections of these essays in revised form.

I
the origins of the Irish question

THE ENGLISH CONQUEST OF IRELAND

English imperialism in Ireland did not begin as a planned adventure, even though Ireland became England's first colony. English or Norman intervention in Ireland began when Dermot MacMurrough went to Wales in search of help to regain Leinster, which he had lost in an Irish civil war. He persuaded Richard fitz Gilbert de Clare, Earl of Pembroke, known as Strongbow, one of Henry II's vassals patrolling the Welsh frontier, to assist him. In exchange, MacMurrough promised Strongbow his daughter in marriage and succession to the Leinster throne.

When the Normans under Strongbow arrived in Ireland in 1169, they confronted an enemy united culturally but not politically. Whereas the rest of Western Europe was developing nation states, Ireland was divided into provincial and petty kingdoms, which in turn were divided into clan territories. Irish clannishness or tribalism assured Norman victories and Irish defeats. Another factor that guaranteed this was the superior Norman military skills, tactics, and weapons—they wore armour, used horses for mobility, and employed castles as fortresses to secure conquered territory.

Since Irish resistance was not effective, Strongbow extended the conquest beyond Leinster. This upset Henry II, who feared that his vassals might establish an independent and rival Norman-Irish kingdom across the

1

Irish Sea. He came to Ireland in 1171 and received homage as Lord of Ireland from his vassals and from a number of Irish chiefs and bishops. An English pope, Adrian IV (Nicholas Breakespear) had originally conferred this title on the King of England in 1156.

Papal interference in Anglo-Irish relations indicates that Ireland was a victim of several kinds of imperialism: political, economic, cultural, and religious. Before the Normans arrived from Britain, Irish society had been in transition and European influences had been at work in the change. Elements of feudalism had become a part of the Irish political system. Petty kings had been vassals of provincial kings, but the powers of the provincial kings were so evenly balanced that no one monarch could unify the country. And Irish Christianity had been experiencing a reformation involving the creation of a diocesan structure and the importation of religious orders from abroad. Although the Viking invasions had resulted in a sharp decline in the quality of Irish learning there was a cultural renaissance of no small significance in the eleventh and twelfth centuries. But despite the changing character of Irish society, from a Continental or English perspective, Ireland appeared a primitive even savage place, with an archaic clan system and a decadent, disorganized, and immoral brand of Christianity remote from the authority of Rome. The Norman English came to Ireland to civilize the country by both Anglicizing and Romanizing it. The English colony in Ireland began with an attitude of superiority toward the natives, one it never abandoned.

In the fourteenth century the tides of battle turned, putting the Norman English on the defensive. There were a number of reasons for this change: Irish clan chiefs learned Norman military tactics and borrowed their weapons; many Englishmen in remote sections of the country married Irish women and adopted the Gaelic life style, and others, tired of the cold and damp of Ireland, returned home. Those who returned home turned the management of their estates over to agents, thus beginning a pattern of absentee landlordism. But because the Irish were divided, politically unsophisticated, and without a concept of political nationhood, they were unable to exploit English weakness and drive the intruder from the country.

From the middle of the fourteenth until early in the sixteenth century, the English colony in Ireland was more concerned with survival than with expansion. This defensive attitude was expressed in the Statutes of Kilkenny, which the Irish Parliament enacted in 1366. An early example of cultural apartheid in Western civilization, the Statutes forbade the English in Ireland to associate with the natives, marry their women, wear their costumes, speak their language, adopt their children, or call on the spiritual services and consolations of their priests.

In 1509 when Henry VIII became King of England, he also became Lord of three Irelands: the Pale or Anglo-Irish Ireland, a miniature England

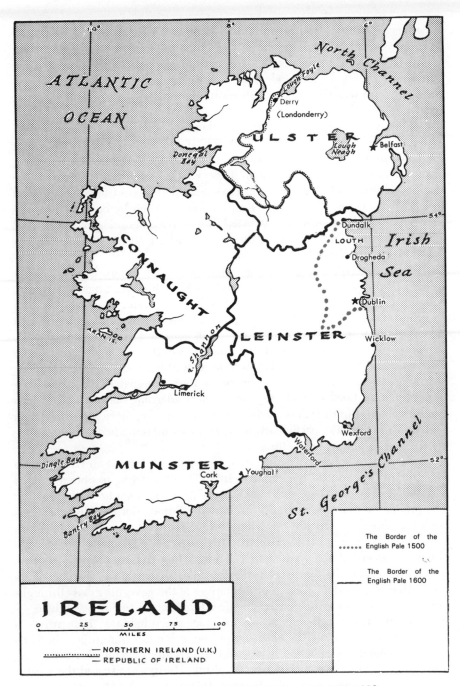

THE BORDERS OF THE ENGLISH PALE, 1500 AND 1600

in language, culture, and institutions; Gaelic Ireland, where Gaelic culture was represented in its purest form; and an ambiguous in-between Ireland, where Irish and English peoples and institutions existed side-by-side and sometimes blended. The Pale was essentially the province of Leinster, Gaelic Ireland was Ulster, the ambiguous in-between Ireland was Munster and Connacht.

During the time of the Tudors, England emerged as a European power with a budding overseas empire. This new status provided the rationale for English imperialism in Ireland. Tudor monarchs decided that they no longer could tolerate the defensive status of the English colony in Ireland or the chaotic condition of that country. They feared that continued anarchy in Ireland beyond the Pale would encourage an invasion by one of England's continental enemies. And they worried that an Ireland under enemy control would endanger England's security by diminishing the significance of her island position defended by sea power.

Instead of spending the large sums of money necessary to conquer Ireland, Henry chose a more subtle strategy for extending English authority beyond the Pale. He persuaded clan chiefs to surrender their lands to him and then receive them back with territorial titles to use and administer as vassals of the King: for example, the O'Neill became Earl of Tyrone and the O'Donnell Earl of Tyrconnell. The foundations of the Gaelic order certainly were weakened and the spread of Commonlaw at the expense of Brehon law encouraged when the Irish Parliament in 1541 designated Henry as King rather than as Lord of Ireland, and when feudalism was introduced into Gaelic Ireland. But the effects of these innovations were more superficial than real. Outside the Pale, particularly in Ulster, Ireland remained Gaelic and decentralized in political structure.

Henry's religious policy had a more significant impact on Ireland than his attempt to feudalize the country. In 1534, after failing to obtain a papal annulment of his marriage with Catherine of Aragon so that he could remarry and produce a male heir, Henry broke with Rome. Both the English and Irish Parliaments endorsed the King's religious rebellion and declared him Head of the Church. Irish bishops, Anglo-Irish feudal lords, and Gaelic chiefs all accepted the new state religion. They did so because Henry's quarrel with Rome had little relevance for the Irish who always had been less papist than the English. Like representatives of the governing class throughout Western Europe, Irish leaders believed that "cuius regio, eius religio"— the principle that the people should embrace the religion of their prince— was a legitimate strategy for securing public order and tranquility. In addition, the change of spiritual leadership from Pope to King did not really touch the religious lives of the people. While Henry confiscated the wealth and property of monastic establishments, retaining much of the spoils for the royal treasury and distributing the rest among loyal Anglo-Irish feudal lords and Irish chiefs, his rejection of papal supremacy did not interfere with traditional Catholic devotionalism.

The total effects of the Reformation did not become apparent until the reigns of Henry's son, Edward VI (1547–1553), and his daughter, Elizabeth I (1558–1603), when the state church evolved into a Protestant one in theology and much of its liturgy. The Irish regarded efforts to make them conform to Protestantism as an attack on the Gaelic nation, in fact, a more pernicious kind of imperialism than previous English political and military adventures in Ireland. Irish leaders negotiated with Catholic powers on the Continent to obtain support for their resistance to English domination. And the religious dimension of the contest between English imperialism and Irish resistance altered the character of Irish Catholicism, gradually transforming Catholicism into the main feature of the Irish identity profile and the nucleus of an incipient nationalism. Jesuits and Franciscans poured into Ireland as agents of Counter-Reformation Catholicism, which was more austere in tone, practice, and content than the easy going, less structured Celtic Catholicism.

Protestantism destroyed the mechanism of cultural assimilation that had for centuries protected Ireland from complete conquest by her stronger neighbor. It created an impassible barrier between the English and Irish identities. Catholicism symbolized beseiged Irish civilization; Protestantism represented Anglo-Saxon aggression. While the Irish rallied behind the standard of Catholicism to defend their cultural and political autonomy, the English justified their effort to conquer, subdue, and control Ireland as a Protestant crusade against the alien, tyrannical, and subversive manifestations of popery.

During the sixteenth and seventeenth centuries, England engaged in wars against Spain and then France, in order first to achieve and then to maintain status as a first rate power. Since Spain and France were both Catholic countries, the English cultivated Protestant nativism as an ideological cause and weapon against the foreign foe. England's war against the Catholic powers added strength to the argument that the Catholic Irish must be conquered and pacified so that their country would not become a back door for the enemy to use to invade England. English leaders warned that a turbulent Ireland was an open invitation to Spanish or French incursion. Military strategy harnessed Protestant nativism to the necessities of English national security, producing the main outlines of an Irish policy that remained firm from the sixteenth into the twentieth century.

Throughout her long reign (1558–1603), Elizabeth had to cope with Irish rebellion. The O'Neills, O'Donnells, and Maguires in Ulster, and the Anglo-Irish Fitzgeralds, Earls of Desmond, in Munster, and sometimes the combined forces from the North and South revolted against England. During the 1590's, the Irish forces, led by Hugh O'Neill and Hugh O'Donnell and assisted by Spanish intrigue and intervention, came close to victory. The guerrilla tactics of O'Neill's troops, trained with the most up-to-date weapons, baffled Elizabeth's generals, Sir Henry Bagenal and the Earl of Essex. O'Neill's startling victory at the battle of the Yellow Ford in August, 1598, frightened the English government and aroused national support in Ireland for independence.

In 1601, Spain sent four thousand troops in support of the Irish rebels. They landed in Kinsale in September and were immediately besieged by an English army. An Irish effort to relieve Kinsale failed. After the defeat of the Irish army, the Spaniards returned home. O'Donnell surrendered shortly after this disaster but O'Neill retreated to Ulster, fighting all the way. Defeat, however, was only a matter of time. On March 30, 1603, he formally submitted to Mountjoy, the Queen's deputy, at Mellifont, County Louth, six days after Elizabeth died. O'Neill's surrender was a fatal blow to Gaelic Ireland and seriously threatened Catholic Ireland.

During the reign of Henry VIII (1509–1547), Lord Leonard Grey, his deputy in Ireland, had suggested that the best way to secure English authority would be to confiscate the property of defeated rebels and transfer it to supporters of the crown. Catholic Mary Tudor (1553–1558) was the first Tudor monarch to employ *plantation* as a strategy. She seized the lands of the O'Moore's of Leix and the O'Connors of Offaly, shired them, renamed the conquered territories King's and Queen's Counties, and gave this property to Anglo-Irish lords friendly to English interests. To the Irish-Gaelic and Anglo-Irish, the Leix-Offaly plantations set a frightening precedent, threatening property in and out of the Pale.

As part of the process of subduing Munster, Elizabeth awarded large estates to English adventurers serving in her victorious army. In addition she shired Connacht and Ulster (Munster and Leinster were previously reorganized), outlining the present-day county borders in those provinces. Under the new arrangement, the authorities, particularly in the years 1606–1608, abolished Irish customs and institutions, including Irish forms of serfdom, replacing Brehon with Common law.

Following O'Neill's surrender, James I (1603–1625), the first Stuart king, permitted him and O'Donnell to retain their properties and titles as Earls of Tyrone and Tyrconnell. But in 1607, fearing an English-directed conspiracy against their lives, the two chiefs fled Ireland for a Continental exile that would only terminate with their deaths in Rome. The Flight of the Earls provided James with an opportunity to pacify and control Gaelic Ulster. Previous plantations in the South and West had been superficial, only transferring the ownership of large estates from rebels to loyalists while the masses of Catholics remained on the land. In Ulster, James employed a policy modeled on the one that the Stuarts used to humble the Gaelic chiefs in the Scottish Highlands. In 1610, he seized O'Neill and O'Donnell territory, which extended over most of the present counties of Armagh, Cavan,

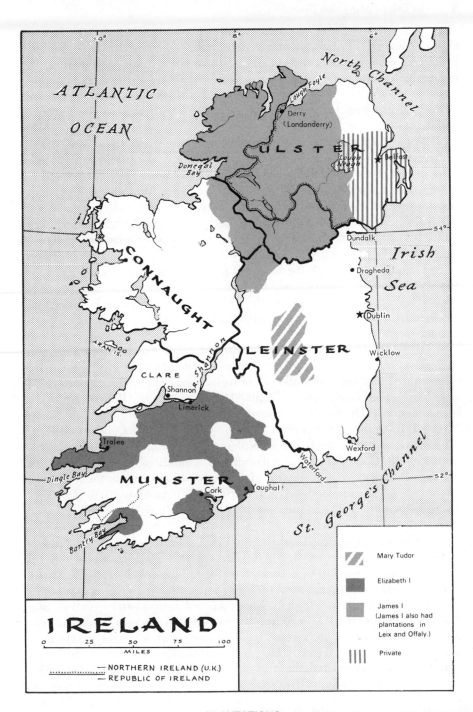

ATLANTIC OCEAN

North Channel

Lough Foyle

Derry (Londonderry)

ULSTER

Donegal Bay

Lough Neagh

Belfast

Dundalk

Irish Sea

Drogheda

CONNAUGHT

Dublin

LEINSTER

Wicklow

ARAN IS.

CLARE

Shannon

Shannon

Limerick

Tralee

Dingle Bay

MUNSTER

Cork

Youghal

Waterford

Wexford

St. George's Channel

Bantry Bay

▨	Mary Tudor
■	Elizabeth I
▨	James I (James I also had plantations in Leix and Offaly.)
‖‖‖	Private

IRELAND

0   25   50   75   100
MILES

—— NORTHERN IRELAND (U.K.)
••••••••• — REPUBLIC OF IRELAND

PLANTATIONS

Derry, Donegal, Fermanagh, and Tyrone, and he planted it with a complete Protestant colony: landlords, tenants, tradesmen, artisans, and merchants. James invited Anglicans from England and Presbyterians from Scotland to settle in Ulster. The thoroughness and the density of the Ulster Plantation made that province the only section of Ireland with a large non-Catholic population.

Not all Catholics in post-Reformation Ireland were natives. Most of the Old English colony had remained Catholic. Their dual loyalties to Pope and King placed them in a difficult and dangerous position. They lost ground to the growing influence of the New English colony of Elizabethan Protestant adventurers who had acquired large Irish estates through conquest and plantation. Although the Old English continued to think of themselves as politically and culturally English, after 1613 they became a minority faction within the Irish Parliament and were liable to heavy resucancy fines for their fidelity to Catholicism. During the reigns of James and his son Charles I (1625–1649), the English government, by insisting on religious conformity as a loyalty test, gradually weakened the cultural and allegiance barriers that separated the Old English from Irish Catholics. The English called both groups "papist."

In 1641, taking advantage of the English Civil War between King and Parliament, Old English and Irish Catholics joined forces in rebellion. By the spring of 1642 they controlled all of Ireland except Dublin, Cork city and large portions of Cork county, Drogheda, Carrickfergus, Belfast, Enniskillen, Coleraine, Derry, North Down, South Antrim, and parts of North Donegal. In October of that year, Catholic bishops, leaders of the Old English colony, and clan chiefs met in Kilkenny to establish a provisional government, the Confederation of Kilkenny. It announced its commitment to freedom of private conscience, the right to worship openly in the church of one's choice, the independence of the Irish nation, and loyalty to the King. These principles were summed up in the motto "Pro Deo, pro rege, pro patria Hibernia unanimis."

Unfortunately for the Confederation, the alliance between Old English and Irish Catholics was too fragile to last. The Old English still considered themselves more English than Irish. They were intensely loyal to the Stuart monarchy and fought to maintain their property and regain their influence in the Irish Parliament. The Irish Catholics wanted a complete revolution, one that would restore the Gaelic order. They never had played a significant role in the Irish Parliament and already had lost most of their property. Giovanni Battista Rinuccini, papal legate, and James Butler, Earl of Ormond, the king's deputy, both manipulated the differences within the Confederation. The former encouraged the native Irish to act as a sword of the Counter-Reformation; the latter attempted to lure the Old English into the Royalist camp in the war against the English Parliament.

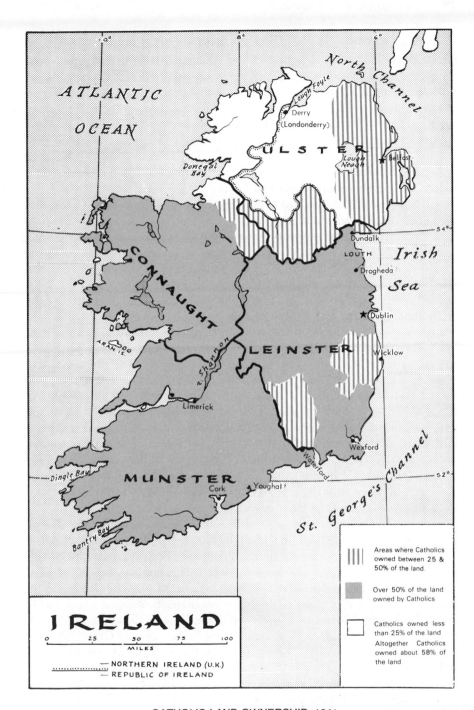

ATLANTIC
OCEAN

North Channel

Lough Foyle
Derry
(Londonderry)

ULSTER

Donegal
Bay

Lough
Neagh

Belfast

Dundalk

LOUTH

Drogheda

Irish

Sea

Dublin

CONNAUGHT

r. Shannon

LEINSTER

Wicklow

ARAN IS.

Limerick

Dingle Bay

MUNSTER

Cork

Youghal

Waterford

Wexford

St. George's Channel

Bantry Bay

| Areas where Catholics owned between 25 & 50% of the land. |
| Over 50% of the land owned by Catholics |
| Catholics owned less than 25% of the land Altogether Catholics owned about 58% of the land |

IRELAND

0   25   50   75   100
MILES

— NORTHERN IRELAND (U.K.)
— REPUBLIC OF IRELAND

CATHOLIC LAND OWNERSHIP, 1641

9

Disputes within the councils of the Confederation, the intrigues of Ormond and Rinuccini, divided military strategy, inadequate weapons and short supplies, and poorly trained soldiers prevented military success. At the same time, antagonism between Ormond and pro-Parliament Ulster Presbyterians divided English interests in Ireland and delayed their victory. By the time Ormond and Confederation leaders agreed on a coalition in 1649, Cromwell already had defeated the Stuart forces in Britain. He then proceeded to Ireland and by the time he left in 1650 he had broken Catholic resistance. Within two years Cromwell's lieutenant, Henry Ireton, completed the task his commander had begun.

Massive confiscations and plantations followed Cromwell's victory. Before his Irish triumph, Catholics, mostly Old English, had managed to hold on to two-thirds of Irish property, despite the Elizabethan and Stuart plantations. But Cromwell reduced this amount to one-fourth. In addition to the punishment of more plantations, the consequences of war had diminished the Catholic population by one-third—some were transported to the West Indies in chains to be sold as slaves, and compelled a large section of the Catholic aristocracy and gentry, along with their followers, to seek new homes west of the Shannon in the rugged, infertile terrain of Connacht.

Following the Stuart restoration in 1660, Irish Catholics supported the monarchy in its quarrels with the English Parliament. They believed that Charles II (1660–1685) was sympathetic to their religious convictions and hoped that he might restore some of the land "stolen" by Cromwell. Although Charles did have a tolerance for things Catholic and did return a small amount of confiscated property, he had no intention of provoking British and Anglo-Irish forces against the Crown by repealing the Cromwellian settlement. His Catholic brother, James II (1685–1688), however, was openly friendly to Irish Catholics. And his Catholic deputy in Ireland, Richard Talbot, Earl of Tyrconnell, employed Irish Catholics in the Irish army and even placed some in important government positions.

James's pro-Irish Catholic attitude and conduct were factors, though not as important as the birth of a Catholic heir to the throne, in the English Parliament's decision to depose him and invite his Protestant daughter Mary and her Dutch husband, William of Orange, to become joint rulers of England. James abandoned England without a fight. He decided to make his stand in Ireland, where he could count on majority support. The war in Ireland between William and James fitted into a wider European context. It was part of the conflict between Louis XIV of France and the Grand Alliance, a coalition led by William. The members of the Grand Alliance attempted to frustrate Louis's maneuvers to seize the Spanish throne for Bourbon power, and his territorial ambitions concerning the Rhenish Palatinate. Louis encouraged James with men and money to fight in Ireland in order to occupy William's attention and exhaust his resources. Because of a dispute with Louis

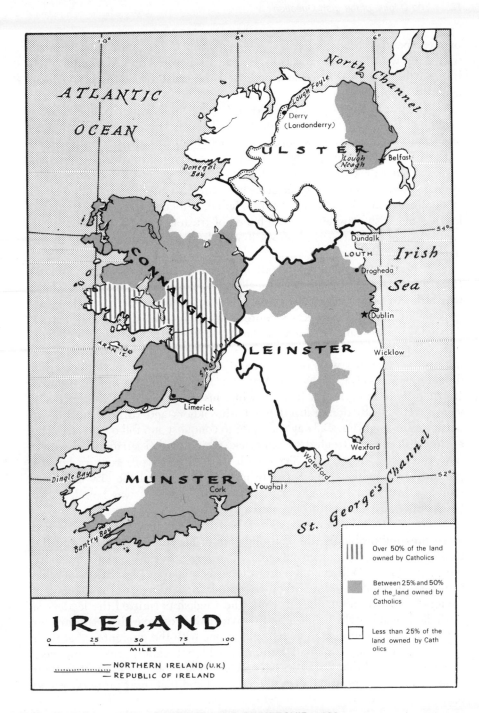

Over 50% of the land owned by Catholics

Between 25% and 50% of the land owned by Catholics

Less than 25% of the land owned by Catholics

IRELAND

0   25   50   75   100
MILES

— NORTHERN IRELAND (U.K.)
········· REPUBLIC OF IRELAND

CATHOLIC LAND OWNERSHIP, 1688

over competing candidates for the Archbishopric of Cologne and His Holiness's friendship with Leopold, the Holy Roman Emperor, Pope Alexander VIII, blessed the Grand Alliance and endorsed the cause of Protestant William against Catholic James.

The war in Ireland was decided on July 12, 1690, when William's army of 36,000 Englishmen, Irish Protestants, French Huguenots, Dutchmen, and Danes defeated James' force of 25,000 Irish Catholics supplemented with French officers, on the banks of the Boyne river. After his defeat James fled to France, leaving his Irish allies to fight on against impossible odds. William attempted to take Limerick, the main Irish outpost, defended by an Irish officer, Patrick Sarsfield. After he failed, William returned to England, leaving the Irish campaign in the hands of trusted lieutenants. Before the conclusion of 1690, the Earl of Marlborough took Cork and Kinsale in the name of King William.

When the war resumed in 1691, the Jacobite (supporters of the Stuarts) army was weakened by feuds and jealousies among its commanders. There was little cohesion among Tyrconnell, James' leading lieutenant, the Marquis de St. Ruth, Louis XIV's representative on the scene, and Patrick Sarsfield, the brilliant Irish leader. On June 30, 1691, Godbert de Ginkel, one of William's skilled generals, defeated St. Ruth and took Athlone, opening up Irish territory west of the Shannon to conquest. St. Ruth decided to defend the accesses to Galway at Aughrim, near Ballinasloe in east Galway. He died there in battle on July 12, while his troops were in the process of victory. His death demoralized the Irish soldiers and turned the tide of battle. After Aughrim, Galway was open to conquest and fell on July 21. The entire Irish army retreated to Limerick, which Ginkel surrounded with a powerful force. In August, Tyrconnell died—there were rumors he was poisoned by enemies—but Sarsfield managed to defend the city and keep morale at a reasonably high level. His cause, however, was hopeless. An English fleet cut off help from or escape by sea.

By this time William considered the Irish situation a nuisance. He had more pressing problems: the consolidation of his rule in England and the Continental campaign against Louis. In order to free his troops for more important duties, William offered Catholics besieged in Limerick honorable terms of surrender, which they accepted. According to the Treaty of Limerick, signed on October 2, 1691, the English permitted the leaders of Catholic Ireland—Old English and native Irish—to leave their country for service with the Catholic monarchs of Europe with the guarantee that their co-religionists who remained behind would not suffer cruel vengence. William promised that Catholics in Ireland would be as free to practice their religion as they were in the days of Charles II and that their property would remain secure. In late 1691, therefore, important members of the Catholic aristocracy and their retainers sailed to France, leaving their dependents under the protection of a vaguely worded document, a written pledge that rested on the integrity and humanity of the King of England, the English government, and the triumphant Irish Protestant planter colony.

THE PENAL LAWS

William of Orange was a politique, not a bigot. He intended to honor the terms of the Treaty of Limerick. His own country, the Dutch Republic, had adopted a policy of religious tolerance as a pragmatic alternative to civil war. William was prepared to apply a similar approach in Britain and Ireland as a path toward reconciliation, peace, and stability, goals he considered more important than Protestant ascendancy. Unfortunately, Irish and British Protestants did not share the King's attitude; they wanted to punish the defeated enemy. Carefully considering the fanaticism of British and Irish no-popery, William decided that it would be impolitic to resist the popular demand and he consented to anti-Catholic legislation in both kingdoms.

Irish Penal Laws were enacted by Parliament during the reigns of William and Mary, Anne, and the first two Georges. They were harsher than those in England and touched every aspect of civil and religious life. They banished bishops and members of religious orders from the country and forbade the entry of secular priests from abroad. Resident secular priests had to register and pay a fee, remain in their parishes, and take an oath abjuring the Stuart Pretender. The Penal Laws disarmed Catholics, excluded them from Parliament and the legal profession, and denied them the franchise. They prohibited Catholics from establishing schools or sending their children abroad to be educated. They stated that Catholics could lease property for as long as thirty-one years but could not purchase it, and that at the owner's death Catholic property existing from pre-Penal days had to be divided among all the sons. At any time, an eldest son could acquire the family estate by turning Protestant, thus reducing his father to the status of life tenant.

British and Irish Protestants considered themselves the most enlightened people in Europe, the possessors of the Whig, representative government, constitutional tradition. They frequently denounced Catholic bigotry, citing the Spanish Inquisition, the repeal of the Edict of Nantes, and the consequent persecution of Huguenots in France as typical examples of Catholic oppression. Since the Penal Laws in Ireland, England, and the American colonies contradicted this claim of enlightment, how did Irish and English Protestants defend programs of anti-Catholicism that exceeded religious persecutions in any of the Catholic areas of Western Europe?

Protestants in England, Ireland, and North America argued that anti-Catholic laws were necessary for security reasons. They insisted that the subversive and malignant nature of popery excluded it from all normal claims for tolerance. To them Catholicism was the epitome of antiintellectualism and superstition, an expression of tyranny, authoritarianism, and treason. Catholics accepted the temporal authority of a foreign ruler, the Pope in Rome, and they had extended aid and comfort to the foreign enemies of England.

Anti-Catholic legislation did not destroy or weaken Irish Catholicism. Government authorities did not have the will, resources, or personnel to systematically enforce all the religious clauses of the Penal Laws. In 1709, Rome began to appoint new Irish bishops. By mid-century, many diocesan priests and members of religious orders—Franciscans, Dominicans, Carmelites, Capuchins, Jesuits—served the Irish Catholic community. Candidates for the priesthood studied at Louvain, Antwerp, Douay, Paris, Nantes, Lille, Barcelona, Santiago, Seville, Salamanca, Rome, and other continental Catholic seminaries. Lay Catholics, members of the aristocracy and affluent middle class, also sent their sons abroad for secular education. Although the Irish Catholic masses were very ignorant of the theology of their religion, and many indifferent to its practice, by 1760 the Catholic church in Ireland was in a far healthier condition than before the Penal era.

The Penal Laws did not result in a significant conversion of people from Catholic to Protestant. Legal pressures, property considerations, concern for the future of sons, the desire for status, and political ambitions did encourage most members of the Catholic aristocracy and gentry to become Protestants. However, adversity did not affect the religious faith of the agrarian masses, and many members of the native and Old English aristocracies held on to the faith of their ancestors.

If the purpose of the Penal Laws was the destruction of Irish Catholicism or mass conversion then they obviously failed. But that was not their main intent. They were designed more as instruments of terror than proselytism. They expressed Protestant fear, insecurity, and hatred. Victories in sixteenth and seventeenth centuries wars left Irish Protestants a privileged minority. They had a monopoly of power but were unsure whether they could maintain it. Like ancient Spartans or present-day whites in Rhodesia or South Africa, they were surrounded by hostile and dangerous natives and constantly feared a helot insurrection. As an English garrison, they believed that the only way that they could maintain their property and power was to degrade and humiliate the Catholic majority. Mass defections of Irish Catholics were not likely or even desirable—somebody had to do the menial labor. What was desirable was to make the natives feel inferior and impotent, to demoralize and degrade them through an environment of terror. The Penal Laws were an updated version of the Laws of Lycurgus and the Statutes of Kilkenny, an early form of cultural apartheid that would become an essential feature of Western imperialism. They were a method of emasculating a conquered people so that they would accept their position as a servile class—"the hewers of wood and drawers of water."

As an instrument of terror, the Penal Laws were a remarkable success. Members of the Catholic aristocracy, gentry, middle class, and peasantry all bowed to Protestant Ascendancy. Toleration rather than equality became the goal of Catholic agitation against the Penal Laws. Petitions emanating from Catholic committees representing the aristocracy, gentry, and middle class, while pleading for the restoration of civil and property rights, humbly renounced any intention of subverting Protestant Ascendancy or the Protestant constitution.

The Penal Laws completed the division of Ireland into two separate societies: Protestant and Catholic, conqueror and conquered. Of course, not all Protestants were members of the aristocracy or gentry. Some were merchants, tradesmen, even tenant farmers and agricultural laborers. And many Protestants were not members of the established church. About fifteen percent of the total Irish population were Nonconformists, most of them Ulster Presbyterians. A Sacramental Test Clause attached to the 1704 Popery Act excluded Protestant Nonconformists from civil and military office. A series of Toleration and Indemnity Acts eased the legal burdens on Nonconformists, but they still resented a position of something less than first class citizenship. During the eighteenth century a large number of them emigrated to North America.

Not all Irish Catholics were poor. A few members of the aristocracy and gentry classes managed to hold on to their property through the travails of the Penal Laws, often with the aid of Protestant neighbors. Anti-Catholic legislation encouraged the growth of a significant Catholic middle class. Denied opportunities to purchase landed property or to pursue careers in politics or law, many bright and ambitious young Catholics entered banking and commerce, particularly the lucrative provisions trade. Many Protestant landlords employed Catholic agents to manage their estates and collect the rents. These agents often acquired wealth and standing in rural Ireland. Also there were a number of Catholic strong farmers, perhaps a hundred thousand, who rented thirty acres or more, often subleased part of their holdings, had tenants of their own, and employed agricultural laborers.

Despite the above exceptions, religious allegiances defined two separate communities, distinguished by property and nonproperty, wealth and poverty, power and impotence. By the mid-eighteenth century, the seventy-five percent Catholic majority owned less than ten percent of Irish landed property and were excluded from the affairs of their own country. Yet despite their political and economic grievances against the Protestant Ascendancy, middle-class urban and rural peasant Nonconformists shared the es-

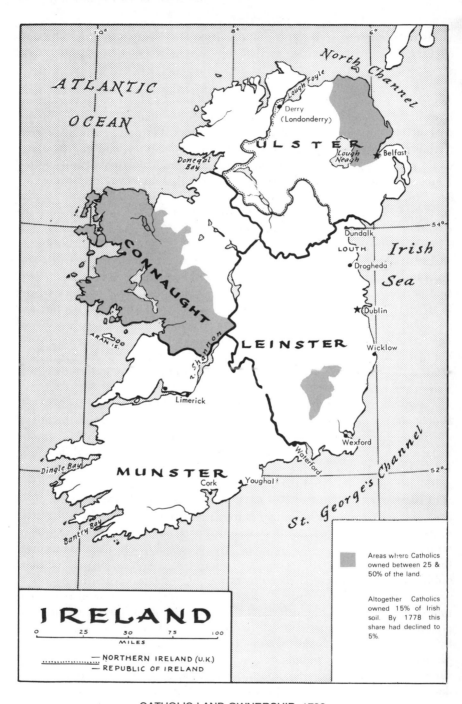

ATLANTIC
OCEAN

North Channel

Lough Foyle

Derry
(Londonderry)

U L S T E R

Donegal
Bay

Lough
Neagh

Belfast

Dundalk

LOUTH

Irish

Drogheda

Sea

CONNAUGHT

ARAN IS.

Shannon

LEINSTER

Dublin

Wicklow

Limerick

Waterford

Wexford

Dingle Bay

MUNSTER

Youghal

St. George's Channel

Cork

Bantry Bay

54°

52°

Areas where Catholics
owned between 25 &
50% of the land.

Altogether Catholics
owned 15% of Irish
soil. By 1778 this
share had declined to
5%.

IRELAND

| 0 | 25 | 50 | 75 | 100 |
MILES

·················· NORTHERN IRELAND (U.K.)
———— REPUBLIC OF IRELAND

CATHOLIC LAND OWNERSHIP, 1703

16

tablishment's hatred and fear of Catholicism. In fact, the rigidity of Calvinist theology tended to make Presbyterians more intense than Church of Irelanders in their no-popery.

The landlord system shaped the personality of the Irish Ascendancy. An irresponsible system bred irresponsible people. Members of the Irish aristocracy and gentry acquired a reputation for charm, gaiety, wit, hospitality, and courage. Yet the charm was restricted to peers, the gaiety was often a feature of inebriation, the wit could be biting and cruel, the hospitality was frequently profligacy, and the courage at times was a euphemism for recklessness. Many landlords were indifferent to the source of their incomes, ignored the welfare of their estates, and wasted their resources on an exorbitant standard of living and decadent life style. Maria Edgeworth's *Castle Rackrent* (1800) is the classic literary description of landlord irresponsibility.

Many members of the Protestant Ascendancy preferred not to live in Ireland. Bright young men who graduated from Trinity College, such as Edmund Burke and Oliver Goldsmith, fled provincial Dublin to seek and find fame and fortune in London. Despite the good hunting and fishing and some attractive big houses, many members of the landlord class abandoned rural Ireland for the more exciting life style of England, leaving behind agents to manage their estates. There is no convincing evidence that absentee landlords as a group were more hard-hearted than those who resided in the country or that their estates were more inefficiently operated. But absenteeism did deprive the country of potential talent and leadership, widen the gap between the two communities—Catholic and Protestant, landlord and tenant—and drain money from the Irish economy. Rents collected in Ireland and spent in England retarded the growth of local industries and crafts.

In contrast to the comfortable existence of resident and absentee Protestant landlords, most Catholic peasants led a life of abject poverty. They were the most miserable example of their class in Western Europe. If a Catholic peasant was fortunate enough to rent a farm—there were more agricultural laborers than tenant farmers—it was usually small, less than fifteen acres. His home was a mud cabin with a thatched roof that harbored a wide variety of vermin and a dirt floor that turned to mire in the frequent Irish rains. He was lucky, indeed, if his cottage had windows for ventilation or a chimney to carry off the smoke from turf (peat) fires that provided warmth and heat for cooking. Large families inhabited these one, two, or three room hovels, often sharing them with a pig or chickens.

As a class, Irish peasants were illiterate, and many, perhaps a majority in the South and West, could only speak Irish, which was another barrier between religions and classes. Tobacco and alcohol—much of it an illegally distilled malt and barley whiskey called poteen (poitín)—was one escape from the pressures of poverty. Frustration was also released in violence. Family feuds led to faction fights. In Ulster, party fights involved Catholic and Protestant tenant farmers. Only the comforts of Catholicism—its rituals, sacraments, and hope of salvation through poverty and redemptive suffering— brought a touch of beauty, a measure of psychological comfort and security, and some discipline to peasant life.

Visitors to rural Ireland frequently commented on the desperate condition of the peasantry and the brutality of an economic and social system that permitted landlords to treat tenants and laborers as slaves. They also described the complexity of the peasant character: on the positive side, generosity, good humor, sexual purity, close family ties and affection, with politeness; on the negative side, irresponsibility, indifference to work, disrespect for law, improvidence, drunkenness, and violence.

Those negative aspects of the peasant personality were formed largely out of economic and social experience. Hunger, cold, pain, oppression, degradation, and ignorance do not produce ambition, sobriety, law and order values, thrift, or inner joy. Peasant vices often reflected the conduct of the aristocracy and gentry. As the master class and leaders of rural society, they established the norms and set the standards of conduct.

Foreign and English observers tended to blame the wretched conditions in rural Ireland on "alien" landlords. Ever since the early nineteenth century Irish nationalists have echoed this accusation. Unfortunately, too many Irish historians have failed to probe its authenticity. Actually, the Protestant planter proprietors were not any more improvident or indifferent to the welfare of the peasantry than the native or Old English Catholics they replaced. Anglo-Irish Catholic feudal lords and Gaelic clan chieftans had been notorious for their drinking, gambling, and hunting; they were far from agricultural experts. It can be argued that the conduct of Protestant landlords in the eighteenth and nineteenth centuries was another example of the English in Ireland becoming more Irish than the natives. It can even be argued that many so called "alien" landlords were actually more interested in their farms and tenants than the Catholic landlords before them. There were many examples of mutual loyalty, even affection, between Protestant landlord and Catholic tenant. And despite the Irish peasants' miserable standard of living, they were not the only members of their class to suffer from hunger, insecurity, and exploitation in Europe. Institutionally, the legal position of tenant farmers and agricultural laborers in Britain was similar to the situation in Ireland, and many of them also existed on the margin of that in Ireland, and many of them also existed on the margin of survival.

In Ireland the essence of the land question was probably more cultural than social or economic. British landlords and peasants belonged to a common Protestant cultural community. In Ireland the relationship between the landowning class and those who worked the soil was complicated by conflicting loyalties: British and Irish, Protestant and Catholic, and colonial and native. Eighteenth-century Irish peasants were not sophisticated concerning politics and economics, and they had not yet acquired a national self-consciousness, but they knew, instinctively and emotionally, that the landlord system in Ireland represented conquest for the landlord and servitude for them.

Although an expanding agricultural and commercial economy increased the wealth of the upper and middle classes, in the eighteenth century a rapid increase in the Irish population lowered the peasant standard of living. From 1687 to 1725 the number of people living in Ireland increased from 2,167,000 to 3,042,000. By 1785 the population had jumped to 4,019,000. By 1821, 6,802,000 people lived off the meagre resources of the country, and by 1841 Ireland was bursting at the seams with a population of 8,175,000.[1] This population explosion was part of a general European phenomenon. Many demographers attribute the rapid increase of people in Britain to the health benefits associated with the Industrial and Agricultural Revolutions. Improved sanitation, fresh water, inexpensive clothing, better and cheaper food, and vaccinations against smallpox prolonged life and reduced infant mortality. But Ireland did not have either an Industrial or an Agricultural Revolution and medical care was primitive and rarely available. Famine and disease were endemic.

This Irish population explosion managed to triumph over infant mortality, famines, plagues, and bad sanitation. It was the result of increased fertility, the fruit of early marriages. Males married at an average age of sixteen, and females at fourteen. Poverty appeared to encourage the satisfaction of sexual urges, and to Irish Catholics this meant the marriage bed. And to people as poor and as miserable as they were, sex and the companionship of wives, husbands, and children, like good and even bad whiskey, were a comfort and an escape. The potato was the most important factor in early marriages and the consequent fecundity of Irish women. It is an easy vegetable to cultivate, flourishes even in bad soil, and provides a nutritious diet. By the early nineteenth century the average Irishman was consuming between eight and ten pounds of potatoes every day; sometimes he would eat them half cooked so they would take longer to digest, and occasionally he might drink a little milk to wash them down. He seldom ate bread, eggs, or meat. He sold his grain harvest, the pig, and the eggs to provide money for the rent. An exclusive potato diet made it possible for a family to feed many children on a small piece of land, encouraging early marriages and the rearing of many children. But the reliance on the potato meant the constant threat and reality of frequent famines.

The population explosion put too much strain on an already weak agrar-

---

[1]These population figures come from K. H. Connell, *The Population of Ireland, 1750–1845*, Oxford: The Clarendon Press, 1950, p. 25. Connell revises previous estimates but warns the reader that pre-census (1821) population statistics are bound to be somewhat unreliable.

ian economy. Since there was no industry in Ireland to absorb the surplus population, tenant farmers subdivided their small plots to accommodate more people and to earn a few shillings and pence in rent. As Irish farms decreased in size, Irish agriculture became more inefficient. Exploiting a land shortage, landlords were able to raise rents far beyond the real value of the land, since they could always find desperate tenants willing to pay. Tenants with larger plots paying inflated rents were anxious to sublease and also to charge excessive rents so that they could meet their obligation to the landlord.

Quite often landlords were more the victims than the promoters of a vicious economic system. Until after the French Revolution, they were reluctant to halt the process of subdivision. Landlords were slow to comprehend that the multiplication of small holdings was responsible for inefficient farming, reducing long-range profit potential. And they had to confront the pressures of peasant needs and, to a lesser extent, British mercantilist restrictions on Irish trade, which prevented the development of a dynamic urban economy that might have siphoned off some of the surplus rural population. An intelligent, efficient landlord, determined to improve the quality of his estate by rational, hard-headed measures, would have inflicted many hardships on the tenantry. By forbidding subleasing, he would have destroyed the social patterns of rural life, and antagonized those not adverse to sharing their poverty with others. The easy way out was for landlords to collect rents without interfering with peasant mores, even if such timidity encouraged a situation that could only lead to eventual disaster.

Land hunger fostered avarice, evictions, class war, and violence. Since the landlords had the support of the authorities and the legal system, peasants often resorted to terror to protect their interest in the land. A number of secret societies beginning with the Whiteboys in the 1760s and followed by the Rightboys, Thrashers, Whitefeet, Blackfeet, Lady Clares, Terry Alts, Molly Maguires, Defenders, and Ribbonmen, expressed a gamut of peasant grievances: excessive rents, evictions, tithes, and the exorbitant dues that some Catholic priests demanded for baptisms, weddings, and funerals. Their tactics included written warnings followed by cattle maiming, destruction of crops, tearing down of ditches and fences, burning ricks and outhouses, and, as a last resort, shooting landlords or their agents and tithe collectors. Members of secret societies would also intimidate other peasants who dared to take the farm of an evicted tenant, and they would drive out agricultural laborers whom landlords imported from other districts.

Some Protestants charged that agrarian secret societies were, in fact, papist guerrilla armies attacking their Ascendancy and their property. But Catholic bishops frequently excommunicated Whiteboys and other rural terrorists, and secret societies threatened and took action against Catholic landlords as well as against priests who charged excessive dues. Members of the Catholic hierarchy condemned agrarian violence because, in principle, they were opposed to secret societies and they feared that any attack on Protestant property would encourage reprisals.

Landlord-tenant relations were more cordial in Protestant Ulster than in Leinster, Munster, or Connacht. Ulster Custom permitted a tenant to sell his interest in the farm on leaving and protected him against arbitrary eviction and unjust rent increases. In contrast, tenants in the South and West who improved their farms by draining, fencing, and fertilizing land or by repairing buildings might be rewarded for their efforts by a rent increase reflecting the escalated value of their farms. If they were unable to meet the landlord's new demand, they could be evicted without any compensation for the contributions they had made to their landlords' property. As a result, tenants in Leinster, Munster, and Connacht were reluctant to improve their farms, and so the quality of agriculture was higher in Ulster. Perhaps landlord-tenant relations in Ulster were more harmonious because many of the tenants were Protestant or Nonconformist, therefore religious differences did not intensify class conflict.

In the North violence was much more likely to occur between Catholic and Protestant tenant farmers than between landlords and tenants. Sectarian tension, particularly west of the Bann river, initiated rival secret societies. During the 1780's, Protestant Peep O' Day Boys terrorized Catholics, who responded by forming the Defenders. The 1795 Battle of the Diamond between Peep O' Day Boys and Defenders in County Armagh resulted in a victory for the former and the beginnings of the Orange Order. This new Protestant organization quickly gained adherents, terrorized Ulster Catholics, and drove many of them out of the province toward the west to Connacht. Realizing the no-popery, Protestant Ascendancy potential of Orangeism, the gentry took command of the movement, armed its members, and persuaded the government that religious bigotry was an effective instrument of law and order. The Orange Order would remain a permanent weapon of Protestant Ascendancy, a divisive irrational hate factor in Irish life, the prototype of future Anglo-Saxon Protestant nativist movements in Ireland, Britain, and North America.

Although the Defenders were mainly concerned with protecting Catholics from violence, they were also involved in protests against excessive rents and tithes. In the early nineteenth century, a new secret agrarian organization, the Ribbon society absorbed the Defenders. Despite its Ulster Catholic origins, the Ribbon society was much more concerned with economic than sectarian matters, and spread into Leinster and Munster.

Ribbonism appealed to agricultural laborers, revealing class divisions within the peasant community. Until the Great Famine of the late 1840's radically reduced the rural population, agricultural laborers outnumbered tenant farmers who often exploited them in the same way that landlords abused tenants. Most laborers worked for tenant farmers rather than for the aristocracy or gentry, and they rented small potato patches (conacre) from their employers. Sometimes the patch was in lieu of wages A shift from tillage to grazing in the eighteenth century to satisfy the meat needs of urban Britain was particularly hard on agricultural laborers. Finding it difficult to find either work or conacre, they turned to the Ribbon society to support their interests against tenant farmer employers.

On occasion, secret societies were strong enough to take to the hills and wage effective guerrilla campaigns against the army and the constabulary. Twice during the early nineteenth century—from 1813 to 1816 and from 1819 to 1822—peasant forces controlled large sections of rural Ireland. Looking back from a twentieth-century perspective, there is a romantic quality about secret societies—the weak fighting the strong, but agrarian terrorists were often cruel and indiscriminate in their violence, maiming and sometimes killing innocent women and children. But at a time when the Irish and British Parliaments and the Protestant Ascendancy in Ireland were indifferent to the Catholic peasant masses, people without civil or legal rights had no option but to counter oppression with terror. And there can be no doubt that the intimidation by secret societies did mitigate some of the economic and social evils of manorialism.

Some nationalist ideologists and amateur historians have seen the embryo of revolutionary nationalism in secret societies. This interpretation distorts reality. Secret societies did not attempt to destroy either Protestant Ascendancy or manorialism. Instead they tried to reform the system through effective regulation. Revolutions are the product of hope and rising expectations rather than despair. The Irish Catholic masses were too demoralized and impoverished to make good revolutionaries. They had not organized the religious commitment, language, customs, and values that separated them from the Protestant Ascendancy into a coherent ethnic identity. Their identity reference was Catholic rather than Irish. Irish peasants sought salvation and significance within the confines of Catholicism. But men angry enough to use a cudgel or pike, to burn a building, to shoot a landlord agent or tithe collector had some revolutionary potential. All the Irish Catholic masses needed to begin to liberate themselves was hope, discipline, goals, ethnic identity, and charismatic leadership. They had to wait until the nineteenth century to find them.

THE RISE AND FALL OF THE PROTESTANT NATION

During the eighteenth century the British colony in Ireland evolved into an Irish Protestant nation. With the Penal Laws' success in degrading and demoralizing the Catholic majority, Protestants felt more secure and less dependent on Britain for their survival. As a result, they began to resent

British political and commercial restrictions. Poynings' law (1494), amended during the reign of Mary Tudor and modified by centuries of practice, limited the legislative role of the Irish Parliament to the submission of bills to the King and his privy Council in Britain for approval, veto, or amendment. The Irish Parliament could only accept or reject English amendments. If it attempted to improve an amended bill, the bill then became new legislation and was resubmitted to the King and Council. In 1720, the British Parliament's Declaratory Act (the sixth of George I) further restricted Irish sovereignty by insisting on the right to legislate for Ireland. The appellate jurisdiction of the British House of Lords in legal cases also pointed to the subordinate position of Ireland *vis à vis* Britain.

Irish commercial interests certainly profited through their association with the world's richest empire. Through most of the eighteenth century, Irish landlords, merchants, and manufacturers prospered and raised their standards of living. But they complained of British mercantilism that regulated the Irish economy to satisfy the needs and interests of the British. Since she was short on basic resources, Ireland probably never would have been a serious trade competitor with Britain, but she did have a few small industries capable of development (i.e. woolen textiles and glass making) that might, if encouraged, have served as useful employment and investment alternatives to a primitive agrarian economy suffering the consequences of over-population.[2]

The English colony in Ireland evolved into a community of Anglo-Irish patriots (a similar process took place in eighteenth-century North America). It complained that absentee landlordism drained Irish talent, leadership, and investment potential. Patriots argued that if more men of property remained in the country that furnished them with their incomes, they might develop a concern for Irish rights and progress. They also protested the expense of a large military establishment and the Hanoverian exploitation of the Irish pension list to reward royal favorites. Both, they said, deprived Ireland of funds that could have been put to better economic uses.

Like eighteenth-century Anglo-Americans, the Anglo-Irish expressed their grievances in Lockean rhetoric. William Molyneux, the first theoretician of Anglo-Irish patriotism, and a friend of John Locke, insisted that only the Irish Parliament could represent the will of the Irish Protestant community because Irish laws and institutions had to reflect an Anglo-Irish, not a British, consensus. Jonathan Swift, Dean of St Patrick's, and the most articulate of the patriot propagandists, argued in *The Drapier Letters* (1724) that

[2]Linen was an exception. Both the Irish and British Parliaments encouraged the growth of an Irish linen industry. Because of the concentration on linen factories in the Belfast area, it was the only part of Ireland to experience the Industrial Revolution, widening the cultural and economic differences between the one region with a majority Protestant population and the rest of the country.

"all Government without the consent of the *Governed* is the *very definition* of *Slavery*." He told the Anglo-Irish "that by Laws of God, of nature, of Nations, and of your own Country, you Are and Ought to be a Free a people as your Brethren in England."

Patriotic sentiment continued to grow among members of the Irish Protestant community, but British influence in Ireland was sustained by forces independent of public opinion. These forces included the Primates (Archbishops of Armagh) of the Church of Ireland who were English appointees, as were about half the members of the hierarchy. These prelates defined the mission of the church as the promotion and advancement of British interests in Ireland. The British cause also attracted many members of the Anglo-Irish aristocracy and gentry. British Lord Lieutenants played a minor role in Irish affairs and spent little time in Ireland. In their absence, three Lord Justices, usually including the Primate and the Speaker of the Irish House of Commons, represented the Crown. These Lord Justices spoke for the landed magnates and controlled a majority of seats in Parliament through the instrument of patronage.[3] As long as British politicians avoided conflict with their Irish agents they could depend on them to pursue British interests as well as their own.

In 1767 the British Government appointed Lord Townshend as Lord Lieutenant and instructed him to diminish the influence of the Anglo-Irish aristocracy and gentry. Evidently, the ministry in London decided that ruling Ireland through Anglo-Irish middlemen was too expensive, inefficient, and humiliating. Under the new policy, Lord Lieutenants had to reside in Ireland and directly control patronage. The promotion of the Lord Lieutenant and the demotion of the Anglo-Irish Protestant Ascendancy clarified Ireland's colonial status, and it persuaded many members of the aristocracy and gentry that there were conflicts between British and Irish interests. But the Lord Lieutenant could still employ patronage to maintain a pro-British parliamentary majority.

Beginning in 1775, the strategies and goals of Anglo-Irish patriotism merged with those of Anglo-American patriots to reduce British influence in their part of the world. In October 1775, the Irish government asked Parliament to approve an address that branded the American patriots as rebels and called for Irish cooperation in a war to preserve the empire. Since so many Irish M.P.s benefited from crown patronage, a parliamentary majority endorsed the address. But the American cause had friends in Ireland, particularly in Ulster, who sympathized with Benjamin Franklin's appeal for Irish support against a common "tyranny." Fifty-four M.P.s had the courage to vote against approving the address.

---

[3] These landed magnates were called Undertakers because they undertook to carry out British policy in Ireland in exchange for their control of Irish affairs.

The American victory at Saratoga in 1777 which brought Bourbon France and Spain into the war on the side of the rebels gave Britain reason to worry about Irish discontent. Now she had to fear Irish Protestant as well as Catholic anti-British sentiment. Irish grumbling grew louder when Britain placed an embargo on exports from Ireland, except to certain specified countries, to prevent supplies from reaching the American enemy. Anglo-Irish patriots blamed the embargo for an expanding Irish debt which had then reached £3,000,000. They argued that the embargo made it difficult for Ireland to find new sources of revenue, eliminated some that already existed, and impoverished a number of tax payers.

Lord North, the British Prime Minister, would have liked to soothe the feelings of Anglo-Irish patriots by making some concessions to their economic grievances, but the leaders of British commerce objected and forced him to abandon the idea. The Anglo-Irish interpreted North's surrender to the pressures of British commercial interests as evidence that Britain would never tolerate a vigorous, varied, or competitive Irish economy.

Since Anglo-Irish patriots could not overcome the patronage-bought pro-British majority in Parliament, they were forced to employ extra-parliamentary pressure, and the war in America gave them an opportunity to do so. Most Irish soldiers were in America while the combined French and Spanish navies commanded the surrounding seas. This left Ireland vulnerable to attack. Lord Buckinghamshire, the Lord Lieutenant, responded to a Belfast citizen petition requesting troop protection against the invasion danger with the frank admission that the American war made it impossible to honor such an appeal. The petitioners then proceeded to organize a volunteer force to defend themselves. Their initiative set an example for other parts of the country. Soon local companies were coordinated into a National Volunteer movement.

A large number of Protestants who could afford to purchase arms enlisted in the Volunteers. Although Anglo-Irish Protestants did not like to see armed Catholics, in 1780 they relented and permitted respectable gentry and middle-class papists to join the Volunteers. The Earl of Leinster and Lord Charlemont commanded the Volunteers, and parliamentary patriots served as officers in local companies. When Leinster realized that patriots had something in mind for the Volunteers beyond the function of a defense force, he reduced his commitment, leaving Charlemont as sole Commander.

Representatives of the British government in Ireland were suspicious of the Volunteers but indirectly armed them by distributing arms and ammunition to Lord Lieutenants of the counties as a precaution against invasion. Since most of them also led Volunteer companies, these weapons found their way into the hands of patriots.

Not only did the American war aid the efforts of Anglo-Irish patriots, it also slightly improved the condition of Irish Catholics. Even before hostilities began in America, the spirit of the Enlightenment, the growth of Irish-Protestant self-confidence, the increase in the size and respectability of the Catholic middle class, and the loyalty of Catholics to the Hanoverian crown during the 1715 and 1745 Stuart disturbances in Scotland increased the prospect for some concessions to Catholic agitation against the Penal Laws. In 1774, the year that the British government extended toleration to French Canadian Catholics, Catholics in Ireland received permission to demonstrate their loyalty by taking an oath of allegiance to the King. While this oath conferred no benefits, it did acknowledge the existence of Catholic subjects, and hinted of future concessions with regard to their grievances.

When the French and Spanish became American allies, the Protestant Ascendancy in Ireland argued against concessions to Catholics since they might encourage treason. English Whigs, however, expressed the opinion that no-popery fostered rather than discouraged Catholic treachery. In 1777, George III favorably received an Irish Catholic petition to mitigate the Penal Laws, and British Whigs suggested to their Irish counterparts that it was time to relax religious tensions.

Fearing that the British might exploit the religious issue to enlist Irish Catholics against the patriot cause, Henry Grattan, leader of the patriot movement in and out of Parliament, decided that it would be good strategy to encourage Catholic civil rights. He told his coreligionists that "the Irish Protestant could never be free until the Irish Catholic ceased to be a slave." At the urging of Grattan and British Whigs, the Irish Parliament passed a Relief Bill that permitted Catholics to lease land for 999 years and to pass on their property through primogeniture. It also eliminated the threat of an apostate son acquiring his father's estate. For all practical purposes a 999 year lease was ownership, although Catholics were excluded from the political influence associated with the direct ownership of property.

In 1779, patriots applied Volunteer pressure to the free trade issue. When the Irish Parliament met on October 12, Grattan moved an amendment to the King's speech, stating that Ireland's economic problems originated in British mercantilism. On November 4, the Volunteers celebrated the birthday of William III with a display of military force. They assembled in College Green with two cannons carrying placards warning "Free Trade or This." Parliament received the message and cooperated with the Volunteers by voting the government only six months supplies. Impressed by the strength and determination of the Volunteers, harassed by the war in America, worried about a potential French invasion, and urged by the Whig opposition to compromise, Lord North persuaded the British Parliament to permit the Irish to export glass and woolen products and trade with British plantations without restriction.

Encouraged by this major concession, Grattan decided to push for the ultimate goal, self-government. Once more he relied on the influence of

Irish opinion and the menace of the Volunteers to convince the Irish Parliament and the British government that an increase of Irish sovereignty was necessary and prudent. On December 18, 1781, Irish M.P.s called for an end to Poynings' Law and the Declaratory Act. Two months later Volunteer leaders met at Dungannon to ratify a set of resolutions demanding (1) an independent Irish Parliament, (2) complete free trade, (3) control of the Irish judiciary by the Irish Parliament, (4) an annual Mutiny Act, and (5) repeal of the Penal Laws.

Repeal of the Penal Laws represented Grattan's conviction that a successful Irish nation demanded full equality between Catholics and Protestants. Henry Flood, his colleague and rival in the patriot movement, led the opposition to repeal. He insisted that it would lead to Catholic power at the expense of the Protestant constitution and the destruction of Anglo-Irish culture. Claiming to be an enlightened advocate of tolerance, Flood argued that Protestant Ascendancy protected liberty against the authoritarianism and bigotry of popery. Subsequent events revealed that Flood's antipathy to Catholicism was more representative of Anglo-Irish opinion than Grattan's inclusive patriotism.

A political change in Britain was as important as Volunteer pressure in advancing patriot objectives. In March, 1782, the Whigs came to power with the Marquis of Rockingham as Prime Minister and Charles James Fox as leader in the House of Commons. Since they shared Locke's ideology, British Whigs had long urged compromise with Irish Whigs, but they were reluctant to abandon all jurisdiction in Ireland. However, the Duke of Portland, the Viceroy in Ireland, informed Rockingham and Fox that Grattan and his friends would accept nothing short of an independent Irish Parliament. Britain's international difficulties added weight to Portland's intelligence.

In the late stages of the American War, the combined French and Spanish fleets controlled and sailed up and down the English Channel and blockaded Chesapeake Bay and the mouth of the York River. This prevented supplies from reaching Marquess Charles Cornwallis, Major General in the British army, who was winter-quartering at Yorktown after a successful campaign in the Carolinas, and led to his defeat. After Cornwallis' surrender in October, 1781, ended the war in the North American colonies, the Bourbon powers still were confident. In 1782, they captured Minorca and laid siege to Gibraltar, but the tide of war changed in April, 1782, when Admiral George Brydges Rodney defeated and captured his French opponent Admiral François Joseph Paul de Grasse, Marquis de Grassetilly in the West Indies. Nevertheless the war against France and Spain (the Dutch also joined the anti-English coalition) had Irish implications that caused anxiety at Westminster. So on May 15, 1782, Fox introduced a series of proposals in the House of Commons that finally received the assent of both houses of Parliament. They amended Poyning's Law and repealed the Declaratory Act. These changes meant that Lord Lieutenants and their advisors no longer could initiate Irish legislation, the King could veto Irish bills but not alter them, the British Parliament could not legislate for Ireland, and Irish judges had secure tenures and Irish courts final jurisdiction.[4]

These British concessions to Anglo-Irish patriotism were far less than those that Anglo-Americans won at the Treaty of Paris (1783). Irish sovereignty was limited in two significant ways: Lord Lieutenants were responsible to the British rather than the Irish government, and the King's veto depended on the advice of British not Irish ministers. Nevertheless, they represented a considerable advance in the direction of Irish independence, and by any standard of judgment the first ten years of the Irish Protestant nation added up to a record of achievement. There was an increase in manufacturing, trade, and the consumption of goods. As a class, only the Catholic peasant masses did not participate in the new prosperity. An expanding economy and the importance of the Irish Parliament improved the quality of Irish culture. The founding of the Royal Irish Academy and the construction of impressive buildings like the Customs House and the Four Courts along the banks of the Liffey indicated a mood of energy and confidence. Dublin began to wear the vestments of a capital city.

Although much Irish talent continued to emigrate, absenteeism declined. Many members of the aristocracy decided that life in Ireland was exciting and Irish politics worthy of their concern. They also found Dublin's social and intellectual climate stimulating. Quite a few members of the affluent landlord class built attractive town houses in or on the fringes of the city. A large resident aristocracy and an affluent middle class encouraged a taste for luxury goods and a skilled artisan class to cater to sophisticated demands.

During the 1780's and 1790's the condition of the Catholic upper and middle classes also improved, though more as the result of British than Irish Protestant initiative. The wars of the French Revolution revived fears of Ireland as a potential danger to Britain, and British leaders pressured the Irish Parliament to make some gesture of good will to Catholic population. In 1792 the Irish Parliament responded by removing disabilities connected with mixed marriages, granting Catholics permission to open schools, and permitting them to become members of the legal profession. A year later, the Irish Parliament extended the municipal and parliamentary franchises to Catholics on an equal footing with Protestants, allowed them to bear arms, and declared them eligible for minor civil and military positions.

Granting the franchise offered the shadow not the substance of political influence. Religious loyalty oaths continued to bar Catholics from Parliament

---

[4]In 1783, under pressure from Anglo-Irish patriots, the British Parliament passed a Renunciation Act abandoning any claim to legislate for Ireland in the future as well as the present.

and urban corporations. Without a secret ballot, the forty shilling freehold suffrage only expanded the political power of the Protestant Ascendancy and encouraged further land subdivision with increasingly inefficient units of agriculture. Subdivision created more forty shilling voters to support the candidates of Protestant landlords. If a tenant did not vote his landlord's preference, he risked eviction.

As French Revolutionary armies swept over the Continent, the Irish and British governments grew concerned over the education of the Irish clergy. Many of the seminaries training Irish candidates for the priesthood had to shut down or bend to the winds of radical, anticlerical, and antireligious Jacobin ideology. Irish Catholic bishops and Irish and British politicians feared Irish priests would return from the Continent as agents of the French Revolution. To prevent this possibility, the Irish Parliament, encouraged by British leaders, in 1795 established a Roman Catholic seminary at Maynooth, County Kildare, and furnished it with an annual grant. No-popery had bowed to expediency.

These successful British efforts to make the Irish Parliament pull back from the extreme frontiers of no-popery revealed that the Irish Protestant nation was in retreat, the victory of 1782 was compromised. In the 1790's, the economic dimensions of the wars of the French Revolution restricted Irish trade and put an end to the economic boom of the 1780's. The Irish government was deep in debt and dependent on the British government for loans. British money meant a revival of British influence in Irish affairs.

Political instability magnified the economic crisis and allowed for British interference. Feuds, disputes, and rivalries had forced both Grattan and Flood from the political arena. Parliament was a cockpit of selfish factions. The aristocracy dominated both the Commons and the Lords, and the Lord Lieutenant manipulated competing Irish cliques. Both Grattan and Flood had believed that the patriot victory would not be complete until the Irish Parliament represented a wider spectrum of opinion, and their disciples continued to urge parliamentary reform. But the stubborn resistance of the landed aristocracy to even moderate constitutional changes drove patriotic reformers farther to the left. In 1791, some of them organized the Society of United Irishmen. Its members admired Rousseau and their organization was an Irish imitation of the Jacobins. They advocated a democratic republic as the most desireable alternative to rule by a Protestant Ascendancy aristocracy. United Irishmen were prepared to use physical force to achieve government by the General Will.

With a middle class Ulster Presbyterian power base, the United Irishmen represented Anglo-Irish patriotism evolving into Irish nationalism. They wanted a democratic Ireland without the divisiveness of sectarianism. Theobold Wolfe Tone, a Dublin Protestant, was the dominant personality in the United Irishmen. From 1792 to 1793, Tone served as Secretary of the

Catholic Committee as part of an effort to wed Catholics and Protestants in a common revolutionary cause. While he had little respect for the timid Catholic gentry and middle classes, Tone did consider the exploited Catholic peasant masses a source of excellent revolutionary material, potential allies of radical, middle class Nonconformists in Ulster.

Sensing a mood of unrest, the Irish government reacted with coercion rather than reform. In 1796, Parliament approved legislation restricting civil liberties, increasing police power, and suspending habeus corpus. Since officials distrusted the loyalty of militia companies containing large numbers of Catholics, they armed Protestant yeomen corps which landlords recruited from the ranks of the Orange Order. But the government had no need to doubt Catholic soldiers; they did their duty. In 1797, Catholic militiamen served General Lake when he moved into Ulster and smashed the United Irishmen organization in Belfast and damaged it in other sections of the province. Since coercion and terror proved effective in the North, it was applied to the rest of the country. Orange yeomen were guilty of numerous atrocities in their zeal to crush "treason" in the Catholic South. Orange terrorism frightened many Catholics, but it also drove others into the ranks of the Defenders, allies of the United Irishmen.

Dublin Castle made its strongest move to prevent revolution in March, 1798, when government agents arrested most of the United Irishmen leaders in the Dublin area. (Tone escaped since he was in France attempting to raise an expeditionary force to support an Irish rebellion.) Although Lord Edward Fitzgerald, the most prestigious member of the Society, escaped the March dragnet, he was mortally wounded two months later while resisting arrest.

Government repression destroyed the efficiency of the United Irishmen but failed to prevent insurrection. On May 26, 1798, Catholic peasants in Wexford, led by Father John Murphy, lifted the standard of revolt. They won some victories but their pikes were no match for the guns of militia and yeomen, and on June 21 government troops crushed their revolt at Vinegar Hill. Although Lake's 1797 excursion into Ulster severely crippled the United Irishmen in the North, in June, 1798, they led risings in Antrim and Down. Ulster rebels fought bravely, but government forces defeated them and executed their leaders.

The original strategy of the United Irishmen called for a coordinated national revolution, but the risings in Wexford, Antrim, and Down were spontaneous assaults on the established order. When the French sailed into Killala Bay, County Mayo, in August, 1798, they came too late with too little. General Humbert's small army of about a thousand men, supplemented by a small contingent of Connacht peasants armed with pikes, for a time outmanuevered and outfought its enemies. But in September, Humbert ran out of supplies and area to maneuver; he surrendered to General Pakenham.[5] In October, Wolfe Tone, with the rank of Adjutant General in the French army, failed in an attempt to invade Ireland. After his capture off the Donegal coast, Tone committed suicide in a Dublin cell when the authorities insisted they would hang him as a traitor rather than shoot him as an enemy officer.

Perhaps the events of 1798 were distorted through the mythology of Irish nationalism more than any incident or series of incidents in Irish history. Events in Northern Ireland since 1968 have perpetuated this mythology. According to the canons of Irish nationalism, 1798 was an ecumenical happening: Protestants from the North joined with Catholics from the South in a crusade for Irish independence and the rights of man. But United Irishmen were not typical Irish Protestants. They were Enlightenment Deists, hostile to all forms of organized religion, and oblivious to the sectarian passions that symbolized the cultural identities that divided Anglo-Irish Protestants from Irish Catholics. In reality, the Orange Order was far more representative of the Protestant North than was the Society of United Irishmen.

In Antrim and Down, Protestant rebels did not feel a community of cause with Catholics who fought in Wexford and Mayo. And those Catholics who murdered Protestants in Wexford, and in turn were slaughtered by Orange yeomen, were participating in a peasant revolt rather then a struggle for an independent, democratic, nonsectarian Irish Republic. Catholic peasants in Mayo joined Humbert to fight for the Pope and the Blessed Virgin rather than for the rights of man. Throughout the violence of 1798, Catholics in the militia remained loyal to the King and the Protestant Irish government. They furnished most of the troops that smashed rebellion.

The year 1798 diminished rather than expanded Irish freedom. Even before the events of that year, the instability of Irish life and politics disturbed the thoughts of British politicians at Westminster. The risings in Wexford, Antrim, Down, and Mayo, plus French involvement convinced the British Prime Minister, William Pitt, the younger, that Ireland would have to become part of the United Kingdom. An influential segment of the Irish aristocracy, led by John Fitzgibbon, Earl of Clare, whose father had converted to Protestantism, agreed with Pitt. Although he was a patriot in his youth, Clare had long since decided that Catholic discontent wedded to Jacobin radicalism could destroy Protestant Ascendancy. He and his friends agreed that Protestant Ascendancy was more important than the existence of an independent Irish Parliament. If Ireland joined the United Kingdom, British military power would preserve the Protestant monopoly in Ireland.

In advocating union with Britain, Clare was candid about class and

[5]In 1812 Humbert had his revenge when he helped Andrew Jackson defeat Pakenham at New Orleans.

religious realities in Ireland. He told his Whig opponents in the Irish Parliament that their reform idealism jeopardized their status. He said that there could never be democracy and civil rights in Ireland because Protestants were the descendents of conquerors who robbed the native population of their property and then enslaved them. It would be unreasonable not to expect that emancipated natives would insist upon the restoration of what they believed belonged to them.

> What then, was the situation of Ireland at the Revolution, and what is it at this day? The whole power and property of the country has been conferred by successive monarchs of England upon an English colony composed of three sets of English adventurers, who poured into this country at the termination of three successive rebellions. Confiscation is their common title, and from their first settlement they have been hemmed in on every side by the old inhabitants of the island, brooding over their discontents in sullen indignation.[6]

Pitt instructed the Lord Lieutenant, Lord Cornwallis of Yorktown prominence and his Chief Secretary, Lord Castlereagh, to prepare the ground for Union. Like Pitt, Cornwallis and Castlereagh were proponents of Catholic emancipation. They told members of the Irish Catholic hierarchy that a union with Britain would advance Catholic liberties because a British Parliament would be more objective than the Protestant Ascendancy Irish legislature. Cornwallis and Castlereagh promised the prelates that they and Pitt would try to persuade the British Parliament to concede Catholic emancipation once the two countries were united. While the Lord Lieutenant and Chief Secretary were courting Catholic bishops, other English politicians were assuring Lord Clare and his friends that the union would sustain Protestant Ascendancy.

Late in 1798 both houses of the British Parliament agreed to the principle of union, but in January, 1799, the Irish House of Commons rejected a pro-union paragraph in the Lord Lieutenant's address. For the remainder of the year, Irish M.P.s and pamphleteers debated the merits and demerits of union in an atmosphere clouded by rumors of French invasion plots and the presence of martial law. Both operated as pro-union intimidation factors.

Advocates of a British Connection argued that the Irish political system had failed to maintain security or stability or to protect the country from foreign intervention. They insisted that integration into the United Kingdom was necessary to defend Ireland from internal chaos, and external enemies, and to guarantee the continuation of Protestant Ascendancy. Led by Grattan, who returned to politics, patriots against a union with Britain replied that membership in the United Kingdom would reduce Ireland to provincial status. They said that Britain would deny Ireland fair representa-

---

[6]W. E. H. Lecky, *A History of Ireland in the Eighteenth Century*, abridged by L. P. Curtis, Jr. (Chicago: The University of Chicago Press, 1972) p. 212.

tion in the United Kingdom Parliament, which would then sacrifice Irish to British interests. They warned that once Ireland lost her independence, the aristocracy would abandon the country, industries would collapse, and trade would decline.

Most Orangemen opposed the Union, anticipating that a British Parliament would make concessions to Catholic agitation. Some Catholic merchants and lawyers shared the Protestant patriot concern that union with Britain would destroy the Irish economy. But most Catholic bishops and lay leaders accepted Pitt's promise that the inclusion of Ireland in the United Kingdom would be a prelude to the repeal of remaining Penal Laws.

While the upper and middle classes were discussing the pros and cons of a union—the issue was irrelevant to the peasant masses—Cornwallis and Castlereagh were busy employing the arts of persuasion and the power of patronage to the construction of a parliamentary majority for union. They concentrated on the large numbers of M.P.s who remained neutral in January, 1799. In February, 1800, after the Lord Lieutenant had distributed peerages, granted pensions, and agreed to compensate the owners of seats in the Irish Parliament, the House of Commons endorsed union by a 43 vote majority, 158 to 115. In the House of Lords, support for union was more substantial, 75 to 26. In March, the Irish Parliament approved specific articles for an Act of Union. The British Parliament did the same two months later. On December 31, 1800, the Irish Protestant political nation ceased to exist.[7]

In the 1920's, infuriated by legislation from a Catholic dominated Irish Dail which discriminated against the private lives and consciences of Protestants, William Butler Yeats described his Protestant co-religionists as one of the great stocks of Europe, the people of Swift, Goldsmith, Burke, Berkeley, Davis, and Parnell. Yeats was right: the Anglo-Irish were "no petty people"; they bred genius, but missed the mark of true greatness. Anglo-Irish arro-

---

[7]Irish nationalists have described the Act of Union as an example of British treachery because with titles and bribes representatives of the Crown seduced a corrupt Anglo-Irish Protestant Ascendancy to sell their nation into bondage. Nationalists claim that the landed oligarchy who controlled the Irish Parliament did not represent Irish opinion so therefore the Act of Union was an illegal contract. By the current standards of liberal-democracy the Act of Union was a corrupt bargain. A majority of Irish opinion probably did oppose the British connection. The Irish Parliament did not adequately represent the wishes of the Irish people, and British leaders did influence Irish M.P.s with peerages and patronage. But according to G. C. Bolton, *The Passing of the Act of Union*, London: Oxford University Press, 1966, Cornwallis and Castlereagh's methods were acceptable political practices in eighteenth-century Ireland and Britain. Despite Whig political principles and theory, the Irish and British Parliaments represented property not people, and it is possible, even probable, that Irish landed property desired the Union. Corrupt politicians occasionally vote their convictions, even if they accept money to do so, and convictions in themselves are neither noble or ignoble. People on both sides of the Union dispute believed their cause honorable, serving the long range interests of their country, and there were others obviously motivated by personal or group ambitions for political power and religious domination.

gance and exclusiveness rejected Irish Catholics as part of the eighteenth-century Irish nation. While a more civilized group than contemporary white Rhodesians and South Africans, they were pioneers in apartheid colonialism:

> They resided in Ireland—their country, never their nation—so that their achievements were, for the most part, so remote from the life of the native Irish (now utterly suppressed) that they ultimately became part of the English rather than the Irish cultural record.[8]

Despite the limitations of the Anglo-Irish, they made important and permanent contributions to the Irish political and cultural personalities. They decorated Irish cities with attractive and graceful architecture, created the first Irish political nation, and endowed subsequent Irish nationalism with liberal and democratic values. The Irish Protestant nation and the patriotism that created it took prominent places in the history and mythology of Irish nationalism, inspiring the imagination and encouraging the deeds of nineteenth and twentieth centuries' constitutional and physical force participants in Irish freedom efforts.

[8]Sean O'Faolain, *The Irish*, Harmondsworth, Middlesex, England: Pelican Books, 1969, p. 88.

2

Daniel O'Connell and modern Irish political nationalism

THE UNION AND THE IRISH QUESTION

When the Westminster Parliament opened on January 28, 1801, one hundred M.P.s represented Ireland in the 658-member House of Commons, and thirty-two peers, four of them Protestant bishops, in a 360-member House of Lords. With the Union, the Church of Ireland became part of the United Church of England and Ireland. But Ireland was not as fully integrated into the United Kingdom as was Scotland or Wales. The preservation of the offices of Lord Lieutenant and Chief Secretary, a large Dublin Castle bureaucracy, separate courts, a local prison system, and a variety of government agencies and bureaus dealing with Irish business were remnants of independence. And the frequent suspension of the constitution, accompanied by coercion and martial law, also indicated that Britain neither treated nor accepted Ireland as an integral part of the United Kingdom.

From the beginning to the end of the Union, the Irish Question ideologically polarized British politics: it defined party principles, programs, and tactics; it made and destroyed political careers; it determined who would govern the United Kingdom; it altered the tone, style, and rules of Parliament; it advanced social democracy in Britain; and, finally in 1914, it brought the United Kingdom to the verge of civil war. Ireland brought a multitude of problems with her into the United Kingdom: an inadequate agrarian economy; a poverty ridden, ignorant, demoralized, but growing peasant population, which was far too numerous for the resources of the country; and a long history of religious tension and conflict, persecution, and Protestant Ascendancy.

Although the Act of Union did not initiate the religious, economic, social, or all of the political dimensions of the Irish Question, British politicians certainly aggravated the situation. But they were more arrogant than vicious toward Ireland. They honestly believed that the "feckless, immature, and emotional" Irish were fortunate to have British masters. This conceit was accompanied by massive ignorance. British politicians who legislated for Ireland knew less about the Irish than they did about people on the Continent or in the remote outposts of the Empire. In fact, few members of the governing or intellectual classes ever had visited Ireland. Benjamin Disraeli never crossed the Irish Sea and William Ewart Gladstone made only one, two-week, police-conducted tour of Ireland.

Prejudice joined conceit and ignorance in shaping Irish policy. Because of George III's insistence that he was the Protestant King of a Protestant country governed by a Protestant constitution, Pitt could not honor his commitment to Catholic emancipation. Tory governments after Pitt pledged themselves to Protestant Ascendancy in Ireland, reflecting the wishes and convictions of no-Popery British public opinion.

As long as the Union lasted, British hostility to Catholicism persisted. English and Scots Catholics were a small, timid minority anxious to be accepted by the Protestant majority. They were certainly Gallican rather than Ultramontane Catholics, much more loyal to King and country than to Pope or church. On the other hand, Irish Catholics were a majority in their own country and comprised a significant minority within the United Kingdom. They satisfied the psychological needs of British nativists for an alien enemy. Anti-Catholicism focusing on the Irish became the most emotional issue in British politics, one that both fanatics and cynics exploited for votes. Conservatives were more likely to use no-popery in the context of the Irish Question than Whigs or Liberals, but under pressure, leftist politicians might also appeal to Protestant nativism to improve the prospects of their party or faction.

It is valid to describe Irish Catholics as the blacks of British history. Already in the first half of the nineteenth century religious prejudice often was expressed in racial terms. In December, 1835, *Blackwood's,* a most respectable and influential Tory periodical, described Irish Catholics as "one hundred years behind their fellow subjects in their intelligence and capacity for freedom." Long discussions of Irish topics in the House of Commons, agitations and agrarian violence in Ireland, and the impact of Irish immigration to Britain sharpened the racial aspect of sectarian bitterness.

Attempting to escape the burdens of poverty in their own country,

Irish peasants arrived in Britain without the skills necessary for success in an urban, industrial society. They had to settle for menial employment. They brought in the harvest, dug the canals, and laid railroad track. Irish women worked with their men as unskilled mine or factory workers or they were servants in upper- and middle-class British homes. In urban Britain, Irish peasants exchanged the misery of thatched roofed, unsanitary mud cabins for the horrors of slum tenements; they drowned their poverty and loneliness in a flood of cheap alcohol. When drunk they often argued and fought. Many of the Irish in Britain became thieves, muggers, juvenile, adolescent, and adult delinquents, alcoholics, and prostitutes. Most of these vices and antisocial behavior patterns were common to the lower levels of the British working class. But since the Irish could be identified by accent, religion, and cultural mores, British public opinion tended to associate urban social problems with Irish immigrants, and the character flaws of the Irish with their Catholicism.

Anti-Irish prejudice was most intense among the British proletariat. British workers claimed that the Irish took low-paying jobs, reducing the general working-class standard of living. No doubt there was more than employment rivalry involved in this proletarian anger. Like poor whites in the United States who hate blacks, British workers received an ego lift in finding someone they could look down on in the same way that the upper- and middle-classes looked down on them.

No doubt, anti-Irish, no-popery nativism in Britain worked as a safety valve, turning attention away from social and economic problems and uniting all classes in a common Anglo-Saxon Protestant patriotism. Thus Irish immigration and the Irish Question established a kind of solidarity in what was a very class-structured British society, contributed to a national consensus, and provided politicians with an emotional lever to manipulate public opinion.

The class, religious, ideological, or party loyalties of British politicians caused them to see Ireland as a menace, or nuisance, or opportunity to experiment, or as some abstract problem in political economy, but seldom as a land of desperate human beings or as a equal partner in the United Kingdom. Consequently the union of primitive, agrarian Ireland with the world's leading industrial power sacrificed the needs and interests of the former to the latter. As predicted by the opponents of the Union, the Irish economy declined, reducing the employment prospects for an already depressed population.

Irish Protestants relied on Tory and Conservative politicians to defend their position in Parliament against the aspirations of Irish Catholics. And the British landed gentry, the leading influence in British Toryism, was bound by compact, religious convictions, class privilege, and property interests to the Irish Protestant Ascendancy. The British right realized that concessions to the demands of the Irish Catholic masses would establish precedents encouraging radical assaults in Britain on the political power and property rights of the aristocracy and gentry.

British Tories considered law and order their prime responsibility in governing Ireland, and they concentrated on suppressing agrarian discontent as represented by secret societies. Beginning in 1807, Tory administrations frequently resorted to Insurrection Acts that permitted the authorities to invoke curfews, search for arms without warrant, and sentence terrorists without jury trials to seven years transportation in a penal colony.

In 1813, Sir Robert Peel, the Chief Secretary and leader of the Tory party in the House of Commons, introduced the Peace Preservation Act. This act created stipendary magistrates in Ireland and a professional, mobile Peace Preservation Force that could move into districts and assume the duties of ineffective resident magistrates and their baronial constabulary. Peel also recommended a county police force to prevent agrarian crime. In 1822, the Tories did establish a special constabulary with provincial inspectors and local chief constables who received appointments from Dublin Castle, leaving resident magistrates to select local constables, a power that the Dublin bureaucracy gradually usurped.

While often expressing enthusiasm for reform and progress in Ireland, Whigs and Radicals were so confined by the dogma of *laissez faire* economics, that they were blind to the realities of Ireland. Despite good intentions, the British left was confused by the complexities of the Irish Question. Since Ireland did not fit into any of the neat categories of their economic dogmas, the Whigs and Radicals chose to establish law and order and defend property rather than change the Irish situation. In 1836, a Whig government improved and reorganized the county constabulary, putting more control in the hands of Dublin Castle. This armed, paramilitary police force, renamed in 1867 the Royal Irish Constabulary—half soldiers, half policemen who lived in barracks—became a model security force, which was imitated in other parts of the empire.

FROM PROTESTANT PATRIOTISM TO CATHOLIC NATIONALISM

After the Union, Protestant patriotism faded away. All segments of the Protestant community united in praise and defense of the British connection. Once the most fervent of eighteenth-century patriots, Ulster Nonconformists emerged as the most enthusiastic friends of Britain. This shift in opinion was related to economics. Belfast linen mills and shipyards directed northeast Ulster into the main stream of the British economy. Ulster businessmen and industrialists joined the landed aristocracy and gentry in their own province and from the rest of Ireland in insisting that the Union was essential to Irish prosperity. Of course they buttressed economic arguments with the passions of Protestant nativism. The Orange Order spoke for Irish Protestant unionism.

With the Protestant community for Union, the Catholic population was the only hope for the patriot tradition. Irish Catholics had the grievances to launch a liberation movement, but they were too depressed and degraded for effective political action. Except for a Defender cell in Dublin that articulated a comprehensive radical program, most secret societies continued to confine their protests to rents, tithes, and excessive clerical dues. Peasants could not depend on members of the Catholic upper- and middle-classes for leadership. These gentlemen were timidly agitating for Catholic emancipation only to better their own social and professional status.

As far as anti-Union activity was concerned, things were relatively quiet in Ireland from 1800 until the 1820's. Only Robert Emmet's 1803 rebellion disturbed the calm. Emmet, the brother of Thomas Addis Emmet, one of the founders of the of the Society of United Irishmen, was a pathetic figure as an insurrectionist. He could not persuade the French to send troops to assist an Irish revolution, he could not keep his mouth shut, he could not keep informers from infiltrating his organization, and he led an insurrection that degenerated into a Dublin street brawl. Following his conviction for treason and before the death sentence, Emmet delivered a speech from the dock that converted his failure into a glorious legend. In his address to judge, jury, and the people of Ireland, young Emmet defended revolutionary nationalism, condemned British rule as oppression, and called on future generations to take up his burden. He asked his fellow countrymen to postpone any memorials to him until their nation was free: "When my country takes her place among the nations of the earth, then, and not until then, let my epitaph be written."

With his death on the gallows, Emmet joined Wolfe Tone at the head of what would become a long list of patriot martyrs. More talented men would serve the cause of Irish nationalism, and many of them would accomplish more for their people, but none would be better loved. Emmet's youth, idealism, zeal, and rhetoric captured the Irish imagination. His portrait became a patriotic shrine in Irish homes. Parents recited the speech from the dock to their children, and often named their sons Emmet or Robert Emmet—this was particularly true of the Irish in America. Thomas Moore, the first popular poet of Irish nationalism, contributed to the Emmet myth:

> *Oh, breathe not his name! Let it*
> *sleep in the shade,*
> *Where cold and unhonored his relics*
> *are laid;*
> *Sad, silent, and dark be the tears*

> *that he shed,*
> *As the night-dew that falls on the*
> *grass o'er his head.*

While Emmet contributed to the inspirational myths of Irish nationalism, Daniel O'Connell created its reality. He was born on August 6, 1775, in County Kerry where the Atlantic pounds the southwest coast of Ireland. The O'Connells managed to maintain their property through the penal period without changing their religion, and they supplemented the family fortune by smuggling luxury goods from the Continent. Like other members of the Catholic gentry, some O'Connells found fame and fortune by serving Bourbons or Hapsburgs. Daniel's uncle, Daniel Charles, was a French count and lieutenant general in the French army.

Daniel's father was Morgan O'Connell, but his childless Uncle Maurice adopted him as his heir. Since the Penal Laws banned Catholic education in Ireland, Maurice sent his nephew to France and then to Belgium for schooling. The advancing armies of the French Revolution forced the young O'Connell to finish his secondary-school studies in England. While he was there the Irish Parliament amended the Penal Laws to permit Catholic entry into the legal profession. O'Connell studied at the Lincoln's Inn, London, and the King's Inn, Dublin in hopes of becoming a barrister. While living in London he began to read William Godwin, Thomas Paine, Adam Smith, and Jeremy Bentham. They converted him to a permanent adherence to political radicalism and, for a time, to religious indifference. Though he returned to the Catholic faith, he remained a loyal friend and disciple of Bentham.

In Dublin, O'Connell continued his study of radical literature, joined and became Grand Master of a Masonic lodge, spoke out for parliamentary reform, became a fringe member of the Society of United Irishmen, attended debates in the House of Commons, and decided that someday he would sit in College Green as the Catholic Grattan, increasing the liberties and ending the serfdom of his people. O'Connell somewhat balanced his left-wing tendencies by enlisting in a lawyer's yeomen corp which was assigned the task of preserving order in a city saturated with the spirit and talk of insurrection.

As rebellion approached, O'Connell left Dublin for Kerry, fearing that his political opinions would lead to arrest. When he learned of Wexford, O'Connell expressed shock. In his diary he wrote: "Good God! What a brute man becomes when ignorant and oppressed! Oh liberty, what horrors are perpetrated in thy name! May every virtuous revolutionary remember the horrors of Wexford."[1] O'Connell's reaction was not a change of heart. In

---

[1] Arthur Houston, *Daniel O'Connell: His Early Life and Journal, 1795–1802*, London: Pitman and Co., 1906, p. 231. Reprinted by permission.

1796, when he learned that Wolfe Tone and a French invasion fleet were in Bantry Bay he commented in his journal:

I know that the victories of the French would be attended with bad consequences. The Irish people are not sufficiently enlightened to be able to bear the sun of freedom. Freedom would dwindle into licentiousness. They would rob, they would murder. The altar of liberty totters when it is supported only with carcasses. The liberty which I look for is that which would increase the happiness of mankind. In the service of this liberty I have devoted my life and whatever portions of talent I may have or acquire.[2]

O'Connell's hostility to Irish revolutionary violence continued after 1798. He did not admire Robert Emmet:

Young Emmet is, they say, certainly arrested in Dublin. If he has been concerned in the late insurrection of which I fancy there is no doubt—he merits and will suffer the severest punishment. For my part I think pity would be almost thrown away upon the contriver of the affair of the 23rd of July. A man who could coolly prepare so much bloodshed, so many murders—and such horrors of every kind has ceased to be an object of compassion.[3]

O'Connell's antipathy to the United Irishmen and to Emmet was not caused by pacifism or a rejection of revolution in every time or place. He often praised the American founding fathers, and proudly sent his son, Morgan, to join Bolivar's liberation movement in South America. In the early 1820's, he volunteered to raise a yeomen corp against secret societies and Orangemen. O'Connell opposed rebellion in Ireland because he feared that it would unleash the passions of men made bitter and ignorant by centuries of oppression and degradation. He felt it would drive them mad, making them kill innocent people and destroy property. Then they would have to face the vengeance of a Protestant Ascendancy that could call on the might of the British army. The events of the year 1798 proved to O'Connell that revolutionary violence would lead to the reduction rather than the increase of Irish freedom. He was convinced that Irish liberty and democracy could only be achieved through constitutional means: the application of mobilized and disciplined public opinion.

O'Connell became the most successful barrister in Ireland, and a folk hero in his own time. To the Irish Catholic population he was "the Counsellor," the man who successfully challenged the Protestant Ascendancy at their own game, British law, in their own arena, the court room. O'Connell employed an alien legal code to defend his own people, and to expose the tyranny of British rule. He told judges and juries that the crimes of his Catholic clients were reactions to poverty and injustice.

[2]Houston, *Daniel O'Connell: His Early Life and Journal*, p. 155.
    [3]Maurice R. O'Connell, editor, *The Correspondence of Daniel O'Connell, Vol. 1, 1792–1814*, New York: Barnes and Noble, p. 99.

CATHOLIC EMANCIPATION

In 1800, O'Connell opposed the Union, insisting that Irish sovereignty was even more important than Catholic emancipation. Four years later he joined the Catholic Committee, and soon he became its leading personality. The Committee annually sent a Catholic emancipation petition to Henry Grattan, who was serving in the United Kingdom Parliament. Grattan then submitted it to the Commons. Emancipation did have friends at Westminster. A number of Whigs and a few Tories thought that political expediency and the welfare of the Union necessitated Catholic civil rights. But most of them disliked popery. In exchange for emancipation they wanted securities that the Pope would never appoint anti-British Irish bishops. Advocates of securities suggested that either a committee of respectable and loyal Catholic laymen or the government should have veto powers over the appointment of Catholic prelates in the United Kingdom.

This demand for securities was not unusual in an age when governments all over Europe and Latin America influenced episcopal appointments, and Rome accepted this arrangement as a way of maintaining cordial relations with the nation states. Cardinals in the Curia looked forward to friendly associations with the British government that could lead to a dual religious establishment in Ireland.

British Catholics were quite willing to sacrifice some of their church's independence to achieve first-class citizenship in the United Kingdom. Upper- and middle-class Irish Catholics were also prepared to allow a large measure of government control over the church because emancipation would bring them respectability, access to political office and influence, and professional opportunities and improved status. However, most Irish Catholic bishops and priests opposed any veto over episcopal appointments. Since it was independent of state interference and financed through the generosity of the laity, the Catholic church in Ireland, though poor, was more vital and less corrupt than the church on the Continent. Common adversities had established a bond of affection and trust between priest and people. There was no reason why the Irish bishops should risk disturbing the relatively healthy condition of Irish Catholicism by endorsing a Rome-Westminster alliance. But Irish prelates, conditioned by the Penal Laws, were accustomed to operating in the shadows. They found it difficult to resist Roman, British, and Irish pressures in favor of securities. They feared that a strong opposition might invite no-popery reprisals. In 1815, the Irish, Catholic hierarchy found an ally and advocate in O'Connell. Bolstered by the weight of ecclesiastical opinion, his influence smashed the securities compromise, seriously damaged emancipation prospects in Parliament, and divided the Catholic Committee into pro- and anti-veto camps.

O'Connell's hostility to securities was caused by a variety of motives.

By 1815 he was once more a practicing Catholic. From that perspective he believed that government interference had a negative impact on religion. As a Benthamite radical he argued that British government influence over the appointment of Catholic bishops violated the principle of church-state separation. But O'Connell's opposition to the veto had nuances beyond Catholic or radical motives. If the British government established any kind of control over the Catholic church in Ireland, it would destroy O'Connell's long range strategy. He had confidence that the agitation for Catholic emancipation contained the seeds of Irish nationalism. Catholicism was the symbol of an independent Irish identity; it was the only thing that commanded the loyalty of the Irish masses. O'Connell intended to use the Catholic civil rights movement as an instrument for creating a mobilized and disciplined Irish nationalist opinion and for converting Catholic identity into an Irish self-consciousness. His sabotage of the veto compromise delayed emancipation and split the Catholic community, but it preserved the independence of the church, thus sustaining the prospects of Irish nationalism.

In 1823 Catholic factionalism came to an end when O'Connell joined proponents of the veto, Thomas Wyse and Richard Lalor Sheil, in a new organization, the Catholic Association. This new initiative was was not particularly successful until 1825 when O'Connell improvised a strategy which brought energy and enthusiasm to the emancipation effort by enlisting the tenant farmer class. He extended an invitation to those who could not afford the one guinea annual dues paid by the gentry and middle class to join the Catholic Association. They could join as associate members for only a shilling a year. They could pay it in a lump sum, or at the rate of a penny a month or a farthing a week. O'Connell's new tactic was designed not only to make the emancipation cause more significant in Ireland, but to demonstrate to the British that the Irish Catholic classes and masses were united in the demand for civil rights, and that they would not be denied.

O'Connell asked the Catholic hierarchy and clergy to help him recruit members of the lower classes for the Catholic Association, suggesting that it was time for the hierarchy and clergy to emerge from the shadows of Irish life and fill the leadership vacuum created by the adhesion of the Protestant aristocracy and gentry to the Union. In making this request, he was aware of the changes that had taken place in the character of the priesthood since the founding of Maynooth in 1795. In contrast to the conservative and timid priests who returned from eighteenth-century Continental seminaries, Maynooth had spawned a generation of clergymen who had remained close to their strong farmer or middle-class origins. Like their lay relatives, they were bitter concerning the servile condition of Catholics and Catholicism. Despite government expectations, Maynooth graduates were not grateful for the mediocre education they received or the stingy grant, only £9,000 a year in 1844, which supported the seminary. And they did not look forward to subsisting on the generosity of a burdened laity. Because of the class background of Irish bishops and priests, Irish Catholicism had a democratic flavor that was missing from Catholicism on the Continent. This closeness between priest and people provided O'Connell with a well-qualified cadre of lieutenants.

At Sunday morning Mass, priests advised that all good Catholics had a religious and patriotic obligation to join the Catholic Association. As the people left the chapel, a local agent was outside to enlist recruits for the Association and to collect the "Catholic Rent." He then forwarded the shillings, pence, and farthings, along with the names of the contributors, to headquarters, the Corn Exchange, Burgh Quay, Dublin. This small fee required to participate in the Emancipation movement was a sacrifice for the ordinary urban or rural Irish Catholic. In order to make his contribution he might have to reduce his enjoyment of the simple pleasures of the poor, liquor and tobacco. But this sacrifice intensified involvement. For the first time since the Penal times Irish Catholics lifted their eyes and their knees from the ground. O'Connell had given them not only a cause, but pride, dignity, and hope. The people became so intensely involved in the emancipation agitation, so keen on victory, that they turned from drink and violence. According to police reports, the activities of secret societies declined, as did faction fighting and drunkenness.

For the first time since the Treaty of Limerick, the British and the Irish Protestant Ascendancy faced a formidable challenge from the Catholic Irish. Under the direction of O'Connell, the Catholic Association had become an unofficial native parliament, where all Irish grievances, democracy, tenant-rights and repeal of the union as well as emancipation could be discussed. In 1826, he decided to demonstrate the Association's power by having it endorse pro-emancipation candidates in the general election. At the urging of their priests, forty-shilling freehold voters defied their landlords' instructions about how to vote. They defeated the mighty Beresford family in Waterford, which inspired similar victories in Louth, Westmeath, Armagh, Cork City, and Galway.

In 1828, the British Prime Minister, the Duke of Wellington, appointed C. E. Vesey Fitzgerald, an Irish Protestant landlord, to the Cabinet as President of the Board of Trade, forcing him to seek re-election from County Clare. Fitzgerald was a decent landlord, and a friend to Catholic emancipation, but the Association was determined to replace a Tory Cabinet minister with a Catholic opponent, and persuaded O'Connell to declare his candidacy. After a bitter campaign, in which both the Ascendancy and the Catholic Association invested their resources, the priest again proved more powerful than the landlord. O'Connell won by a large majority. Sir Robert Peel, the Home Secretary and the Tory leader in the House of Commons, admitted that the Clare election demonstrated that tenant farmers no longer supported their landlords or were intimidated by them.

In deliberating their response to O'Connell's victory, emancipation opponents Wellington and Peel had to ponder a number of unpleasant alternatives. By conceding Catholic emancipation they might encourage further Irish agitations, antagonize British no-popery opinion, and perhaps open the door to political reform in Britain. By ignoring the Clare results and continuing to exclude Catholics from full civil rights, they would give credence to the charges that Ireland was not fully integrated into the United Kingdom, perhaps promote an alliance between the forces of Catholic Emancipation and parliamentary reform, and possibly provoke insurrection. While O'Connell emphasized law and order and constitutional methods, he still presented an implied threat of violence associated with the emancipation effort. O'Connell frequently reminded government ministers that if they did not want to come to terms with him, a reasonable man, they would have to deal with men of violence. If they frustrated the constitutional endeavors of his followers, Irish Catholics would have no choice but to turn to the pike and the gun.

In an April 3, 1829 letter to Sir Walter Scott, Peel revealed government fears of revolution in Ireland:

> We were watching the movements of tens of thousands of disciplined fanatics—abstaining from every excess and every indulgence, and concentrating every passion and feeling on the single object—with hundreds of police and of soldiers, half of whom were Roman Catholics. That half, faithful and prepared, I have no doubt, to do their duty, but is it consistent with common prudence and common sense to expect such scenes and to incur such risk of contagion?[4]

What "risk of contagion"? There was always the possibility that an Irish insurrection might stir fires of discontent in Britain where the urban masses suffered the economic, social, and psychological assaults of the Industrial Revolution. And Whig and Radical M.P.s in the House of Commons might extend sympathy to Irish rebels denied civil rights, making it difficult for the government to get full parliamentary support for repressive measures in Ireland.

Of course Britain had the strength to cope with Irish rebellion, and the events of 1798 indicated that she could depend on Catholic soldiers and constables to do their duty. But in addition to the potential consequences to Britain of violence in Ireland, the suppression of an Irish rebellion would be costly in terms of lives and property and it would inflict wounds, perhaps mortal, on the Union. After smashing the Catholic Association without rec-

---

[4]Peel Papers, British Museum, Add. MS 40399 quoted in Galen Broeker, *Rural Disorder and Police Reform in Ireland, 1812–1836*, Toronto: University of Toronto Press, 1970, p. 179.

ognizing its constitutional victory, Britain would have to abandon hope for reconciling Catholics to the British connection. She would have to station troops in Ireland not as a security force but as a permanent army of occupation. Bitter Ireland would exist as an open sore, draining away the energy, and straining the resources of the United Kingdom.

Wellington and Peel chose prudence over principle. They were not, however, gracious losers. Previous to introducing a Catholic Relief Bill into the House of Commons, the government outlawed the Catholic Association. The Bill also disfranchised the forty-shilling freeholders and made Catholics subscribe to an oath of allegiance they found insulting before taking their seats in Parliament. Since O'Connell's victory in Clare took place before the Relief Bill, the House of Commons made him go through the time and expense of another election.

Following the March, 1829 Relief Act, Catholics were eligible to sit in both houses of Parliament and qualified for all offices in the United Kingdom except Regent, Lord Chancellor, Lord Lieutenant, and Lord Chancellor of Ireland. The loss of the forty-shilling voters reduced the Catholic electorate from around 200,000 to close to 16,000. Still, the nervous Duke of Wellington feared the return of sixty Catholic M.P.s. This was a ludicrous assessment of political reality. Most Catholics could not afford to play the game of aristocratic British politics. Election expenses were forbidding, costs of London residences were high, and salaries for M.P.s were nonexistent. As late as 1874, after considerable extensions of the franchise, adoption of the secret ballot, and an increase in Catholic wealth and position, only forty-nine Catholic M.P.s represented Ireland in the House of Commons. Until Parnell organized a strong, democratically flavored Irish party in the 1880's, Protestant Irish nationalists and liberals joined with Catholic Whigs and nationalists to defend Irish Catholic interests at Westminster.

Many critics of O'Connell have said that the surrender of the forty-shilling vote in exchange for emancipation betrayed Irish nationalism and democracy. O'Connell tried to save the forty-shilling voters but was unable to do so. His effort reflected a sense of honor rather than conviction. He honestly believed that a reduction of the franchise might aid rather than hurt Catholic influence. O'Connell feared peasant voters who could be intimidated by landlords, and he doubted that they could continue to act on the courage of their convictions. And O'Connell feared that landlords might retaliate for the rebellion of the forty-shilling voters in 1826 and 1828 by clearing their estates. He also had to consider the wishes of British Catholics. Upper- and middle-class British Catholics had no interest in defending the political influence of Irish tenant farmers. Because they were contemptuous of Irish Catholics, O'Connell did not like them as a group, but he did not want to divide United Kingdom Catholic opinion during the emancipation crisis.

Catholic emancipation had almost as much impact on the course of British as it did on Irish history. During the 1828–1829 crisis, ultra-Tories rallied British no-popery in a furious attempt to preserve Protestant Ascendancy and Catholic servility. When defeated, they turned the rage of their frustrations on Wellington and Peel, particularly the latter. Peel lost his Oxford seat and had to find a new constituency, Westbury. Catholic emancipation drove some ultra-Tories to embrace parliamentary reform, since they felt public opinion had been sounder on the popery question than the cowardly compromisers in Parliament.

In 1830, bitter Tories collaborated with Whigs, Radicals, and Irish Repealers to bring down Wellington's government, clearing the way for parliamentary reform. In their blind rage, Tory extremists lost their political perspective. They realized too late that the British masses, no matter how anti-Catholic, posed as much of a threat to aristocracy as did emerging Irish Catholic nationalists. Their flirtation with reform was a brief deviation from normal conduct, but their distrust of Peel remained a permanent fixture of the Tory mind. In time, the pressures of Irish discontent combined with other issues would widen and deepen the fissures in the Tory party, finally splitting it into moderate and reactionary wings.

While Catholic emancipation sowed seeds of discord among the British right, it instructed the left. British Radicals, in their successful campaign to broaden the base of parliamentary government, applied O'Connell's tactics for mobilizing and disciplining public opinion, collecting funds, and intimidating the power structure with the threat of reform or revolution. During the 1830's and 1840's, a variety of British reform organizations resembled the Catholic Association.

Beyond precedent and tactics, Catholic emancipation contributed to the advance of British democracy. George IV had put the prestige of the monarchy behind the opposition to Catholic civil rights. Therefore, the Catholic Relief Bill was a defeat for the crown. And in 1829 the House of Lords lost an important skirmish with the House of Commons; an important early episode in a continuing conflict that would not end until the victory of the latter in the Parliament Act of 1911, legislation also associated with an Irish crisis.

Although Wellington and Peel made concessions to Irish agitation to avoid various dangers, one historian has described their actions as "strategic withdrawal rather than surrender," a way of rallying support behind law and order. The Prime Minister hoped "Emancipation, passed into law with proper safeguards, would check the insidious growth of democracy in Ireland, strengthen the ministry by rallying English 'Catholics' to it, and thus enable Wellington to get the support from Parliament necessary to halt agitation and deal with possible revolution."[5] These concessions did maintain peace, but Irish Catholics were not as grateful as many Englishmen thought they should be. They properly interpreted the results of their agitation as a hard earned victory against a surly foe, not as a generous gift from their British partners in the Union.

Although Catholic emancipation bestowed few benefits on the Catholic peasant masses, it was a major victory for Catholic solidarity. Its success contributed to the growth of Irish nationalism by convincing the people that mobilized Irish opinion could influence the decisions of British politicians. From a negative perspective, Catholic emancipation intensified tensions between the Protestant and Catholic communities. Catholic Irish nationalism speeded the demise of Protestant Irish patriotism. Throughout the nineteenth century, O'Connell and subsequent popular leaders insisted that Irish nationalism exclude sectarianism and pleaded with Protestants to join with Catholics in seeking self-government. These appeals fell on deaf ears because Protestants remained convinced that Irish nationalism represented the ambitions of a Catholic democracy intent on destroying Protestant privilege and seizing Protestant property. Certain that the Union protected them, during the nineteenth century Irish Protestants once more became the British colony in Ireland.

O'CONNELL AND THE WHIG ALLIANCE

Mounted on a Premier's back
Lash the Ministerial pack,
At thy nod they hold their places,
Crack their sinews, grind their faces,
Tho' thy hand has stabbed their mother,
They would fawn and call thee brother...
          (The *Times*, London, November 26, 1835)

When O'Connell entered the British House of Commons he was approaching fifty-five years of age. Since he could not afford to abandon his law practice, which provided him with an annual income of about £9,000, his friends organized an annual tribute from the Irish people. During the first year they donated £13,000, but they never contributed that much again. O'Connell's enemies ridiculed the tribute, and described him as the "Big

[5]Galen Broeker, *Rural Disorder and Police Reform in Ireland*, pp. 180, 181.

DANIEL O'CONNELL
1775–1847

Daniel O'Connell built modern Irish nationalism on the foundations of the Catholic Emancipation agitation. As a champion of human rights and freedom throughout the world, he implanted the values of liberal democracy in the soil of Irish nationalism. (Photo painted and engraved by R. M. Hodgetts, courtesy of the National Gallery of Ireland.)

Beggarman," claiming he had a vested interest in agitation. He replied that his contribution of time and talent and his sacrifice of career prospects earned him the gratitude of the people. To him, the tribute was as Charles Greville said in his *Memoirs*, "alike honorable to the contributors and the recipient; it was an income nobly given and nobly earned."

Few British political pundits expected O'Connell to make the transition from successful Irish agitator to influential parliamentarian. They said that the sophistication of Westminster was a different world from the crudity of Irish mass meetings or the halls of the Catholic Association. Many of them expected "the uncrowned King of Ireland" to be revealed as just a vulgar blarney man. O'Connell quickly proved them wrong by making his mark as an effective and conscientious M.P., a superb debator, a tough advocate, and a wily negotiator.

During the early 1830's, O'Connell sat in the House of Commons in a dual capacity: as leader of an Irish national movement dedicated to repeal of the Union, and as a prominent Benthamite Radical advocating prison and legal reforms, black and Jewish emancipation, and political democracy. In the former role he commanded the first Irish parliamentary party, in the latter he led the forces of change. Bentham expected O'Connell to be the floor leader of his reform program. O'Connell responded by assuring the father of Utilitarianism that he was "your zealous if you will not allow me to call myself your humble disciple." He said that he was proud to be Bentham's "mouthpiece" in the House of Commons, and instrument for the "greatest possible good to the greatest possible number."[6]

O'Connell was a sincere Benthamite. In fact, his nationalism was more ideologically flexible than his radicalism. His radical rigidity limited his effectiveness as an Irish nationalist because the radical creed was designed for the problems of industrial Britain, not agrarian Ireland. O'Connell's *laissez faire* evangelicism led him to attack many of the practices of Dublin trade unionism, thus antagonizing the Irish urban proletariat. His demand for free trade promoted British industrialism to the neglect of Irish agriculture. O'Connell helped author the democratic program of Chartism in its initial stages. Later he attacked the movement, partly because he believed Chartism contained elements of violence. O'Connell's frequent denunciations of Chartism damaged the prospects of an alliance between Irish nationalists and British working-class protesters.

O'Connell's radicalism did contain qualifications. Although he opposed the House of Lords, he revered the monarchy. His sentimental affection for "the little Queen" often made him appear groveling and silly. Continental

---

[6]Although much of the O'Connell-Bentham correspondence has been published in John Bowring, editor, *The Works of Jeremy Bentham*, Edinburgh, 1943–1959, MS 5769, the National Library of Ireland, contains additional letters between the two men.

radicals praised O'Connell as a great tribune of the people, a man who had defied aristocracy and advanced democracy. But he was reluctant to identify with the Continental left because it included enemies of organized religion and promoters of revolution.

By papal standards, however, O'Connell's opinions were dangerous: the denial of the Pope's temporal power, support for religious toleration and freedom of conscience, and insistence on the principle of church-state separation. But Rome never officially condemned O'Connell as it did French Catholic liberals like Lamennais, Montalembert, and Lacordaire. As the leader of the Irish Catholic masses, he was untouchable. O'Connell never intellectually confronted the paradoxes of his conflicting loyalties—Rome and Bentham. He told the latter that his faith and politics supplemented each other, both working to purify man's physical environment.

O'Connell never had any confidence in the Union. His intellectual ancestors were the Irish Protestant Whig patriots of the eighteenth century. He argued that only an Irish legislature could respond to Irish problems; only Irish politicians could comprehend Irish needs. O'Connell believed that without the British presence, Irish Protestants and Catholics would be forced to resolve the religious and class antagonisms that divided the country and retarded her progress. He was certain that the British Parliament would never bring peace or prosperity to Ireland:

> It is vain to expect any relief from England. All parties there concur in hatred to Ireland and Catholicity; and it is also founded in human nature that they should, for they have injured us too much ever to forgive us.[7]

Despite his hatred of the Union, his desire for the restoration of the Irish Parliament, and his profound insight into the psychology of prejudice, O'Connell was prepared to cooperate pragmatically with British politicians to achieve some improvement in the Irish situation. His support kept the Whigs in office during the 1830–1832 Reform Bill crisis, but he was disappointed in the results. He had hoped that a reformed Parliament would reflect Ireland's population growth, but the 93,000 post-Reform Bill Irish electorate was less than the one that preceded emancipation, and the number of Irish M.P.s only increased from 100 to 105 (a subsequent Reform Bill reduced that figure to 103). A £10 household franchise had a smaller check on the power of the landed aristocracy and gentry in Ireland than it did in Britain. One person in 115 voted in Irish county elections compared to one in twenty-four in England, one in twenty-three in Wales, and one in forty-five in Scotland. In the boroughs the ratio was as follows: Ireland, one

[7]O'Connell to Archbishop John MacHale, July 25, 1840, W. J. Fitzpatrick, editor, *The Correspondence of Daniel O'Connell*, Vol II, London: John Murray, 1888, p. 246.

in twenty-two; England and Wales, one in seventeen; and Scotland, one in twenty-seven. As a democrat. O'Connell insisted that population should determine parliamentary representation. This would have increased Irish M.P.s by more than fifty. British leaders, however, insisted that Parliament represented property not public opinion, and that 105 M.P.s adequately represented Irish property.

Although O'Connell received little benefit for Ireland from the Reform Bill, the Whigs did give his country a national system of nondenominational elementary education. Disputes between Anglicans and Nonconformists blocked state-supported mass education in Britain, but British politicians were less reluctant to experiment in the satellite island. At first Irish Protestant leaders denounced "Godless education", while Catholic spokesmen welcomed the opportunity to lift the cultural level of their people. Later, nudged by Catholic bishops, Irish nationalists condemned the national schools and demanded a state financed system of denominational education. Protestants then switched to a defense of the national schools as preferable to an educational system dominated by popery.

No doubt British politicians expected the national schools to Anglicize the Irish, and many Irish nationalists have judged them to be instruments of British cultural imperialism destroying the Gaelic language and tradition. But even before the national schools began to function, the Irish language was dying. In 1851, before the schools had acquired much influence, only ten percent of the Irish people could not speak English, and only thirty percent could speak Irish. (Very few people could both read and write Irish, probably less than a thousand). Although the national schools did emphasize English cultural values, by teaching the Irish how to read they exposed them to nationalist as well as British propaganda, and many schoolmasters taught from a nationalist perspective. National schools did not long remain nondenominational, except in theory. Gradually the British government turned local schools over to clerical managers. In Catholic areas priest managers and Catholic teachers expressed nationalist and Catholic viewpoints.

O'Connell could not afford completely to abandon the agitation in Ireland to concentrate on parliamentary strategy. In 1832, he took command of a widespread movement against the payment of tithes to support the Protestant church. He did so to prevent a revival of secret agrarian societies that were attempting to exploit a volatile situation in an effort to undercut constitutional efforts to remedy Irish grievances.

In 1834, Fergus O'Connor and other impatient nationalist M.P.s persuaded a reluctant O'Connell to bring Repeal before the House of Commons. When he did so, only one British M.P. voted to restore the Irish Parliament. This massive defeat convinced O'Connell that Repeal, like Catholic emancipation, would result from agitation in Ireland rather than from arguments in the British Parliament. He then turned nationalist strategy at Westminster toward collaboration with the Whigs. O'Connell's parliamentary strategy polarized British politics, defining left and right and encouraged the evolution of factions into parties. His opposition to coercion bills and the tithe split the Whigs into conservatives and moderates, similar to the process by which Catholic emancipation divided the Tories in the 1820's. In 1834, powerful Whigs like Edward Stanley and the Earl of Ripon, the Duke of Richmond, and Sir James Graham resigned from the Cabinet rather than accept the idea that the government could violate property rights and reduce the influence of the Protestant church by using the surplus revenue of the church in Ireland for general public services. By the end of the 1830's, these defectors joined the Tory party, renamed the Conservative party.

Whig leaders were reluctant to embrace the Repeal party, considering it "a species of a foreign body lodged in the entrails of the British Parliament."[8] But in the mid-1830's, the political winds shifted and the Whigs were forced to court O'Connell to remain in office. In the 1835 Lichfield House Compact, they promised him reform and good government for Ireland in exchange for the cessation of agitation against the Union and support for Whig policy in the House of Commons. O'Connell then asked the Irish people to be patient while the Melbourne administration attempted to prove that the Union could bring justice, sound and equitable government, individual freedom, and prosperity to Ireland.

O'Connell soon became disenchanted with his bargain. The government commuted the tithe to a land tax without appropriating surplus church revenue for public needs, gave Ireland a Municipal Reform Bill with a franchise more restricted than the one in Britain, and imposed an Irish Poor Law. The Poor Law did most to convince O'Connell that there was no salvation for Ireland within the confines of the United Kingdom.

An Irish Poor Law Commission recommended a Poor Law for Ireland but rejected the workhouse system then operating in Britain. Commisioners defined one-third of the Irish population as paupers. They said that taxes collected to provide workhouse space for that many people would damage an already fragile Irish economy and push many more Irish men and women below the poverty level. Instead of the British solution, the Commission recommended public works to provide employment, at the same time increasing the potential of the Irish economy, and government sponsored and financed emigration. Loyal to the dogmas of *laissez faire*, the Whigs rejected the advice of Irish experts, insisting that the government could not interfere with the Irish economy. They argued that since the workhouse system had

[8]Elie Halevy, *The Triumph of Reform*, London: Ernest Benn, 1965, p. 65.

curbed mendicancy in Britain, it would no doubt do the same in Ireland. So Ireland got a poor law based upon British precedents rather than Irish needs.

The Whigs kept one promise to O'Connell. They gave Ireland good government. Thomas Drummond as Under-Secretary in Dublin Castle took significant steps to carry out the implications of Catholic emancipation. He informed landlords that property had duties as well as rights, and he appointed Catholics to government, magisterial, and legal offices. He also outlawed the Orange Order, temporarily driving the forces of bigotry underground.

3

repeal, revolution, and famine

REPEAL

After threats to resume agitating against the Union failed to prod a floundering Whig government into substantial Irish reform, O'Connell created the National Association of Ireland, which he rechristened the Loyal National Repeal Association the following year. The Repeal Association closely resembled its Catholic predecessor with its one-shilling associate membership, wardens, rent collectors, and emphasis on constitutional agitation. It also met at the Corn Exchange, Burgh Quay, Dublin. At first there was not much enthusiasm for the new agitation. No doubt O'Connell's association with the Whigs encouraged both apathy and cynicism among many of his followers. And now that emancipation had provided them with social, economic, professional, and political opportunities, many members of the Catholic upper and middle classes had lost interest in nationalism. A large number of Catholic bishops, particularly in Leinster and Munster, also thought that the Union presented possibilities for the improvement of Catholic life in Ireland, and that agitation against Ireland's participation in the United Kingdom could have negative results. British politicians and journalists enjoyed O'Connell's failure to stimulate Repeal enthusiasm. *Blackwood's* taunted him:

What can you any longer do or affect to do old gentleman to earn your honorable wages? Is there not (as the lawyers would style it) a failure of consideration? If you go on any longer collecting "the rent" may you not be liable to an indictment for obtaining money under false pretences? Poor old soul, his cuckoo cry of Repeal grows feebler and feebler, yet he must keep it up or starve.[1]

British gloaters spoke too soon. O'Connell still had the energy, talent, and ingredients for a successful agitation. The people were embittered by a meager harvest and the Poor Law. Many refused to pay poor rates; some resisted with violence. When soldiers confiscated a farmer's cattle in lieu of rates, other farmers refused to bid at auction on the livestock of their neighbors. While O'Connell had been holding hands with the Whigs at Westminster, Father Theobold Mathew's temperance crusade had kept the spirit of mass meeting alive in Ireland. As the Franciscan friar traveled the country asking the people to give up the Irish curse, drink, he signed up five million people as teetotalers. He set up local temperance organizations with reading rooms and uniformed marching bands.

The most popular newspaper in the temperance reading rooms was the *Nation*, first published in October 1842. Charles Gavan Duffy, John Blake Dillon, and Thomas Osborne Davis founded the *Nation*. Dillon and Duffy were Catholics; Davis was Anglo-Irish Protestant. Davis and Dillon had gone to Trinity College; Duffy was largely self-educated. Duffy's roots were in Monaghan; Davis was born in Cork but raised in Dublin; Dillon came from Mayo. While all three had journalism experience, Duffy was the real professional. He had been editor of the *Vindicator*, a Belfast Catholic nationalist newspaper. Dillon and Davis, already friends, met Duffy at the King's Inn where all three were preparing for admission to the Irish Bar. The young men often strolled in the Phoenix Park while discussing the prospects of Irish nationalism and the direction it should take. They decided that the time was propitious for them to communicate their ideas in a weekly newspaper.

The *Nation* was an unusual Irish nationalist newspaper. It did more than just criticize Britain, praise O'Connell, and demand Repeal. In it, Duffy, Dillon, and Davis defined and taught an Irish cultural nationalism. They wanted to make Irish opinion "racy of the soil" and to purify the Irish mind and soul through a process of de-Anglicization. What good would it be, they asked, if Ireland had her own Parliament, while the Irish people remained enslaved by the materialistic values of British culture? The *Nation* published editorials and articles on Irish history and culture, original stories and essays on Irish life, and poems on patriotic themes. It urged the Irish people to learn the history of their own country, to patronize art and literature with an Irish spirit, and to think and to speak Irish. The last objective

[1]*Blackwood's Magazine*, 53:142 (ca. 1840).

THOMAS OSBORNE DAVIS
1814–1845

Thomas Osborne Davis co-founded the Young Ireland Movement. In his editorial columns and his ballad poetry published in the *Nation,* he helped define the spirit and contents of Irish cultural nationalism. (Photo taken from Sir Charles Gavan Duffy, *Thomas Davis: The Memoirs of an Irish Patriot, 1840–46,* London, 1890.)

meant that Irish men and women should preserve the native language against the inroads of English.[2]

The *Nation's* cultural nationalism was an Irish expression of the European romantic movement, a reaction against the rationalism of the Enlightenment and the materialism and ugliness of the Industrial Revolution. To Duffy and his friends, Britain represented industrialism threatening a more spiritual Irish agrarian way of life. They argued that the dogmas of Utilitarianism, so dear to O'Connell, embodied the coarseness and materialism of British urban, industrial culture.

[2]In contrast, O'Connell, a native speaker—Dillon, Davis, and Duffy were not—thought that the preservation of Irish limited the intellectual and economic progress of the Irish people.

In many ways, the *Nation* expressed an Irish Catholic, middle-class identity crisis. This group was increasing in numbers and influence but was psychologically insecure. Snubbed by the Anglo-Irish Protestant Ascendancy, ashamed of the manners of the Irish Catholic peasantry, and desperately trying to find something of significance in the Irish historical experience, the Catholic bourgeoisie found their pride and identity in the columns of the *Nation.* Now they knew they were an important people.

About eight thousand people bought the *Nation* every week (at 6d a copy, half a day's wages for a laborer), making it the most widely circulated newspaper in the country. Its influence extended beyond its subscription list. People consulted the *Nation* in Repeal and temperance reading rooms. Throughout the country they crowded into peasant cottages to hear the local "scholar" read the new scripture of Irish nationalism. Many intelligent and idealistic members of the Irish middle class followed Davis, Dillon, and Duffy and contributed to the *Nation.* This new generation of Repealers acquired the name Young Ireland, which associated them with other European nationalist movements—Young Italy, Young Poland, even Young England—distinguishing them from O'Connell, the voice of Old Ireland and its Whig political patriotism.

In their efforts to liberate Ireland from British political and cultural bondage, Young Irelanders subordinated art to nationalism. They were journalists rather than artists, but first-rate journalists and they did advance art. Although he made his reputation publishing in Protestant papers like the *Christian Examiner,* William Carleton, the first Irish writer to penetrate the mask of Catholic peasant Ireland, and James Clarence Mangan, the most talented modern Irish poet before Yeats, contributed to the *Nation.* Young Ireland's patriotic ballads have had a lasting quality. They are still sung in Irish pubs and at Irish parties all over the English-speaking world.

Young Ireland's theoretically inclusive, nonsectarian nationalism was best expressed in Thomas Davis's *Anglo-Saxon and Celt:*

> *What matters that at different shrines*
> *We pray unto one God?*
> *What matters that at different times*
> *Our fathers won this sod?*
> *In fortune and in name we're bound*
> *By stronger links than steel;*
> *And neither can be safe nor sound*
> *But in the other's weal.*

But in contrast to the tolerant attitude expressed in this poem, Davis's emphasis on the Celtic past and the Irish historical experience, and his constant belittling of Anglo-Saxon materialism actually encouraged and perpetuated ethnic, religious, and class division in Ireland. The message of Young Ireland was far more attractive to Catholics than it was to Protestants who felt that they had a vested interest in the Union and who considered themselves the British colony in Ireland.

Although the nineteenth-century romantic nationalism of Young Ireland contrasted with O'Connell's eighteenth-century Whig patriotism, Duffy, Dillon, and Davis became active members of the Repeal Association, filling the vacuum left by the lawyers and businessmen who deserted nationalism after emancipation. And O'Connell made an alliance with Archbishop John MacHale of Tuam which gave the Association the support of a number of bishops, most of them from the West. This arrangement outlined what was to become the terms of a Catholic-nationalist alliance which has survived into the twentieth century. MacHale agreed to endorse Repeal in exchange for O'Connell's pledge to defend the educational interests of the Catholic hierarchy.

From the autumn of 1841 through the fall of 1842, O'Connell played down Repeal to concentrate on his duties as the first Catholic Lord Mayor of Dublin. But in January, 1843, he announced the Repeal Year, promising that by December the Tories once again would surrender to the demands of disciplined and mobilized Irish nationalist opinion. O'Connell assimilated the enthusiasm and discipline generated by the temperance movement, the hostility to the poor law, and the spirit of Young Ireland into a formidable agitation, despite the wishes of Father Mathew, who wanted to keep his movement nonpolitical. The Dublin Corporation and a number of town councils and Poor Law Boards of Guardians voted to petition for Repeal. Money flowed into the Repeal treasury, a considerable amount from the Irish in America and Britain. Hundreds of thousands of people gathered on hillsides all over Ireland on Sunday afternoons to listen to O'Connell tell them that they soon would be a free people. The Repeal Association functioned as an Irish parliament, promising that Repeal would be followed by a democratic suffrage with a secret ballot, tenant-right, and national prosperity. O'Connell established arbitration courts, which in some places took over the functions of British judges and juries, and he announced plans to assemble a Council of Three Hundred as a step toward forming a parliament. Anglo-Irish Protestants pleaded with the British government to rescue them from impending massacre and falsely told the authorities that French soldiers were drilling Irish rebels in the mountains.[3]

In 1843, as he did in 1828, O'Connell challenged the British govern-

---

[3]O'Connell refused to accept money from Irish-Americans who supported slavery, saying that he would not liberate Irish slaves with money earned from the blood of black slaves. English and Irish newspapers claimed that a million people gathered at Tara to hear O'Connell. The *Times* (London) called the large outdoor Repeal gatherings Monster meetings. O'Connell embraced the description.

ment with the alternative of reform or revolution—either British politicians would make concessions to constitutional agitation or the Irish people would turn to physical force. This time, Sir Robert Peel, now Prime Minister, did not flinch. O'Connell did not seem to comprehend the essential difference between Catholic emancipation and Repeal. To British politicians, granting Catholic civil rights was an unpleasant concession they might make to save the Union. Repeal would destroy the Union which the British believed essential to their national security and the maintenance of the Empire. Peel said that he would fight a civil war if necessary to preserve the Union, and then flooded Ireland with troops in anticipation of insurrection. All shades of parliamentary opinion backed the Prime Minister. This time O'Connell retreated, slowing down the pace of the agitation and instructing his followers that Irish freedom required patience and obedience to the law.

In October, when the authorities banned the last scheduled outdoor Repeal rally scheduled for Clontarf on the very eve of the day it was to take place, O'Connell sent his lieutenants out on the roads to turn the people back from a confrontation with soldiers. His ability to prevent violence in 1843 indicated O'Connell's hold on the emotions of the Irish people. Fortunately for all concerned, an abundent harvest diminished the possibility of revolutionary mischief.

Shortly after banning the Clontarf meeting, the government arrested O'Connell and a few of his lieutenants and successfully tried them for sedition. O'Connell and his associates paid their fines and went off to serve their year's sentence in prison, but the Law Lords, by a three to two verdict, reversed the Dublin conviction on the grounds that the prosecution drew up an improper indictment and tried its case with a packed jury that excluded Catholics. O'Connell's release from Richmond prison set off a national celebration—bonfires were lit on the hills of Ireland. But O'Connell, now approaching seventy, was too weary to resume mass agitation. The Repeal Association continued to hold meetings but a rapidly declining Repeal rent reflected a lack of nationalist enthusiasm.

The year 1843 was not a total defeat. The massiveness of the Repeal agitation convinced Peel that the Union was not working. But he did not believe that Irish nationalism had taken firm root in the Irish soil. Instead, he was convinced that Repeal enthusiasm was more an expression of Irish discontent than a determination to secede from the United Kingdom. Peel decided that remedial legislation would break up the "unnatural" coalition of priest, peasant, and middle class, and preserve the Union. But he would not make any concessions to Irish grievances as long as the Repeal movement was in full bloom, because such action might indicate government weakness and encourage the enemies of the British connection.

When Peel was sure that O'Connell had been defeated, he began preparations for an extensive revision of the Irish status quo by seeking the aid of Rome in curtailing clerical support of nationalism in Ireland. Through the agency of Metternich, William Petre, the government's unofficial British agent in Rome, convinced Roman authorities that Irish bishops and priests were contributing to a state of unrest in the United Kingdom. He suggested that if the Pope took steps to harness the hierarchy and clergy in Ireland, the British government would ease the financial burdens on the church in Ireland, perhaps even to the point of endowment. Impressed with the prospects of cooperation and friendship with the world's greatest power, Cardinal Fransoni, Prefect of Propaganda, sent a letter to Archbishop Crolly of Armagh asking bishops and priests to cease political activities and "to cherish among the people the quiet tranquility, and peace, which is the bond of Christianity and constantly teach by example, precept, or deed, submission to the temporal power in those matters which pertain to civil affairs. . . ." Since the Irish church in the 1840's was still Gallican in spirit, with the bishops divided into factions that followed either MacHale or Archbishop Daniel Murray of Dublin, most of the hierarchy preferred to treat the Cardinal's message as a counsel in prudence rather than a command.

With the groundwork laid in Rome, in 1844 Peel initiated the parliamentary phase of his Irish policy with a bill removing most of the restrictions on charitable bequests to Catholic institutions. This bill also established a Charitable Bequests Board, which the Prime Minister intended to employ as a means of communication between the Irish hierarchy and the government. The following year, Peel asked Parliament to increase the annual grant to Maynooth and to convert it into a permanent endowment. He expected that improved seminary education, along with a more prosperous Catholic church in Ireland, might improve the quality of the clergy, might induce more members of the Catholic gentry and upper middle class to enter the priesthood. This would diminish the peasant and provincial shopkeeper tone of Irish Catholicism. In time, an affluent church, served and led by sophisticated and well educated prelates and priests, might disengage Irish Catholicism from anti-Union activities. It would then be as politically bland and harmless as Anglicanism in the United Kingdom.

Peel also concocted a juicy morsel for the Catholic middle class. Since Trinity College was a Protestant institution, Catholics were discouraged from seeking a university education, increasing the inferiority complex that tied them to nationalism. Peel attempted to remedy this situation by creating a new, non-denominational Queen's University with constituent colleges in Belfast, Galway, and Cork. The campus in Belfast would serve Presbyterians, the ones in Cork and Galway would appeal to Catholics. University education would increase the sophistication of the Irish Catholic middle class, giving them interests and ambitions transcending nationalism.

Peel included tenant farmers in his vision of a reconstructed Ireland happily assimilated into the United Kingdom. Since he realized that poverty and insecurity fed agrarian discontent, he decided to reform the Irish land system by limiting landlord prerogatives and increasing the security of tenant farmers. Peel appointed Lord Devon, an Englishman with an Irish estate who sympathized with the plight of Irish peasants, as chairman of a commission to investigate landlord-tenant relations as preliminary to reform legislation. The Devon Commission accumulated valuable information, but when the government introduced a moderate tenant-right bill based on its findings, both Whigs and Tories opposed the measure as a violation of property rights, forcing Peel to abandon this portion of his Irish policy.

Parliament did pass the Colleges Bill, the Charitable Bequests Act, and the Maynooth Bill. O'Connell praised the government for its generosity to Maynooth, but attacked the Bequests Act as insufficient and as a menace to the liberty of the church. In opposing the Bequests Act, O'Connell, through information he received from Paul Cullen, Rector of the Irish College in Rome, exposed Peel's negotiations with the Holy See, interpreting them as an effort to arrange a concordat between the Pope and the British government at the expense of Irish nationalism and Catholicism. He accused those bishops serving as commissioners on the Bequests Board of being agents of British intrigue.

O'Connell also attacked the establishment of the Queen's University as anti-Catholic in intent, and insisted that the Catholic hierarchy should have a voice in curriculum planning and faculty appointments. His vehement criticism of the Queen's University surprised many Repealers, who thought it contradicted his liberal political principles. He had always championed separation of church and state, favored the mingling of Catholics and Protestants in one Irish community, and condemned sectarianism as divisive.

O'Connell's endorsement of separate Catholic education was not necessarily a revision of former opinions. Catholics who defend separation of church and state have never accepted the notion that this principle excluded religious schools from public funds. But O'Connell's attack on the Colleges Bill had more to do with tactics than ideology. He was honoring his commitment to Archbishop MacHale to support the educational demands of the hierarchy. During the 1840's, MacHale was at the center of the campaign against the national schools, insisting that they endangered the faith of Catholic students and served as instruments of Protestant proselytism. He declared that Catholics could never accept an educational program without a religious foundation and that the bishops had a right and a duty to form and shape the the intellectual and moral values of the Catholic community.

In opposing the Bequests Act, O'Connell scored some points against Peel's effort to diminish the Catholic component in Irish nationalism. His exposure of British negotiations in Rome forced Archbishop Crolly to publish Cardinal Fransoni's letter to the hierarchy. The contents of this letter antagonized Irish nationalist opinion and persuaded many bishops to announce publicly that they were opposed to any concordat between Rome and Westminster that would regulate Irish Catholicism. In attacking the Colleges Bill, however, O'Connell created dissension within the Repeal Association. Young Irelanders understood that Peel intended the new colleges to wean the Catholic middle class away from nationalism, but they were convinced that a university situation involving dialogue between Catholics and Protestants would increase and strengthen nationalism by developing an ecumenical Irish cultural community.

In the long run the Catholic hierarchy succeeded in frustrating the hopes of both Peel and Young Ireland. Despite some government concessions to Catholic interests, at the Synod of Thurles in 1850, the bishops warned Catholics about enrolling in the colleges, and forbade the clergy from accepting teaching or administrative positions in them. Rome approved this policy, and though a considerable number of the Catholic middle class were unhappy with the decision, Archbishop Paul Cullen's forceful and unrelenting hostility to the Queen's Colleges in the next decade made Rome's will effective on the matter.

Although all sections of Irish Catholic opinion were pleased by the Maynooth Bill, the majority of British opinion was anti-Catholic, and it was furious that its government would support heresy and treason in Ireland. The Maynooth Bill revived Tory distrust of Peel, first planted when he conceded Catholic Emancipation in 1829. And the Prime Minister already was in trouble with the right wing of the Conservative Party for expressing approval of free trade in agriculture represented by the Anti-Corn Law League.

Benjamin Disraeli, a bright young man in a hurry, with talents insufficiently regarded or rewarded by Peel, decided to pin his political future on the coattails of Tory agricultural and no-popery interests. In the House of Commons, Disraeli described Peel as a "Machiavelli with dirty hands, legislating Whig measures with Tory votes," accusing the Prime Minister of sacrificing his party to satisfy his personal ego and ambitions. Peel managed to overcome Tory opposition to the Maynooth Bill with Whig and Radical votes. In defeat, the Tory faction within the Conservative Party licked its wounds, nursed a bitter hatred for "Judas" Peel, and patiently waited for revenge.

If one can assume that most Britons wanted to completely assimilate Ireland into the United Kingdom, even though such an assumption rests on shaky ground, then one could argue that given twenty years of economic prosperity, Peel's Irish policy had a reasonably good chance of reversing the momentum of Irish nationalism. By the mid-1840's, the values and ideas of O'Connell's political nationalism and Young Ireland's cultural nationalism had influenced only the middle and strong farmer classes. Many Catholics were far more loyal to O'Connell, the man, than to his principles. By reducing the religious grievances of Irish Catholics and by providing them with opportunities for economic, social, and professional mobility, British politicians might have created a situation in which Irish Catholics would have become as integrated into the United Kingdom as the Scots or the Welsh.

The anti-Maynooth furor that swept through Britain indicated that British public opinion was not particularly interested in integrating the Catholic Irish, and this certainly limited the impact of Peel's Irish strategy. Then in 1845, famine descended on Ireland, interfering with the Prime Minister's hopes for a British-Ireland. Peel reacted in a humane fashion. He fed starving people with maize imported from America, exploiting the food shortage in Ireland as an argument against the Corn Laws. Peel balanced his generosity to the suffering Irish with the introduction of a tough Coercion Bill to cope with an agrarian crime wave provoked by famine hardships.

The Coercion Bill gave Tories an opportunity to settle their score with Peel. On the evening of June 26, 1846, a few hours after the House of Lords assented to the repeal of the Corn Laws, Tories joined with Radicals, Whigs, and Irish Repealers to kill the Coercion Bill, forcing Peel to resign. The Irish Question had finally wrecked the career of the most talented British politician of the first half of the nineteenth century. Ireland would have to wait twenty years for another British leader with the courage to confront the Irish situation. By that time, the roots of political and cultural nationalism would be too deep to be eradicated by concessions short of self-government. Irish nationalism would have assumed an existence independent of the religious, economic, social, and political grievances that gave it birth.

REVOLUTION

The Repeal Association debate between O'Connell and Davis over the terms of the Colleges Bill brought to a head a feud that had been festering for some time. Differences between Old and Young Ireland involved more than a generation gap or varieties in the style and contents of romantic cultural nationalism and Whig patriotism. Young Irelanders were contemptuous of O'Connell's Benthamite Utilitarianism. Following the lead of one of their idols, Thomas Carlyle, they referred to it as "a pig philosophy." Young Irelanders also criticized O'Connell's political pragmatism, his willingness to collaborate with British Whigs.[4] They believed that his association with Catholic prelates like MacHale made it impossible for Irish nationalism to enlist Protestants. On the other hand, O'Connell thought Young Irelanders

---

[4]After the failure of Repeal in 1843, O'Connell said that he would be willing to support Federalism as an alternative if Irish Protestants would accept such an arrangement. Although Davis once expressed the same opinion, Duffy blasted O'Connell in the *Nation* for compromising Irish nationalism.

were intellectually pretentious. He belittled their literary style, indicating his preference for Charles Lever, Samuel Lover, and Charles Dickens. Some of his friends and his son John convinced him that Young Ireland's objections to the Catholic-nationalist alliance was an expression of either anti-clericalism or secularism. And he could not understand their nationalist rigidity, their all or nothing at all attitude, their unwillingness to compromise if accomodation would lead to Ireland's progress. O'Connell believed that freedom could come in short steps and that some improvement was better than none at all.

When the famine increased the level of agrarian violence, O'Connell feared that articles in the *Nation* praising the United Irishmen and the heroes of 1798 were incendiary. They could provoke hot-headed people into acts of violence, and force British authorities into cruel reprisals. In July, 1846, O'Connell introduced a resolution at a Repeal Association meeting which insisted that all members must reject physical force as a means to Irish independence or leave the organization. Young Irelanders objected to the resolution, insisting that they were constitutionalists, but refused to take an absolute stand against a future need for revolution. They argued that there were legitimate revolutions, the American for example, and that it might be necessary for the Irish to defend their rights and fight for their freedom with more than words. After a passionate defense of justified revolutions, led by Thomas Francis Meagher, Young Ireland seceded from the Repeal Association.

Shortly after this, O'Connell's health rapidly deteriorated. His concern over the Irish masses suffering the torments of hunger and fever no doubt hastened his decline. In February, 1847, he made his last speech in the House of Commons. In a voice reduced to a whisper, he pleaded for justice and mercy for his famine-wracked constituents. The Irish leader then set out on a pilgrimage to Rome. When he reached Paris, leaders of the French left came to the railway station to honor the foremost European champion of liberal-democracy. But the old man was really too ill to appreciate the tribute. O'Connell resumed his journey but died in Genoa, leaving his country in the throes of hunger and despair and the Repeal Association in the hands of his incompetent son, John. At his request, O'Connell's heart was buried in Rome and his body in Ireland.

Meanwhile, in January, 1847, Young Irelanders established the Irish Confederation to rival the Repeal Association. Its central office was in Dublin, but it had branch clubs in many cities and towns. Young Ireland continued to appeal to many members of the middle class. But rural people tended to remain loyal to the memory of O'Connell, their Liberator, following the advice of the priests who suspected that the *Nation* was the voice of anti-Catholicism, anticlericalism, and secularism.

Charles Gavan Duffy was the dominant personality in the Irish Confederation. Thomas Davis had died suddenly from scarlet fever in 1845, and John Blake Dillon was frequently incapacitated with tubercular symptoms. With one of his old colleagues dead and the other ill, Duffy turned to William Smith O'Brien for friendship and advice. As a Whig member of the Protestant aristocracy, O'Brien had championed Irish reform in the House of Commons. Ignoring the objections of his family—his mother disinherited him—he joined the Repeal Association in October 1843, in reaction to the government's ban on the Clontarf meeting and the arrest of O'Connell. While O'Connell was in prison, O'Brien presided over the Repeal Association. Later, he attempted to mediate the differences between Old and Young Ireland. By the middle of 1845, however, O'Brien had come to distrust O'Connell's dealings with British Whigs, and resented his arbitrary control over the Repeal movement. He admired the manners, intelligence, and idealism of Young Ireland, and warmly approved of its emphasis on recruiting Protestants for Repeal.

Shortly after its inception, the Irish Confederation became involved in a tactical conflict between Duffy and John Mitchel, an Ulster Nonconformist who had taken Davis' place on the *Nation*. Mitchel, stylistically an excellent journalist, was more influenced by the romantic, racist, elitist views of Thomas Carlyle than other Young Irelanders. He articulated the ideological dichotomy between liberalism and nationalism, the distinctions that separate national sovereignty and individual freedom, group solidarity from personal liberty. Like his disciple, Arthur Griffith, Mitchel could never place the Irish struggle for freedom within the context of human rights or as a universal critique of imperialism and colonialism. His post-Ireland journalistic career as an American defender of white racism and elitism revealed the kind of nationalism Mitchel represented, the antithesis of O'Connell's liberal democracy.

During 1847, Mitchel came under the influence of James Fintan Lalor, a recluse hunchback from Kilkenny, the son of Patrick Lalor, an anti-tithe agitator of the 1830's. Lalor ridiculed the Repeal movement as a distraction from the essential issue, the land. At the height of the 1843 Repeal agitation, Lalor wrote Peel advising him that O'Connell could be destroyed and the Union preserved by government concessions to the demand for tenant-right. He soon moved, however, beyond a rather modest proposal for tenant-right to a total condemnation of the landlord system.

Duffy invited Lalor to present his views on the agrarian situation and his proposed solutions in the *Nation*. In a series of letters to that newspaper, Lalor argued that Repeal was an irrelevant abstraction at a time when the reality of famine was killing people and driving them out of the country. He said that an Irish parliament would be meaningless if alien colonists continued to own most of the property of the country. He claimed that landlordism was the institution that represented British imperialism and Irish servitude. Landlordism must be destroyed; the land of Ireland must be restored to the people of Ireland. Only when Irish farmers became peasant proprietors would they be free and Ireland liberated.

Lalor urged Young Ireland to concentrate its intelligence, influence, and energy on a campaign against landlordism. He also recommended a strategy to destroy Irish manorialism: civil disobedience in the form of nonpayment of rents to landlords. Lalor warned that his tactics could lead to British coercion, which in turn might provoke revolution, but he insisted that it was a noble risk for a necessary purpose.

Mitchell accepted Lalor's analysis of the Irish situation and his strategy but went even further in advocating the nonpayment of rates as well as rent. Duffy and O'Brien rejected Mitchel's suggestion. Young Ireland's analysis of the agrarian question had always been to the left of O'Connell's—in 1842 John Blake Dillon had proposed peasant proprietorship in the *Nation*, but Duffy and O'Brien had considered it irresponsible for Mitchel to urge nonpayments of rates in the midst of famine with millions of people dependent on the Poor Law system. And O'Brien feared that the economic radicalism of Lalor and Mitchel would alienate the Protestant aristocracy, gentry, and middle class from Young Ireland by raising the specter of property confiscation and class war.

Duffy and O'Brien concentrated on a political offensive in attempting to present an alternative program to those of Lalor and Mitchel. They recommended an independent Irish party in the House of Commons, supported by nationalist-controlled agencies of local government in Ireland— municipal corporations, town councils, and Poor Law boards of guardians. O'Brien and Duffy planned that if the British Parliament refused to concede Repeal, members of the Irish party should leave Westminster, return to Dublin, establish a national legislature, and rely on the support of the Irish people to sustain them. This plan, mainly the brainchild of Duffy, included the possibility of civil disobedience to British rule. It did not exclude the possibilities of coercion followed by revolution, but it made no threats on Protestant property.

After a heated debate in the Confederation, a majority accepted the Duffy plan. Mitchel withdrew from the organization, and in January, 1848, began publishing his own newspaper, the *United Irishman*. He and his associate, Devin Reilly, advised their readers to purchase arms, instructing them in the manufacture of pikes, clubs, and an early version of the Molotov cocktail. They described how the narrow streets of Dublin could be used to ambush British soldiers. Despite all this guerilla war advice, Mitchel was a novice at revolution. He scorned secret societies and underground conspiracies. He was a romantic without any real plans, believing that an emotional, spontaneous, public reaction against hunger, injustice, and misgovernment, plus the spirit of nationalism, would generate a revolution that would spread from Dublin throughout the country. Mitchel believed that in their passion the people would liberate themselves from the alien scourge. Men like himself could only counsel and inspire with their own courage and example.

Until February, 1848, a majority of Young Irelanders dismissed revolution as hopeless, realizing that hungry peasants concerned with the basic problem of survival were not good revolutionary material. But then the successful revolution in France inspired enthusiasm among the left all over Europe. Nationalism and liberalism seemed to be marching hand-in-hand to the dawn of freedom, and Ireland certainly had to join the procession. William Smith O'Brien led a three-man delegation to Paris to congratulate leaders of the Second Republic on their victory over Bourbon tyranny and to beseech their support for the liberation of Ireland. Confederation leaders also pondered the possibility of raising an American-Irish brigade for duty in the homeland. In an effort to repair the rifts in the nationalist movement, they invited Mitchel back into the fold and began discussions with John O'Connell.

Duffy and O'Brien hoped to avoid a violent confrontation with the British. Instead, they wanted to repeat 1782. Perhaps Britain, faced with the pressures of a revolutionary plague on the Continent, Chartism at home, and aggressive nationalism in Ireland, might find it prudent to restore the Irish Parliament. If necessary, Young Ireland would fight, but not until after the harvest.

Although the potential for a successful revolution in Ireland was almost negligible, Lord Clarendon, the Viceroy, persuaded the government that insurrection was imminent. Fearing that violence in Ireland might ignite Chartist fires in Britain, the government flooded Ireland with troops and military supplies. It placed a Treason Felony Act on the statute books, followed by a Crime and Outrages Bill. The government also suspended habeus corpus throughout Ireland and applied martial law to Dublin, Waterford, and Cork.

French Republicans, eager to obtain official British recognition of the Republic, refused to aid Irish nationalism. Irish Catholic bishops and priests, for a long time suspicious of the message of the *Nation*, were further alienated from Young Ireland's nationalism when the June Days in Paris exhibited the anti-clericalism of the extreme left in France, and when Mazzini drove Pius IX from the papal states. Measuring clerical opinion and British coercion, John O'Connell broke off discussions with Young Ireland, closed down the Repeal association, and left the country.

In May, the authorities arrested O'Brien, Meagher, and Mitchel and indicted them for sedition. Meagher and O'Brien escaped conviction, but a packed jury and the new coercion acts sentenced Mitchel to Australia for fourteen years. Shortly after, the government arrested Duffy and some other nationalist journalists. Coercion finally produced revolution. Government harrassment convinced O'Brien, Dillon, and Meagher that they had no choice but to fight. They tried to raise an army in Munster, but the people there were too depresed by famine, and they had no weapons. Their priests told them to stay home and not answer the call of reckless men. O'Brien had as little talent for revolution as Robert Emmet. His conservative respect for property and fear of class war would not let him employ the guerrilla tactics that might have resulted in some success. O'Brien, rejecting the notion that a revolutionary army should live off the country, told potential recruits they must bring their own food when for many there was no food. He even told his rag-tag army not to cut down trees for barricades unless they had the permission of the owner of the land on which the trees were growing.

In late May, Young Ireland's revolution came to a pathetic conclusion when the constabulary routed O'Brien's small force in Widow McCormick's Ballingarry cabbage patch, County Tipperary. The authorities arrested, convicted, and transported O'Brien and many of his comrades. Other Young Irelanders went on the run, eventually escaping to France or America. Exiles from this comic-opera revolution joined refugees from famine in the United States, creating a new nationalist movement in the New World to liberate the Old Country.

FAMINE

The conflicts between Young Ireland and O'Connell, Mitchel, and Duffy, and the revolution of 1848 were important episodes that shaped the character, ideology, and strategy of Irish nationalism. But at the time they seemed insignificant to millions of people whose sole concern was finding enough food to stay alive. In 1845, an American potato fungus spread to Europe, making its greatest impact in Ireland, where the vast majority were dependent on that vegetable for nourishment. Blight destroyed almost the entire potato crop. The following year it did and the winter was so severe that the people had a hard time foraging under snow drifts to find nettles, weeds, or cabbage leaves to feed themselves. In 1847, the fungus did not return, but many farmers and conacre agricultural laborers were too demoralized to plant seed, did not have the money to buy seed, or had eaten the seed for sustenance. The absence of the potato disease in 1847 encouraged heavy planting in 1848, but the blight returned. The year 1849 saw the last of the fungus, but the effects of famine were felt as late as 1851.

When the famine struck Ireland, the population for the country was about eight-and-a-half million. By 1851 at least 800,000 and probably a million people had perished from famine-related causes: hunger, scurvy, fever, and cholera. Many of them had died and been buried without record. Cats, dogs, and rats devoured rotting corpses. Over a million desperate souls tried to escape death by fleeing to Britain or North America. They streamed into Cardiff, Glasgow, and Liverpool, the most important refugee center. Most of those who went to Liverpool took passage from there to the United States or Canada, sailing in over-crowded, unsanitary ships, without adequate provisions, often navigated by rapacious captains and crews. Many of the refugees carried fever with them, passing it on to other voyagers.

During a typical crossing, a third or more of the passengers might die and be buried at sea. Half of the remainder would land with fever, many to perish in jammed, makeshift infirmaries at disembarkation ports. Most immigrants arrived in Britain, Canada, or the United States without employment potential, financial resources, food, or clothing, sometimes literally entering naked into a new world. Some Irish landlords of the O'Connell stamp spent their incomes and devoted their energies in efforts to feed their tenants. But there were others less responsible. In order to avoid the tax burden of famine relief, many landlords evicted their tenants or rented ships to transport them to North America. Some of the most desperate arrivals were the victims of landlord emigration projects. Immigration and sanitation restrictions limited refugee access to the United States, but many of those who landed in Canada walked across the border at any point from Michigan to Maine.

Many Britons, including royalty, responded generously to the calamity in Ireland. The British Association collected close to £400,000 for famine relief. British civil servants and physicians worked alongside Irish doctors and clergymen to help famine victims, and many caught the fever themselves and died. Some Protestant organizations, but not Quakers, offered food as the price for conversion (the source of the term souper). Quakers earned a good reputation among Irish Catholics by their generosity. Private philanthropy, however, was unable to cope with a disaster on the scale of the great famine.

During the course of the famine, the British government spent millions of pounds to supply food and to provide public works employment. Although the dogmas of political economy were applied inconsistently, government relief generally was administered within the context of *laissez faire*. British civil servants in charge of famine-relief efforts worked on the premise that charity and government aid should not destroy private initiative or interfere with private enterprise. This kind of dogmatism was more apparent in the Whig response to the famine than in Peel's effort to cope with Irish hunger. He had purchased American maize, distributing it as a way of regulating prices on other grains. He also had initiated public works projects so that the Irish could earn money to buy food. Theoretically, Irish taxes were supposed to finance public works but the Irish economy could not bear such a burden.

Therefore, most government relief expenditures had to be written off as a total loss.

Laissez faire doctrines were only one factor preventing public works from providing the Irish economy with permanent benefits. Many British economists thought it unwise to prop up the Irish agrarian system because it was both inefficient and unproductive. They urged complete reformation that would discourage subdivision and encourage larger units of cultivation. These experts also recommended that the surplus population should be urged to emigrate. Since the economists advised against patching the collapsed Irish agrarian economy, the government, instead of financing useful draining and irrigation schemes, used public works projects to give Ireland miles and miles of country roads, some of them leading nowhere.

Salaries on public works projects were low: 8d to 10d a week for men and only 4d for women. With such a meagre wage, it was almost impossible to purchase food at prices inflated by shortage. When the Whigs came to power in 1846, they applied *laissez faire* more rigidly to famine relief. In 1847, the government started to phase out public works, shifting the burden of relief to the Poor Law in a country without sufficient workhouse space and with citizens lacking money to pay rates. Under these conditions, workhouses had to shut down, forcing the government to switch to outdoor relief in the form of soup kitchens. In 1847 the government decided to terminate the soup kitchens and to reapply the work house system, although the untainted potato harvest of 1847 was insufficient to feed the people.

The famine intensified anti-British, anti-Union sentiment in Ireland, contributing to the mythology and passion of Irish nationalism. Even more than those who remained at home, emigrants and their descendents interpreted the famine as the fruits of the Union. Some went so far as to accuse the British government of genocide. At the time of and even after the famine, Irish nationalists argued that Ireland could have fed her starving masses if only the government would have kept greedy landlords from shipping food to Britain. Both O'Connell and Mitchel complained that while millions of people were dying or leaving the country, ships departed from Irish harbors laden with wheat, barley, oats, rye, cows, sheep, and pigs.

No doubt some nationalist grumblings against Britain's famine relief measures expressed symptoms of acute paranoia. The sources of the famine existed in Irish social and economic institutions long before the Act of Union. Hunger was the harvest of overpopulation, the backward agrarian system, and an exclusive potato diet. Even the closing of Irish ports would not have provided adequate amounts of food for over eight million people or have kept prices at reasonable levels, and during the famine Ireland imported more food than she exported. Even if the Union had never happened, there is no reason to assume that a native Parliament, controlled by the same landowning class in charge of the United Kingdom Parliament, would have demonstrated the will or applied the resources to cope with the great famine.

While the famine was a product of nature abetting a sick economy and social system, guilt for the calamity that hit Ireland must rest with Britain, despite her relief efforts. Since Ireland was a reluctant partner in the United Kingdom, she had a right to expect that the richest and most powerful government in the world would not permit its Irish citizens to perish from hunger and related diseases. Millions of urban and agricultural laborers in Britain were unwilling victims of *laissez faire* principles, but it was unlikely that their government would have permitted close to a million of them to die and another million or so to flee an accident of nature in a rather short period of time without a response more generous and enthusiastic than the one exhibited in Ireland.

During the famine, Ireland was a victim of religious and racial prejudice and ideological violence. Charles Edward Trevelyan, Under-Secretary of the Treasury, the bureaucrat in charge of famine relief under the Whig administration, represented the ignorance of British politicians concerning Ireland and their dislike of her Catholic people. To Trevelyan, the Irish were victims of their own stupidity and indolence, vices bred by popery. He believed that the famine was a divine judgment on a wicked and perverse people.

Trevelyan and other prominent Englishmen, notably the editor of the *Times* complained of Irish ingratitude. They said that the Irish people refused to appreciate the generosity of the English toward them in their time of need or their good fortune in living under the guidance of Anglo-Saxon Protestant wisdom. Instead, these miserable creatures repaid British kindness with insults and sedition, demands for more government handouts, and finally rebellion. In 1848, the influential Tory *Quarterly Review* concluded that the Irish were victims of their own inferior natures.

> . . . all of civilization, arts, comfort, wealth that Ireland enjoys she owes exclusively to England . . . all of her absurdities, errors, misery she owes to herself . . . this unfortunate result is mainly attributable to that confusion of ideas, that instability of purpose, and above all, that reluctance to steady work which are indubitable features of the national character.

While the famine was decimating the Irish people, British politicians, advised by economists, applied ideology that was of some relevance to a sophisticated, British, urban industrial economy but of no practical use to primitive, agrarian Ireland. They spoke of maintaining normal commerce in places without transportation facilities, limited trade, and few, if any, markets. They insisted on self-reliance among a people burdened with excessive rents and demoralized by serfdom. Although British economists correctly diagnosed the illness of the Irish agricultural system, they chose a particularly inappropriate time, famine, to experiment with new theories. During a harvest of death and evictions, Lord Brougham told the House of Lords that the rights of property took priority over the Irish peasants' right to survive. And Nassau Senior, an economic advisor to Whig leaders, pleased that the famine was reducing the surplus Irish population, was disappointed that perhaps only a million people would die in 1848.

The Famine was the Irish holocaust. As the Jews were in the Third Reich, the Irish were victims of ideological murder—no-popery and *laissez faire*. But the British, unlike the Germans, did not plan genocide, although their Irish policy inflicted pain, brought death, and forced exodus. An Irishman walking the roads looking for a bit of weed, leaf, or root to chew; or lying on a cottage dirt floor dying of hunger or fever and watching other members of his family perishing around him; or on his way to the workhouse; or maybe crowded into a foul-smelling, disease-ridden coffin ship sailing to America would not have been consoled to learn that his misery was not planned, and that he was only a sacrifice on the altars of free trade and self-reliance.

4

parliamentarians and fenians

POST-FAMINE IRELAND

With the great famine, the land question began to emerge as the most important motivating factor in nationalist agitation and a vital issue in Anglo-Irish relations. Following the lead of James Fintan Lalor, nationalists attacked the landlord class as the agents of British colonialism and the landlord system as an instrument of British oppression. In Britain, Irish landlords were almost as unpopular as they were in Ireland. They became scapegoats for the failure of the Union. A large section of influential public opinion viewed them as greedy, selfish, heartless men, exploiting poor tenant farmers and agricultural laborers. Fearful of violating the sacred dogmas of political economy, British politicians decided to change the landlords rather than the system. In 1848 and 1849, Parliament passed Encumbered Estates Acts, forcing hopelessly indebted Irish landlords to sell their property. The authors of this legislation expected investors from Britain, solid men of finance, to take advantage of the opportunity to purchase estates in Ireland.

Under the provisions of the Encumbered Estates Acts, five thousand purchasers bought one-seventh of Irish landed property over a ten year period. Until recently, Irish historians described these new landlords as insensitive seekers of profit without concern for Ireland or her people. This description is myth. Very few of the new landlords were British capitalists. Ninety-five percent of them were Irish, including a large number of Catholics, often the younger sons of landlords, lawyers, and shopkeepers who had made money during the famine. As a group, the new proprietors were probably no better or worse than the people they replaced. At least they were residents who spent their rent incomes in Ireland rather than Britain.

One indicator of the importance of the land question was the increase in tenant-right activities during the 1850's and 1860's. This effort to reform the agrarian system expressed rising expectations rather than abject poverty. Except for Connacht, where Irish agriculture retained most of its pre-famine patterns—small farms, subdivision, high population density, and a potato diet—the rural standard of living improved between 1850 and the mid-1870's. British economists had been right, despite the coldness of their logic; the famine did alleviate many of Ireland's social and economic problems. Death and emigration reduced the 1851 population from the expected nine million plus to a more manageable 6,552,385. This decline reduced pressure on the land. From 1847 to 1861, holdings of more than one to less than five acres fell from 139,041 to 85,469. Larger but still subsistence level farms of more than five and less than fifteen acres also were reduced from 269,534 to 183,931. More reasonably sized holdings of more than fifteen and less than thirty acres also declined from 164,337 to 141,251. But farms over thirty acres grew from 157,097 to 157,833. And the number of over thirty acre farms continued to increase, reaching 159,834 in 1881.[1] During the famine years 300,000 cottages disappeared, most of them small, unsanitary, and uncomfortable. Many of them had housed agricultural laborers, the class most affected by the consequences of hunger and disease.

On larger farms the shift from tillage to grazing that had been apparent since 1815 continued. Farmers bought cattle, sheep, and pigs, raised chickens, and profited from rising meat, butter, and egg prices throughout the United Kingdom. Ireland provided badly needed food to urban industrial Britain. From 1851 to 1878, prices for agricultural goods rose much higher and quicker than did rents, allowing for a tidy little profit margin. Emigrant dollars sent home as gifts also lifted the rural standard of living. Tenant farmers improved their lot: they changed their eating habits to include meat, cereals, and other vegetables besides potatoes; they wore better, cleaner, and more comfortable clothing; they lived in neater and more spacious cottages; they invested money in rural savings banks; and they contributed generously to the construction of Catholic churches, convents, rectories, and

[1]Emmet Larkin, "Church, State, and Nation in Modern Ireland," *The American Historical Review*, Vol. LXXX, No. 5 (Dec., 1975), p. 1247. Reprinted in Emmet Larkin, *The Historical Dimension of Irish Catholicism*, New York: Arno Press, 1976.

schools. Evictions became rare incidents. In a twenty-five year period, 1855–1880, only 17,771 tenants left their farms, a rate of less than 3 percent, and many of them were not the victims of eviction.

A rising standard of living did not result in peasant complacency. Their memories of the famine discouraged either enjoyment of the present or trust in the future. Although prices were rising and rents were stable, the Irish farmer still felt insecure. Secure tenure, a demand that had nationalist as well as economic dimensions, was more important to them than rents. The work of O'Connell, the message of Young Ireland, and the ideas of Lalor had persuaded tenant farmers that they were the Irish nation and that their landlords were alien oppressors. Demands for tenant-right only articulated the surface of peasant discontent and ambition. Landlordism was the issue. They wanted "the land of Ireland for the people of Ireland." Agrarian protest mounted in intensity during the last half of the nineteenth century, moving from demands for secure tenures at fair rents, to dual ownership, and finally to peasant proprietorship.

The post-famine transformation of Irish society also influenced the structure, expression, and practices of Catholicism. During the first half of the nineteenth century, Catholicism in Ireland was quite different from that on the Continent, where the church was part of the Old Regime resisting liberalism and nationalism. In Ireland there was a close association between clergy and laity. They shared a common poverty and they protested a common oppression. Bishops and priests had joined and led agitations against the British government in an effort to transform their country into an independent peasant democracy. By the time Peel got around to a policy of trying to separate the Catholic clergy from anti-Union activities, Irish nationalism and Irish Catholicism had become too closely linked to permit that.

There never was, however, a complete consensus in the Irish Catholic hierarchy concerning its relationships to the British government and to Irish nationalism. Some bishops were prepared to accept compromise concessions from the British government if they would benefit the financial position of the church. Others, more militant, insisted on British reform legislation as a response to Irish grievances, but they, in turn, would not pay any attention to British public and parliamentary opinion. In 1838, the militants made it clear that they would no longer tolerate the nondenominational national school system. They demanded Catholic schools for Catholic children.

Divisions between the moderate and militant factions within the hierarchy clearly were revealed during the discussions and debates over Peel's Irish policy, particularly the Charitable Bequests Act and the Queen's Colleges Bill. Archbishop John MacHale of Tuam led those who insisted that only the Catholic hierarchy could set the terms for educating the Catholic laity. Archbishop Daniel Murray of Dublin represented the prelates who were willing to negotiate with the British government. They tolerated mixed, nondenominational education as a road to Catholic opportunity in the United Kingdom.

Neither the moderates nor the militants could be described as either Ultramontanes or Gallicans. MacHale and his friends opposed and obstructed negotiations between Rome and Westminster because they might reduce the power and independence of the church in Ireland. But they constantly petitioned the Pope to condemn the national schools and the Queen's Colleges. While Murray sympathized with Rome's attempt to establish friendly relations with the British government, he rejected the Pope's opinions on education.

In 1849, when Pius IX appointed Paul Cullen Archbishop of Armagh, Primate of the Irish church, and Apostolic Delegate to Ireland, the Murray and MacHale factions were at equal strength. Cullen came from the rectorship of the Irish College in Rome where he had enjoyed the friendship and confidence of the Pope. During the 1840's he had kept O'Connell informed about British moves at the Vatican. He never ceased to be a patriot, but like his friend, Pius IX, his experiences with the Revolution of 1848 in Italy shook his confidence in the benefits of liberal nationalism. His perceptions of Irish affairs were distorted by what he observed in Rome. Cullen honestly believed that Young Ireland was a Celtic copy of Young Italy and that Charles Gavan Duffy was the Irish Mazzini.

Cullen came back to Ireland to Romanize thoroughly the Celtic fringe of Catholicism. He represented the aggressive clericalism of Pius IX. At the Synod of Thurles in 1850, Cullen sided with the militants, placing the Murray faction in a minority position. The new majority condemned the Queen's Colleges and forbade Catholics to have anything to do with them. After Thurles, the Irish bishops concentrated their energies on education, never ceasing to demand that the British government endow Catholic schools from the elementary through the university levels. Their pressure gradually transformed the national education system into sectarian components.

Lord John Russell's Ecclesiastical Titles Bill in 1851, which prohibited Catholic bishops from assuming territorial titles taken from any place in the United Kingdom, helped the militant majority in the ranks of the Irish Catholic hierarchy. This imprudent legislation was a crude Whig bid for the British no-popery vote, which was incensed by Rome's decision to create a diocessan structure in Britain to meet the needs of a Catholic community enlarged by massive Irish immigration.

When Archbishop Murray died in 1852, Cullen was transferred to Dublin, a more influential base of operation. Once installed as Archbishop of Dublin, Cullen found it as difficult to get along with the irascible MacHale as had Murray, but their differences involved more a question of power than policy. Despite MacHale's efforts, Cullen dominated the Irish church until

PAUL CARDINAL CULLEN
1852–1878

Paul Cullen's primary commitment to the interests of the Catholic church made him
unpopular with Irish nationalists, but as Archbishop of Armagh (1849–1852) and
Archbishop of Dublin (1852–1878) he led the "Devotional Revolution" that shaped
the spirit, content, and structure of modern Irish Catholicism. (Courtesy of the National
Library of Ireland.)

his death in 1878, and there was no lay leader with O'Connell's ability to
counter-balance the enormous influence of the Archbishop.

Under Cullen's leadership, the church launched a tremendous building program financed by the contributions of a laity enjoying a rising standard of living and emigrant dollars. New churches, rectories, convents, and
schools expressed the confidence of a prosperous and aggressive Irish
Catholicism. The bishops began to develop policy positions independent of
nationalism. Cullen's patriotism was "faith and fatherland"; what was good
for Catholicism was good for Ireland. As Murray did, he negotiated with
British politicians to advance Catholic interests. But he was more aggressive
than his predecessor, demanding denominational education for Catholics
and the disestablishment of the Protestant church.

Because of his conflicts with Charles Gavan Duffy in the 1850's and his
war against Fenianism in the 1860's, Cullen has been portrayed by na-

tionalists as a reactionary foe of Irish freedom. This distorts the Arch-bishop's motives and goals. While a Romanizer in doctrine and discipline, and a supporter of Pius IX in political matters, Cullen maintained a tra-ditional Irish independence. He could adjust Roman principles to Irish situa-tions, distinguishing between reform and revolution. Cullen preferred to deal with British Liberals than Conservatives and accepted the traditional nationalist preference for the separation of church and state, although such a position contradicted the wishes of Rome. Cullen was quite concerned about the conditions of the urban poor and he opposed emigration. Like other bishops, he feared that the Irish who settled in urban Britain and America risked the loss of faith through contacts with materialistic and secular cul-tures. The Irish hierarchy thought of Ireland as a spiritual haven in a corrupt world. They wanted to improve conditions in rural Ireland through agrarian reform so that the people would not have to abandon their country or their faith.

Although Irish Catholicism in the 1850's assumed a stance somewhat independent of nationalism, bishops and priests retained the role in Irish life that O'Connell had bestowed on them. The Catholic church was more pros-perous than in pre-famine days, and bishops and priests were still closer to the laity than their Continental counterparts. They continued to be sympa-thetic to the economic needs and national aspirations of the people. The hierarchy and clergy still asked nationalist politicians to agitate Catholic issues in the British Parliament, and nationalists still wanted clerical support for their efforts to repeal or amend the Union. The more enthusiastic the clerical endorsement, the more successful the nationalist movement.

Until recently, historians have concentrated on Cullen's relations with nationalism, neglecting his role as a force in changing Catholicism. Pre-famine Irish Catholics were not particularly devout. In some parts of the country only about one-third of the Catholic population attended Mass on Sunday. A shortage of chapels encouraged such a situation. Clerical disci-pline was also a serious problem. Hard-drinking and sexually promiscuous priests were not rarities, and many priests were insubordinate to their bishops. Many of these misfits were exiled to the American mission.

Cullen not only built churches; he filled them. He insisted that the laity honor their religious obligations and encouraged the spread of practices popular in Rome—novenas, forty-hours devotions, and the rosary. The Arch-bishop also improved the quality of the clergy and tightened discipline within the church: laymen obeyed their priests, priests their bishops, and the bishops Rome. Beginning with Cullen's leadership, Ireland earned the reputation as the most Catholic country in the world. Laymen were devout, consistent in the practice of their religion, and extremely generous in their contributions to the church. Many young men and women became priests, brothers, and nuns, serving the church at home, throughout the English-speaking world, and in mission posts all over the British Empire.

The national school system greatly expanded literacy, spreading the message of Irish nationalism among all segments of the population. And the close association between Catholic and Irish identities contributed to the success of Cullen's "Devotional Revolution." As the Irish became more consciously nationalist, they became more consciously Catholic. The energy of the new church and emigration made Irish Catholicism the Catholicism of the English speaking-world. Ireland, a victim of imperialism, had become the capital of a vast new spiritual empire. The "Devotional Revolution" and the results of the national school system combined to civilize and discipline the Irish masses, improving the quality of Irish emigration, and adding to the effectiveness of nationalist agitation and political movements in Ireland.

THE INDEPENDENT IRISH PARTY
AND THE NATIONAL ASSOCIATION

British courts and the pursuit of the Irish Constabulary scattered the Young Ireland leaders around the globe. Only Charles Gavan Duffy remained in Ireland after 1848. The government arrested and tried him for sedition. After five hung juries, the defense tactics of the brilliant Tory barrister, Isaac Butt, returned Duffy to the world of nationalist journalism. He resumed publishing the *Nation* and began to search for techniques to rekindle the flames of hostility to the Union.

Despite the fiery contents of the *Nation's* patriotic ballads and his fling with revolution, fundamentally Duffy was a constitutional nationalist. Just before the ill-fated insurrection he published the objectives of Young Ireland in the *Nation*: an independent Irish Parliament, with ministerial responsibility, under the British monarchy, represented by an Irish-born Viceroy. Duffy said that revolution was an extreme option that could only be justified when it was clear Britain would make no concessions to reasonable Irish demands.

In his effort to reconstruct Irish nationalism, Duffy combined the strategies that he and Mitchel had debated before the Irish Confederation in late 1847. He recommended the creation of an independent Irish parliamentary party that would concentrate on the grievances of Irish tenant farmers. Duffy believed that the tenant-right issue would link together Catholic farmers in the South with Protestants in the North in support of an Irish party at Westminster. It would destroy regional and sectarian biases and promote an ecumenical patriotism that would eventually evolve into an all-Ireland demand for Repeal of the Union.

Dr. John Gray, Protestant proprietor of the *Freeman's Journal*, the most influential nationalist daily newspaper, and Frederick Lucas, owner and editor of the *Tablet*, a Catholic weekly, endorsed Duffy's new strategy. In 1849, Lucas, an English convert from Quakerism to Catholicism, had moved the *Tablet* from London to Dublin. He immediately became immersed in Irish politics, becoming an even more ardent supporter of tenant-right than Duffy. In 1850, Duffy, Lucas, and Gray joined forces with William Sharman Crawford, M.P., an Ulster Protestant advocate of justice for Catholics and of a federal contract between Britain and Ireland, and the most articulate spokesman for tenant-right in the House of Commons. They consolidated tenant-right organizations in Ireland into a Tenant League. This new organization, representing the interests of the more prosperous Irish farmers, did coalesce Protestants and Catholics in one cause. The Tenant League demanded secure tenures at fair rents decided by impartial evaluation, and the right of a tenant to sell his interest in the farm on leaving or eviction, thus compensating him for the improvements he made. Compensation for improvements would have legalized Ulster custom, extending it throughout the country, and discouraged evictions by making them too expensive for landlords.

In 1851, Duffy, Lucas, Crawford, and Gray completed their strategy by forming the Independent Irish Party, a coalition of M.P.s committed to tenant-right and members of the Irish Brigade. George Henry Moore, M.P. Mayo, had organized the Brigade to defend Catholic interests in response to the threat of the Ecclesiastical Titles Bill. The Catholic Defense Association provided the Irish Brigade with its constituency support. Because of its associations with the Catholic hierarchy and militant Catholicism, detractors referred to the Irish Brigade as "the Pope's Brass Band." Duffy admired Moore but doubted the integrity of many Brigade members. Lucas and Crawford persuaded him to accept an alliance between Catholic and tenant-right organizations.

The Irish Party got off to a flying start. In the 1852 general election, Irish voters returned forty-eight M.P.s pledged to support Crawford's Tenant-Right Bill, to independence from Whig, Tory, and Peelite factions, and to opposition against any government unwilling to adopt Crawford's proposal. Members of the Irish Party held the balance of power in a House of Commons divided into factions. They were able to prevent Lord John Russell, the author of the Ecclesiastical Titles Bill, from forming another Whig administration. The result was a coalition of Whigs and Peelites with Lord Aberdeen, the leader of the latter group, as Prime Minister. In order to attract Irish Catholic opinion and its parliamentary forces, Aberdeen indicated a willingness to entertain Irish grievances. To demonstrate his sincerity, he offered ministerial positions to two members of the Brigade wing of the Independent Irish Party, John Sadleir and William Keogh, who then broke their pledge of independent opposition and joined the government. Their defection received the blessing of two members of the Catholic hierarchy, F. Haly, Kildare and Leighlin and G. J. Browne, Elphin. Archbishop Cullen, who had helped launch the Catholic Defense Association and was a friend of tenant-right, made no public comment on the conduct of Keogh and Sadleir, but it was well known that he opposed independent opposition. Cullen was convinced that Irish MPs should use every opportunity to exert influence over British policy in Ireland. He believed that they could do far more for Ireland in the government than in independent opposition.

Cullen's hostility to independent opposition was also partially a function of his poor opinion of some Irish Party leaders. He initially liked Lucas but feared Duffy as an agent of Mazzini-style secular and radical nationalism. The Archbishop was convinced that the editor of the *Nation* was manipulating tenant right and independent opposition strategy to seize control of the Irish nationalist movement and to channel it toward revolution.

In 1854, at a Dublin synod, Cullen persuaded other members of the hierarchy to frame regulations limiting the political activities of the clergy. Duffy and Lucas complained that the Archbishop was attempting to destroy the Independent Irish Party, but the new rules applied to all political activities and Cullen enforced them against friend and foe of independent opposition. There was no doubt, however, that the hierarchy's ban on clerical politics damaged the prospects of the Irish Party. Priests were active recruiters and leaders in the tenant-right agitation. Without their energy and influence the Party suffered in the constituencies.

Lucas journeyed to Rome in a futile effort to persuade the Pope to rescind the hierarchy's ban on clerical involvement in Irish politics. In 1855, he died after composing a long brief against Cullen. That same year, Duffy, facing severe financial problems and convinced that clericalism had defeated Irish nationalism, sold the *Nation* and emigrated to Australia where he finally became Prime Minister of Victoria and attained knighthood. Duffy's spirit remained to shape the character and values of Irish nationalism. His books on Young Ireland and the Independent Irish Party became part of the canon of Irish history and the mythology of the Irish freedom movement.[2]

Duffy insisted that the treachery of Sadleir and Keogh and the antinationalism of Cullen and his clerical friends destroyed the Irish Party and the coalition of Protestant and Catholic tenant farmers. The defection of the two Pope's Brass Banders and Cullen's enmity to independent opposition and Duffy, the untimely death of Lucas, and Duffy's despair and emigration did combine to undermine the Independent Irish Party. Twenty-five M.P.s followed Keogh and Sadleir over to the government benches, leaving the Irish Party with only twenty-three members. By 1856, this number was

---

[2]Charles Gavan Duffy, *Young Ireland*, London: T. Fisher Unwin, 1896; *Thomas Davis*, London: Kegan, Paul, Trench, and Trubner & Co., 1890; *The League of the North and the South*, London: Kegan, Paul, Trench, and Trubner & Co., 1886; *My Life in Two Hemispheres*, London: T. Fisher Unwin, 1898.

reduced to a dozen. When the Party was dissolved in 1859, most of the twelve joined the Whigs, and a few remained independent. Since there was such a strong connection between the Party and the Tenant League, when the former disappeared, the latter ceased to meet.

While treachery and clerical opportunism wounded the Independent Irish Party, it was a victim of more than Sadleir, Keogh, and Cullen. The quality of the Irish Party was low. Politics in the United Kingdom during the nineteenth century was to some extent a game, hobby, or diversion for the aristocracy and gentry requiring large sums of money. M.P.s did not receive salaries, and the costs of elections and London residences were high. Since the ownership of landed estates did not need the close day-by-day supervision demanded by commerce or the professions, members of the aristocracy and gentry were in the best position to follow parliamentary careers. In Ireland, landed proprietors were either Whig or Tory, mostly the latter. From the time of O'Connell's Repeal Party in the 1830's until Parnell took charge of parliamentary nationalism in the 1880's, many nationalist M.P.s were adventurers. At election time they shouted patriotic slogans, but once seated at Westminster they courted the Whigs to obtain office or patronage jobs. Sadleir, Keogh, and their colleagues were examples of a certain breed that pervaded Irish politics, representing nationalism in the British Parliament for opportunistic reasons.

Duffy exaggerated the bonhomie between Protestant and Catholic tenant farmers in the 1850's. The alliance quickly proved to be more artificial than real. During the 1850's bountiful harvests, rising agricultural prices, emigration, and stable rents meant relative prosperity for most parts of rural Ireland. Good times revived regional and sectarian bitterness, destroying the solidarity of Protestant and Catholic tenant-righters. In the North, the Orange Order once more spoke for all sections of the Protestant community.

The resurgence of the Conservative Party under the leadership of Benjamin Disraeli in the House of Commons and Lord Derby in the House of Lords also influenced the fate of the Independent Irish Party. In Ireland, it increased landlord power. The aristocracy and gentry managed to return a Conservative majority from Irish constituencies at the general election of 1859, the same year that spelled the end of the Irish Party, by exploiting their significant pressure over the votes of their tenants who remained without the protection of a secret ballot, the divisions within Catholic nationalism, and the forces of Orange bigotry.

After the demise of the Irish Party, Cullen and the bishops attempted to fill the void in constitutional nationalism with a movement to agitate the interests of tenant farmers and the Catholic church. They used Irish reactions to Cavour's seizure of the papal states in 1859 to establish a militant Catholic public opinion. With the encouragement of the hierarchy, an Irish Brigade went to Rome to defend the temporal power of the Pope against the designs of Italian nationalism. Although it was inconsistent for Irish nationalists to protest Italian unification efforts, the Irish still had difficulty separating their Irish and Catholic identities.

In 1864 a committee of priests and laymen were discussing plans to place a statue of O'Connell at the foot of Sackville Street, Dublin. During the course of their conversations they decided to establish a National Association to urge Catholic and popular causes in the House of Commons and throughout the United Kingdom. Cullen managed to recruit quality talent for the National Association, prominent and respected M.P.s such as John Blake Dillon, John Gray, George Henry Moore, Myles O'Reilly, former Commander of the Irish Brigade in Rome, and John Francis Maguire, proprietor of the *Cork Examiner*. They spoke for the objectives of the National Association: tenant right, denominational education, and the disestablishment of the Protestant church.

Cullen's ambitions and the talents of Association M.P.s, however, did not generate much public support. Events of the 1850's had made many Irish cynical about parliamentary nationalism. Some of the disillusioned had joined the revolutionary Irish Republican Brotherhood. Others who had remained loyal to the constitutional tradition considered themselves disciples of Repeal and Young Ireland. They frowned on the National Association as a clerical front. And not all members of the hierarchy were thrilled about the National Association. More out of spite than principle. Archbishop MacHale refused to cooperate with Cullen. Thomas Nulty, Bishop of Meath, a strong voice for tenant-right, suspected that the agrarian platform of the National Association was just a technique for swelling the denominational education lobby. He asked Dillon, Maguire, and the other parliamentarians to adopt the principle of independent opposition and to emphasize tenant-right. But Cullen rejected any tactics that would restrict negotiations with the British government concerning Catholic education demands. When the National Association turned down Nulty's request, he withdrew his support, and concentrated on revitalizing and restructuring the tenant-right movement.

The National Association balanced its failures in Ireland with its successes in the United Kingdom. Through the diplomatic skills of its Secretary, William J. O'Neill Daunt, one of O'Connell's ablest and most trusted lieutenants, the Association concluded an alliance with two important British organizations: John Bright's Reform League, which advocated a democratic suffrage with a secret ballot, and the Society for the Liberation of the Church from State Patronage and Control. Founded in 1853, the Liberation Society represented Nonconformist efforts to disestablish the Anglican church in England and Wales. Friends of disestablishment realized the value of attacking the church at its most vulnerable point, Ireland. They hoped that the precedent of disestablishment in Ireland would lead to the separation of church and state throughout the United Kingdom. Census figures for 1861 showed only 693,357 members of the established church in Ireland compared to 4,505,265 Catholics.

The alliance between Irish Catholicism, British radicalism, and United Kingdom Nonconformity temporarily overcame a variety of personality and ideological differences and ancient animosities. It also brought the Irish Question to the attention of William Ewart Gladstone, the dominant personality in the Liberal Party, persuading him that Britain had a moral obligation to pacify Ireland. Gladstone became the first Prime Minister since his mentor Peel to risk his career to make the Union work on the basis of equality and justice for Irish Catholics.

In 1869, Gladstone introduced a bill to disestablish the Protestant church in Ireland. Cullen accepted the Prime Minister's offer over Rome's suggestion that dual establishment would be a better alternative than Protestant disestablishment. Cullen remained true to the O'Connell tradition, maintaining the separation of church and state principles of Irish nationalism.

Not long after the Irish Protestant church was disestablished, the alliance between the Liberation Society and the National Association came apart at the seams. The papal infallibility pronouncement of the 1870 Vatican Council and the Irish hierarchy's uncompromising demand for state supported denominational education offended British Liberals and Nonconformists, who were also irritated by the lack of enthusiasm among Irish Catholics for the disestablishment cause in Britain. Despite the collapse of the Irish-Liberal alliance, this experiment in collaboration followed the precedents of O'Connell's cooperation with the Whigs and previewed the future relationship between British Liberalism and Irish Home Rule.

One clause of the Disestablishment Act indicated the direction of future Liberal Irish reform. The government offered loans to tenant farmers on church property to purchase their holdings. This section of the Disestablishment Act created six thousand peasant proprietors. Land sale was also part of Gladstone's second important Irish reform measure, the Land Act of 1870. John Bright added an amendment to the bill offering tenants loans up to two-thirds the purchase price of their farms.

Gladstone and his Cabinet colleagues were still too ideologically orthodox to violate property rights by legislating secure tenure. But they were prepared to curtail evictions by forcing landlords to compensate tenants evicted for any cause save nonpayment of rents. The Prime Minister believed that if landlords had to compensate for improvements and disturbance, they would hesitate to evict. His conviction that security of tenure could exclude a limitation on property rights was naive. Under the provisions of the Land Act, a landlord could still evict by raising rents to a point where tenants could not afford to pay. Even the Bright Clause proved a disappointment because the large down payment and the loan terms were unattractive.

When the Land Act went into operation, the agrarian mood in Ireland was rather placid because of continuing good harvests and rising prices. But starting in 1877, inclement weather and declining markets brought agricultural depression. In the West of Ireland rainy and cold summers ruined crops and created another potato shortage. The spread of industrialism in Europe and the United States, accompanied by economic nationalism in the form of protective tariffs and competition for markets, damaged British commerce, increasing unemployment. People had less money to spend for food. Inexpensive grains from the vast prairies of Canada and the United States flooded the United Kingdom market, inflicting tremendous hardship on British and Irish farmers unprotected by tariffs. The loss of farm incomes in Ireland made it difficult to pay rents and led to a sharp increase in evictions.

Agricultural depression revealed the inadequacies of the 1870 Land Act and moved the land question to center stage, nudging denominational education into the background of Irish concerns. Nevertheless, Gladstone's effort to achieve tenant security established new patterns in Anglo-Irish relations. A British government had decided that property rights were not immune from legislative direction.

Gladstone's last assault on the Irish Question during his first government was a response to the denominational education demand. In 1873 he introduced a bill transforming Protestant Dublin University into a nonsectarian, degree-granting institution without courses in controversial subjects with religious connotations—moral philosophy, theology, and history. The bill included Trinity College and the Catholic University as constituent colleges within the university. Subjects excluded from the university curriculum could be taught in the constituent colleges. Trinity College opposed the new legislation because it reduced its control over Dublin University, and the Catholic hierarchy criticized the proposal because it did not specifically charter and endow the Catholic University. Cullen and his colleagues hoped that their criticisms would lead to government revisions, but Irish Liberal M.P.s misread the bishops' intentions. They voted against the University Bill, placing Gladstone in an impossible political position. Shortly after its defeat, he called for a general election which resulted in a Conservative government with Disraeli as Prime Minister.

THE AMERICAN CONTRIBUTION TO IRISH NATIONALISM

The great famine escalated rather than inaugurated emigration as a major dimension of Irish life. During the eighteenth century a large number of

Ulster Presbyterians sailed to North America to escape religious discrimination and the economic restrictions of British mercantilism. Most of them possessed the intellectual and technological skills to contribute to the development of a new nation. A few Catholics of means and ability also journeyed to the New World. More came as indentured servants or transported prisoners. But most Irish Catholic emigrants went to Britain rather than the New World to work the harvest or as unskilled laborers in the factories started during the Industrial Revolution. Once they earned enough money to pay rents to Irish landlords, migrant harvest workers were inclined to return home; industrial workers, teamsters, navvies, and gandy dancers tended to remain in Britain. Before the great famine, Irish-town ghettos already had taken shape in the urban jungles of Liverpool, Manchester, Birmingham, Leeds, Cardiff, London, and many other cities.

Beginning with severe but short duration famines in the 1820's, the trickle of Irish Catholic emigration to North America became a steady stream. The events of 1845–1849 turned it into a deluge, institutionalizing emigration as a depressing feature of Irish life. In the years from 1845 to 1901, about four million Irish immigrants entered the United States. Britain, Canada, and Australia also attracted Irish refugees from hunger and poverty.

In Ireland, the native culture had always been associated with a rural environment: "the whole nature of Gaelic society was opposed to urban living... the town in Ireland is the mark of the invader..."[3] But in Britain and America the Irish became urbanites. Although the vast majority of the early immigrants did not have the money to travel and purchase land in the American West, their choice to live in cities was more than a surrender to poverty. Irish spade and hoe farmers did not have the skills to meet the challenges of large-scale tillage in the United States or Canada.

Added to their inadequacies as farmers, extrovert and clannish personalities inclined the Irish to city living, where they became the pioneers of the American urban ghetto. In Ireland, small farms were so close together that people could talk over fences and ditches. At night neighbors exchanged visits and sat and gossiped before turf fires. In rural America farms were miles apart and visiting was rare. This isolation was unattractive to the Irish. In cities the work was hard and dirty, and the social conditions were appalling, but the Irish were together, keeping each other company in a strange new land.

Neither British nor American cities were hospitable to the Irish. They moved in on the bottom of a political, economic, and social structure controlled by anti-Catholic and anti-Irish Anglo-Saxon and Anglo-American Protestants. To the upper and middle classes the Irish posed the threat of a

[3]E. Estyn Evans, *The Personality of Ireland*, Cambridge: Cambridge University Press, 1973, p. 82.

barbarian culture; to the native working classes they were cheap competition in a tight labor market. Coarsened by poverty and oppression in Ireland, immigrants were brutalized further by the competitive, merciless industrial systems in Britain and America and by their struggle to survive against prejudice, unemployment, and disease. They reacted to their situation by over-indulgence in drink, which often led to violence. Too many Irish boys became petty thieves; too many Irish girls became prostitutes. In Britain and the United States the Irish filled jails, poorhouses and workhouses, hospitals and sanitariums, seeming to confirm the anti-Irish opinions that they were an inferior species unfit for civilized society.

The Irish did, however, bring one skill with them, politics. Under O'Connell's tutelage they learned the art of mass agitation and how to manipulate Anglo-Saxon political institutions. The openness of American democracy offered them more opportunity to practice their political expertise than did the aristocratic British system. The Irish joined the Democratic Party that embraced the egalitarian principles of Jefferson and Jackson. Democratic politicians exchanged patronage jobs for Irish votes and opposed Whig, Know-Nothing, and Republican politicians who catered to Anglo-American fears by attempting to restrict immigration and Irish political influence.

Despite political successes, Irish assimilation into the main stream of American life was slow. At first they organized for control over their own ghettos and then moved on to dominate urban government. Irish political machines provided jobs, coal, and food baskets; Catholic schools with Irish teachers inculcated American patriotism and preserved the Irish heritage through the Catholic identity. In time, Catholic parochial schools, secondary schools, colleges, and universities educated the priests, teachers, lawyers, doctors, and tradesmen to provide for the spiritual, cultural, political, and physical self-sufficiency of Irish neighborhoods. Starting with the Irish, American Catholicism became more of an ethnic identity badge than an international religion.

A leading expert on Irish nationalism has observed, "The beginnings of the Irish revolution—that is, the revolution of the Catholic Irish—are as much in America as in Ireland."[4] This shrewd judgment is an understatement: the nationalism and the revolutionary spirit of the Catholic Irish gained greater strength in America than in Ireland. Irish nationalism jelled in American ghettos before it did in Ireland. Nativist persecution and the cohesive forces of Catholicism diminished the county and parish identities that people brought with them from Ireland, and gave them a consciousness of Irishness: "for in the alembic of America the parochial peasant was trans-

---

[4]Conor Cruise O'Brien, *States of Ireland*, New York: Vintage Books—Random House, 1973, p. 45.

formed into a passionate Irish nationalist."[5] Irish-Americans hated Britain with an intensity far beyond their kinsmen in the Old Country. They provided the energy and the funds that sustained every constitutional and revolutionary expression of Irish nationalism from Fenianism in the 1860's to the events of Easter Week, 1916.

In many instances, Irish-American nationalism revealed more hate for Britain than love of Ireland. Exiles in the United States blamed Britain for the conditions that made them leave Ireland and settle in a country where they again had to experience poverty and Anglo-Protestant prejudice. Many of the American Irish felt like John Mitchel:

> I have found that there was perhaps less of love in it (Irish nationalism) than hate— less of filial affection to my country than of scornful impatience at the thought that I had the misfortune, I and my children, to be born in a country which suffered itself to be oppressed and humiliated by another . . . and hatred being the thing I chiefly cherished and cultivated, the thing which I specially hated was the British system . . . wishing always that I could strike it between wind and water, and shivor its timbers.[6]

Not all Irish-American nationalism was due to love of Ireland, hatred of Britain, or a case of acute paranoia; some of it was an expression of anti-British American patriotism and much of it represented a search for respectability in the United States. While the United States was culturally an Anglo-Saxon Protestant nation, the American Revolution and the War of 1812 caused considerable Anglophobia. Britain's pro-Confederacy stance during the American Civil War tended to increase and prolong this attitude. Irish immigrants fitted in nicely with the anti-British consensus of American foreign policy. Irish-American nationalists praised the United States as the cradle and fortress of liberty, and they insisted that America had a moral obligation to emancipate Ireland from British imperialism. They attempted to use Irish political power to frustrate rapprochement between the United States and the United Kingdom. The Irish were the first Americans to make ethnic demands affecting foreign policy, a precedent that other minority groups would follow.

Isaiah Berlin has defined nationalism "as an expression of the inflamed desire of the insufficiently regarded to count for something among the cultures of the world."[7] During the nineteenth and early twentieth centuries,

[5]Thomas N. Brown, "Nationalism and the Irish Peasant," *The Review of Politics*, XV (October, 1953), p. 445. This essay has also been republished as a volume in Emmet Larkin and Lawrence J. McCaffrey, editors, *The American Committee for Irish Studies Reprint Series*, and in Lawrence J. McCaffrey, editor, *Irish Nationalism and the American Contribution*, New York: Arno Press, 1976.

[6]Thomas Flanagan, "Rebellion and Style: John Mitchel and the Jail Journal," *Irish University Review*, I (Autumn, 1970), p. 4–5. Flanagan took this quote from William Dillon's two-volume biography of Mitchel, which was published in London, 1888.

[7]"The Bent Twig—A Note on Nationalism," *Foreign Affairs*, 51 (October, 1972), p. 30.

Irish Americans certainly were among the "insufficiently regarded" members of American society. With the exception of those who lived in the demoralizing New England urban ghettos, most Irish Americans experienced economic and social mobility. They entered the skilled working and lower-middle class—some even advanced into the professional and upper-middle classes. But as a national community, Irish Americans suffered from a nagging inferiority complex. Many concluded that Ireland in bondage to Britain accounted for their "insufficiently regarded" status. They decided that an Irish nation state would earn them the respect of other Americans. Their conviction that there was a link between a free Ireland and their success in America encouraged Irish Americans to promote and sustain a variety of efforts to liberate Ireland involving moral and physical force. In equating an emancipated homeland with American respectability, the Irish previewed an attitude that would be shared by other religious and ethnic minorities that followed their trail into the urban ghettos of the United States.

The Irish Republican Brotherhood

During the 1820's Irish-American Catholics and some Protestants encouraged the Catholic emancipation effort in Ireland, but their nationalism really was aroused by the Repeal movement of the 1840's. In almost every Irish-American community there was a Repeal club that sent dollars to Dublin. In his speeches, O'Connell told the British that contributions from America indicated that the Irish of the Diaspora would be a key factor in Anglo-Irish relations. Irish Americans pursuaded many American politicians to express support for a free Ireland. President John Tyler and Governor William Seward of New York were two prominent elected officials who spoke for Repeal. But O'Connell's attacks on American slavery, his reluctance to accept money from Repeal clubs south of the Mason-Dixon line, and his insistence that Irish and black liberation were linked in principle shattered the harmony of the Repeal movement in the United States.

Famine and revolution in Ireland had profound implications for Irish Americans. Increased Irish immigration intensified American nativism, necessitating a greater need for Irish ethnic pride. Famine deaths and the exodus convinced Irish-Americans that the British were attempting to exterminate the Irish race, and they vowed that genocide would be avenged. The events of 1848 gave the Irish American community leaders and an ideology. The ideas of Young Ireland found fertile soil in the Irish ghettos of America. Later, T. D. Sullivan's *Speeches From the Dock* inspired Irish-Americans with the eloquence most Irish rebels seem to possess on the eve of execution. Narrowback children listened to greenhorn parents and grandparents recite Robert Emmet's defiance of Lord Norbury, and his appeal to future generations to take up the cross of Irish freedom. In parish halls all over the United States, Irish Americans listened to Thomas Moore's *Irish Melodies,* and they read and memorized portions of Charles Kickham's *Knocknagow,* a story of Tipperary peasant life that showed the Irish as a much more hospitable, spiritual, and generous people than Anglo-Saxon Protestants.

Charles Kickham was a Fenian and Fenianism best represented the American contribution to Irish revolutionary nationalism. The failure of the Repeal agitation in the 1840's, the great famine, the treachery of Sadleir and Keogh, and the collapse of the Independent Irish Party convinced many Irish nationalists, at home and abroad, that constitutional movements led to compromise and corruption. They believed that British politicians and the seductive spell of the British Parliament always persuaded Irish M.P.s to abandon the interests of their country for personal gain.

John O'Mahony, James Stephens, and Michael Doheny, three veterans of 1848, created the Irish Republican Brotherhood. After escaping a police dragnet, Doheny came directly to the United States. Stephens and O'Mahony fled to Paris where they learned the tactics of revolutionary conspiracy from those who had opposed reaction in Italy, the Hapsburg Empire, Germany, and Russia. O'Mahony earned his living as a translator; Stephens taught English. In 1851, they served at the barricades in the short-lived resistance to Louis Napoleon's overthrow of the Second Republic.

In Paris, Stephens and O'Mahony planned a revolutionary movement dedicated to the achievement of a democratic Irish republic. Although sympathetic to socialism, they decided against emphasizing the economic features of the Irish Question in order not to alienate potential Protestant recruits. Like nationalists before and after them, O'Mahony and Stephens were caught up in the delusion that Irish Protestants would sacrifice their Ascendancy position in Irish life to follow the risky paths of nationalism. This fantasy limited the potential of Irish nationalism by depriving it of an economic basis and appeal.

In 1856, O'Mahony joined Doheny in the United States where they launched the Emmet Monument Association. Stephens concentrated on organizing the Irish in the United Kingdom. In 1858, he created the Irish Republican Brotherhood, and O'Mahony converted the Emmet Monument Association into its American wing, called the Fenian Brotherhood, a name which reflected O'Mahony's interest as a Gaelic scholar in the Fianna sagas. Because of its romantic appeal to the Celtic heritage, Fenianism became the popular term for Irish Republicanism on both sides of the Atlantic.

In Britain and Ireland, Republicans took oaths of allegiance to the Irish Republic, of obedience to their officers, and of secrecy. Anticipating clerical opposition to a secret society, O'Mahony asked American Fenians to take pledges rather than oaths. Both brotherhoods were organized into Circles commanded by a Centre (A). Each circle was divided into smaller cells led by captains (B) who commanded sergeants (C) who supervised privates (D). Those in the lower ranks knew only their immediate comrades and the activities of their own cells. Stephens was Head Centre in Ireland and Britain, O'Mahony in the United States.

Instead of maintaining secrecy, the complicated machinery of the Irish Republican Brotherhood (IRB) invited subversion and treachery. British agents infiltrated the movement; many became officers. Agent Pierce Nagel worked in the Dublin office of the IRB newspaper, the *Irish People*; Colonel F. F. Millen almost succeeded as Head Centre when Stephens was in prison; and Agent Godfrey Massey was a prominent figure in the 1867 insurrection. But infiltration was a two way street. Fenians penetrated the police force and prison staffs in Ireland—guards aided jail breaks, and IRB recruiter John Devoy attempted to create a fifth column among Irish soldiers in the British army. He enlisted many, including John Boyle O'Reilly, into the IRB.

The IRB attracted working class people in Ireland—shop assistants and agricultural laborers, the Irish proletariat in Britain, and some members of the Irish middle class in the United States, Britain, and Ireland. At the height of its strength in the mid-1860s, there were about 45,000 Fenians in the United States, and many other Irish Americans contributed money to the cause. But most of the surviving Young Irelanders stayed aloof from Republicanism. John Blake Dillon, William Smith O'Brien, and John Martin in Ireland; Thomas Francis Meagher in the United States; and Thomas D'Arcy McGee in Canada refused to endorse Fenianism.[8] A. M. Sullivan, the owner and editor of the *Nation*, denounced the IRB as the direct descendent of violent, agrarian secret societies.

Irish Catholic bishops were the chief foes of Fenianism. While they objected to the secret society character of the IRB, they also feared that revolution would destroy Irish property and lives and antagonize British Liberals, thus discouraging government concessions to Irish grievances, particularly in matters of education. To Archbishop Cullen, the IRB was even more dangerous than Young Ireland. He saw Stephens and O'Mahony as the Irish Cavour and Garibaldi and the Fenians as the Irish Carbonari. In the IRB Cullen also saw American paganism, materialism, violence, and anarchy. David Moriarity, the Whig Bishop of Kerry, described IRB leaders as parasites living off the ignorance of their followers, men who "lost their Irish character in the cities of America." He said that God's "withering, blasting, blighting curse" was on Fenianism, and that "eternity is not long enough, nor hell hot enough to punish such miscreants."

---

[8]McGee, a minister in the Canadian government, was assassinated in Ottawa by a Fenian.

In the *Irish People*, Charles Kickham answered the bishops. As a pious Catholic, he professed loyalty to the church, recognizing the rights of the clergy to guide the spiritual formation of the people. However Kickham insisted that the authority of priests stopped on the frontier of politics. He reminded his readers that some members of the Catholic hierarchy had defended the arch-scoundrels Sadleir and Keogh, and he warned that many prelates were prepared to compromise the independence of their country in exchange for British concessions to denominational education. The Irish laity should not run to the parish priest for advice on the best way to serve Irish nationalism. Why, asked Kickham, did bishops ask young Irishmen to join the Irish Brigade for duty in Rome, and then decry a similar sacrifice for Ireland?

Irish bishops remained firm in their opposition, ordering priests not to administer the sacraments to unrepentent Fenians. They also supported British diplomacy at Rome which finally resulted in an explicit papal condemnation of the IRB. Nevertheless, some parish priests and a larger number of curates continued to hear Fenian confessions and to give them communion without asking questions. While opposed to the spirit of Fenianism, American bishops realized that the liberal American climate of opinion made it imprudent for them to dictate the politics of the laity.

In 1861, Fenians decided to bury in Ireland Terence Bellow MacManus, a veteran of 1848, who had escaped from Van Dieman's Land and later died in San Francisco. When MacManus' coffin reached New York, Archbishop John Hughes, a native of Fermanagh, said a funeral Mass in St. Patrick's Cathedral. While the body was en route to Ireland, Cullen announced that no Catholic church in Dublin would be available for funeral services. Dr. Keane, the Bishop of Cloyne, was not so rigid. He allowed the corpse to repose in a Queenstown (Cobh) church. In Dublin, the Fenians held MacManus' wake in the Mechanics Institute. Fifty thousand people marched with the body to Glasnevin cemetary while hundreds of thousands lined the route. At the graveside, Fenians, including Stephens, eulogized the dead revolutionary, and Father Patrick Lavelle of Mayo defied Cullen's orders by blessing the coffin before it was lowered into the ground. This successful challenge to the authority of the bishops was probably the high point of the Fenian movement.

The American Civil War delayed revolution in Ireland. Majority Irish opinion, like British opinion, was pro-South, but for different reasons. British Liberals and Conservatives identified with the Confederacy as an aristocratic society resisting the aggression of a Northern urban democracy. They looked forward to buying cotton from and selling industrial goods to an independent South. British leaders also welcomed the possibility that a divided America would eliminate a potential menance to their interests in Canada. On the other hand, most Irish people thought that the Southern effort to leave the Union was analogous to their desire to sever Ireland's British connection. Although they deplored slavery, they were not convinced it was an important issue in the American struggle. They shared Irish-American hostility to anti-Irish, anti-Catholic American reformism which contained the abolition movement. And the War between the States caused a severe economic pinch in rural Ireland. During the conflict, Irish Americans sent less money to Ireland. Heavy Irish casualties in battle and the unethical methods which Union recruiters used to enlist the Irish in Ireland and America also caused pro-South Irish opinion.

Although most Fenians in the United States regretted that the Civil War diverted Irish-American attention away from Ireland, leaders supported the Union because they wanted a strong United States to serve as an arsenal of Irish freedom. Many Fenians enlisted in the two armies to gain military experience for the inevitable conflict with British imperialism. At least 150,000 Union and about 40,000 Confederate soldiers were born in Ireland, and of course, second and third generation Irish Americans added to the Irish military contribution.[9]

After Lee surrendered to Grant at Appomattox on April 9, 1865, Fenians got down to the work of Irish revolution. Combat-trained Irish Americans arrived in Ireland to teach members of the IRB soldiering, but a feud in American Republicanism dimmed the prospects for a successful insurrection. At the 1865 Fenian convention in Philadelphia, delegates restructured the organization in imitation of the American political system. A General Congress, divided into a Senate and House of Delegates, limited the authority of the President who replaced the Head Centre. This new structure led to a clash between the President, O'Mahony, and the leader of the Senate, Colonel William D. Roberts, who insisted that Irish Americans should strike at British power in nearby Canada rather than in far off Ireland. He wanted to invade and capture Canada and hold it hostage until Britain freed Ireland. Quarrels over the Irish and Canadian attack strategies delayed the shipment of guns and ammunition to Ireland. Reluctant to repeat the fiasco of 1848, Stephens postponed the scheduled 1866 rising.

Meanwhile, the British government took steps to destroy the IRB. After Nagle, the British agent in the office of the *Irish People,* supplied the authorities with incriminating documents, the government shut down the newspaper and arrested its staff, along with Stephens. With the aid of Republican guards in Richmond prison, John Devoy arranged Stephens' escape. Stephens sailed for New York after a short stop in Paris, with the intention of reconciling the Fenian factions and persuading the American

---

[9]These figures come from Joseph M. Hernon, Jr., *Celts, Catholics, and Copperheads,* Columbus, Ohio: Ohio State University Press, 1968, p. 11.

Irish to abandon the Canadian strategy. By the time he arrived in the United States, Stephens found that the Senate group had already deposed O'Mahony, and his haughty disposition and abrasive personality promoted rather than halted division.

In May, 1866, about 600 Fenians crossed the Canadian border, defeated a company of volunteers, and then retreated when they learned that regular British soldiers were about to attack them. Since Roberts was committed to pursue the Canadian strategy and was reluctant to give arms to Ireland, Stephens again postponed revolution in Ireland. American Fenians accused him of cowardice and deposed him as International Head Centre, chosing one of their own, Colonel Thomas J. Kelly, to take his place. Early in 1867, a humiliated Stephens departed New York for another Paris exile.

While Stephens was in the United States, the British government transferred Irish soldiers serving in their own country to British posts, suspended habeus corpus in Ireland, and arrested IRB leaders. In a futile gesture of defiance, outnumbered and inadequately equipped Fenian companies in Kerry, Cork, Tipperary, Limerick, Clare, and Dublin attacked Irish Constabulary barracks and other symbols of British authority. During the snowy months of February and March, 1867, the constabulary aided by the army easily routed small rebel bands and arrested their leaders.

Republican violence was not confined to Ireland. In February, 1867, Fenians in Manchester managed to rescue Colonel Kelly and Captain Thomas Deasy, another Irish American, from a police van. But in doing so they accidently shot and killed a constable. Although there was no solid evidence that any of them had fired the fatal bullet, three members of the rescue party—W. P. Allen, Michael Larkin, and Michael O'Brien—were executed for the policeman's murder. Later in 1867, in an unsuccessful attempt to free Richard O'Sullivan Burke from Clerkenwell prison, a Fenian dynamite charge killed twelve people and wounded 120. IRB violence in England intensified anti-Irish British sentiments. But the defeat and imprisonment of Fenians and the executions in Manchester brought the Republicans a large measure of public sympathy in Ireland. Many bishops, priests, businessmen, and nationalist politicians joined an Amnesty Association that petitioned the government for the release of Fenian prisoners. Allen, Larkin, and O'Brien became "the Manchester Martyrs," victims of British hate masquerading as justice. Bishops, including Cullen, and priests offered prayers for the souls of the martyrs, and throughout Ireland people participated in mock funerals for the three heroes. Inspired by Allen's speech from the dock, which ended with "God Save Ireland," T. D. Sullivan of the *Nation* composed a lyric to the American Civil War melody "Tramp, Tramp, Tramp the Boys are Marching," which he called "God Save Ireland." It quickly became the anthem of Irish nationalism.

God save Ireland said the heroes
God save Ireland, say we all.
Whether on the scaffold high
Or on the battlefield we die,
What matters where for Erin dear we fall.

With the Feninans enshrined in the pantheon of Irish martyrs, Cullen found it difficult to restrain the clergy from swarming into the Amnesty Association. Many priests argued that the original objections to the IRB were no longer valid. The split between the Irish and Irish American Republicans had cleansed the I. R. B. of American violence and secularism. When the Pope in 1870 issued an explicit censure of the IRB, it irritated Irish nationalist opinion.

As Fenianism began to achieve an honorable place in the history and legend of Irish nationalism, Republicanism declined as a significant force. American Fenians remained divided by personality and policy disputes. For a time, many politicians in the United States, courting the Irish vote and protesting pro-Confederacy British public opinion and conduct, refused to hinder or condemn Fenian assaults on Canada. In fact Fenians carried surplus U.S. army weapons. The United States government used the Fenians as a weapon to intimidate the British into settling the Alabama claims and accepting the American naturalization of former British subjects. In 1870, after the Alabama claims and the citizenship issue had been resolved in favor of the American position, President Grant announced that his administration would no longer tolerate an Irish government in exile functioning in the United States or violating the frontiers of a friendly neighbor.

Following Grant's statement, American Fenianism declined. Many members of the Brotherhood joined the Clan na Gael, a new revolutionary, Republican organization. Jerome J. Collins, who became the Science Editor of the *New York Herald,* founded the Clan in 1867, but John Devoy, who came to the United States in 1871 after release from a British prison and also went to work for James Gordon Bennett's newspaper empire, became its dominant personality. The Clan had more discipline and maintained greater secrecy then the Fenian Brotherhood.

In Ireland, the Irish Republican Brotherhood continued to exist and received financial support from the Clan na Gael. In 1877 the two organizations joined in a seven-member Revolutionary Directory—three from the Clan, three from the IRB in the United Kingdom, and one Republican representative from Australasia. But by the end of the 1870's, the IRB had little influence over the direction of Irish nationalism, which was again flowing on a constitutional course flying a Home Rule banner.

5

home rule

BUTT VERSUS PARNELL

During the 1830's and 1840's, Isaac Butt, the son of a Protestant clergyman, barrister, and former economics teacher at Trinity College, was the bright young star of Protestant Ascendancy Ireland. He co-founded and edited *The Dublin University Magazine,* the *Blackwood's* of Irish Toryism, led the opposition to Whig reform in Ireland, and debated O'Connell on the subject of Repeal in the Dublin Corporation. Butt's incipient nationalism was rooted in the conviction that the British Parliament discriminated against the Irish economy. He wanted protection for Irish industries. In 1848, Butt defended Young Irelanders in the court room, arguing that they were intelligent and idealistic young men driven to desperation by British misgovernment of their country. During the 1850's, he sat as a liberal Conservative in the House of Commons, expressing a friendly interest in the education demands of the Irish-Catholic hierarchy and the welfare of Irish tenant farmers. But mismanaged finances and a rather undisciplined and unsavory life style led Butt to debtor's prison for a brief period in the 1860's. While there, he wrote pamphlets urging denominational education and tenant-right as two conservative solutions to basic Irish problems. In the late 1860's, Butt defended Fenian prisoners without charge and then became President of the Amnesty Association seeking their release.

With the failure of Fenianism, Butt and George Henry Moore decided the time was right to exploit Protestant anger against Gladstone's Irish policy by inaugurating a constitutional nationalist movement based on the principle of federalism. After the Northern victory in the American Civil War, many British political theorists wrote in respectable newspapers and periodicals, extolling the virtues of federal constitutions. And the British government had applied a federal solution to the conflicts between English and French cultures in Britain's North American colony in 1867 by creating the Dominion of Canada with its own constitution. When Moore died in the early months of 1870, Butt took the initiative in launching the new movement. In May, 1870, he founded the Home Government Association.

In a small booklet, *Irish Federalism* (1870), Butt spelled out the principles and objectives of Home Rule. He told Irish Protestants that their failure to identify with the legitimate national aspirations of the Catholic majority encouraged class and religious conflict and a mood of instability in the country. He said that Catholic peasants would follow the leadership of an enlightened, Irish-minded aristocracy. And he promised that Irish Protestants would be an important body in an Irish House of Commons and the dominant force in an Irish House of Lords. Butt emphasized that Irish-Protestant opinion would carry far more weight in an Irish Parliament than it did in the legislature of the United Kingdom, reminding his readers that Liberals had ignored Irish-Protestant concerns and that Conservatives had only exploited them in the game of British politics. Butt warned his co-religionists that Home Rule was their last opportunity to shape the future of their country; if they rejected this invitation to participate in Irish nationalism, they could become outcasts in an independent Ireland achieved through the exclusive efforts of the Catholic majority.

Butt assured Irish and British Protestants that Home Rule would strengthen rather than weaken the ties between the two islands. An Irish Parliament would continue to contribute to the defense and expansion of a common empire. He said that the religious values of Irish Catholics made them natural conservatives, respectful of monarchy, aristocracy, and private property. According to Butt, it was not inherent radicalism or anarchism that drove Irish Catholics into the "eddies and whirlpool of revolution," but the frustrations of persecution, serfdom, social injustice, and misrule. Like Grattan and O'Connell, Butt argued that Irish problems demanded Irish solutions. If Britain permitted the Irish to manage their own domestic affairs, she would be rewarded with the friendship of a congenial neighbor. However, if she refused to listen to the cries of an anguished people for local control, she would be punished by a constant threat of revolution. The end result of continued tensions between Ireland and Britain could end in complete separation and permanent animosity between the two islands.

Butt's Home Rule program involved a long-range restructuring of the

United Kingdom. He looked forward to the day when there would be legis-latures in England, Scotland, and Wales as well as Ireland. All of these assemblies would exist in a subordinate position to a United Kingdom Parliament at Westminster that would manage the common affairs of the British Isles. The Westminster Parliament would also be responsible for the defense of the United Kingdom and the empire.

Butt also addressed some remarks to the Catholic hierarchy. He told the bishops that Home Rule represented the constitutional demands of O'Connell's nationalism. He said it would turn Catholics away from secret conspiracies that end in violence. And he assured the prelates that cooperation with Protestants would result in an Irish Parliament that would harmonize class, economic, and religious differences in Ireland.

The Home Rule leader did not intend to use the Home Government Association as the nucleus of an O'Connell-style mass agitation. He feared that a popular movement might alienate Protestant support. For the same reason he forbade the discussion of Catholic or agrarian issues in Home Government Association meetings. He did, however, continue to lend his personal support to demands for denominational education and tenant-right, and he advised nationalist M.P.s to speak out in favor of causes that enjoyed the support of Catholics.

At the beginning of its existence, a significant number of Protestant businessmen, newspaper proprietors, and even a few landlords joined the Home Government Association. Some Irish Liberal M.P.s declared a conversion to Home Rule, and quite a few Home Rule candidates, including Butt, won parliamentary by-elections. Many of these by-elections were marked by controversy between Home Rulers and Catholic bishops and priests who insisted that the Home Government Association was a Protestant Tory front more interested in destroying Gladstone than winning a measure of Irish freedom. In most of the confrontations between Home Rulers and the Catholic clergy, nationalism triumphed over clericalism.

In its early phase, the Irish in America and quite a few of the refugees in Britain remained true to the Republican tradition and condemned the Home Rule movement as a revival of opportunism and compromise. There were, however, many urban Irish in England and Scotland who admired Butt for defending the Fenian prisoners and for his work in the Amnesty Association. They organized Home Rule clubs in most British cities. In 1873 these clubs merged into the Home Rule Confederation of Great Britain with Butt as President. Confederation leaders, many with IRB connections, promised to preach the Home Rule gospel in Britain and to mobilize the Irish vote in England and Scotland behind British politicians friendly to Irish freedom.

Gradually, many Protestants felt uncomfortable in the Home Government Association and left. At the same time, Catholic bishops and priests, disappointed with Gladstone's University Bill, began to favor Home Rule. Many clerics and Catholic laymen, previously friendly to the Liberal Party, joined the Home Government Association. They insisted that the organization should have a more popular appeal. At the November 1873 National Conference, delegates decided to replace the Home Government Association with the Home Rule League. They invited the masses to join the League as associate members, paying a shilling in dues, and they decided to form an Irish Parliamentary Party in the British House of Commons, a party committed to only one issue, Home Rule.

In January 1874, before the Home Rule League was properly organized, Gladstone called for a general election. The Liberals lost the election in Britain but Home Rule won in Ireland. Although it lacked campaign funds, proper candidates, and effective constituency organizations, Home Rule returned fifty-nine M.P.s to the House of Commons. Shortly after the election, nationalist M.P.s met in Dublin, created the Irish Parliamentary Party, and elected Butt as its first Chairman.

Members of the Irish Party agreed to vote as a unit on the question of Home Rule, but they gave each M.P. the right to express personal opinions on other issues. Hoping to persuade Irish and British Protestants that Home Rule was not synonymous with Catholic power or agrarian radicalism, Butt established a loose party structure. He did, however, suggest to his colleagues that prudence demanded their concern with the grievances of the Irish-Catholic majority. Butt was playing a delicate and almost impossible game: he was trying to present Home Rule as inoffensive to Irish Protestants while at the same time making it attractive to Catholic nationalists.

Butt described his parliamentary strategy as a policy of conciliation between Ireland and Britain and between classes and creeds within Ireland. He instructed Home Rule M.P.s to be logical, moderate, and patient in debate, always respecting the dignity of the British Parliament and the sensitivity of British M.P.s. He said that their civilized behavior would help demonstrate that the Irish people could govern themselves.

In 1874, Home Rule M.P.s went to Westminster, enjoying the endorsement of nationalist newspapers and the confidence of the nationalist electorate. Only two years later the Irish Party faced a survival crisis. Both the Catholic and agrarian wings of Irish nationalism came to the conclusion that Home Rule was an inadequate expression of Irish wants and needs. The *Nation* and some other nationalist newspapers complained of the lethargic performance of Home Rule M.P.s, blaming them for the narrow defeats of several Irish reform measures. Frequent absences of the Irish Party members from critical votes on Irish issues suggested that parliamentary nationalism still suffered from the cynicism and opportunism that had afflicted O'Connell's Repeal Party and Duffy's Independent Irish Party.

Despite the deficiencies of its membership, perhaps the Irish Party might have performed more convincingly with better leadership. Butt was an intelligent and sincere nationalist, but he was too gentle and reluctant to order and discipline indifferent colleagues. And serious financial problems made it difficult for him to concentrate on parliamentary duties. Friends donated money so that he could direct his attention to politics, but it was not enough, and the Irish people failed to support a national tribute, based on the O'Connell precedent, probably because they were disillusioned by the puny efforts of most Home Rule M.P.s. So when Butt should have been at Westminster, he was in Dublin working at his law practice, trying to pay off his considerable debts.

Irish Party failures at Westminster were not completely attributable to the poor quality of its membership or Butt's weak leadership. Despite Butt's confidence in a policy of conciliation, most British politicians were disinterested in the Irish case for Home Rule or reform, no matter how reasonably or moderately presented. Their anti-Irish, no-popery prejudices were impervious to rational arguments. And the Irish Party was presenting a case for self-government at a time when imperialism was emerging as one of the most important and emotional issues in British politics. Many Englishmen, particularly Conservatives, were committed to the Union as the foundation of British security and imperial unity. They were convinced that Home Rule for Ireland would initiate a process that would lead to the dissolution of the Empire. They advised the Irish people to abandon the silly notion that Britain would voluntarily dismantle the United Kingdom.

In July, 1876, T. D. Sullivan wrote an editorial for the *Nation,* arguing that the policy of conciliation had failed to capture the attention of British politicians. He urged a new parliamentary strategy based upon obstruction. Sullivan recommended that Home Rule M.P.s should prevent the discussion and solution of British and Empire problems until British politicians were ready to consider the Irish situation. Why, he asked, should Irish M.P.s stand in awe of a political system that oppressed their country?

Obstruction or conciliation? This was the topic of a lively newspaper debate with most nationalist newspapers agreeing with the *Nation.* This same subject was discussed when the Home Rule Confederation held its annual convention in Dublin in August, 1876. Like Irish Americans, the Irish in Britain tended to be more aggressive nationalists than the Irish in Ireland. Convention delegates voted to censure the Irish Party and endorsed a policy of parliamentary obstruction. When Butt addressed the convention, he promised that in 1877 Home Rule M.P.s would pursue a more active policy in the House of Commons.

But when Parliament met there was no discernable improvement in the performance of the Irish Party. Considering its personnel, Butt probably could not have kept his promise to the Home Rule Confederation. However, two members of the Irish Party did answer the call for action. During the parliamentary session of 1877, Joseph Biggar, M. P. Cavan, and Charles Stewart Parnell, M. P. Meath, began to obstruct systematically British and imperial legislation with long lists of amendments, prolonged discussion of alterations, quorum calls, and motions for adjournment.

The tactic of obstruction was not new to Biggar, a Belfast pork merchant and former member of the Supreme Council of the Irish Republican Brotherhood. In 1874 and 1875 he had experimented with that tactic to impede Irish coercion bills and to expand the freedom of the press in reporting parliamentary debates. In 1875, he had teamed with A. M. Sullivan to force the Speaker to eject the Prince of Wales and his society friends from the visitors gallery in order to demonstrate how some M.P.s exercised this parliamentary privilege to prevent journalists from covering debates. Although Biggar and Sullivan had infuriated Disraeli and other British politicians, they made their point and won a victory for a free press. On several occasions in 1874 and 1875, Biggar's tactics had brought forth a censure from Butt.

Charles Stewart Parnell came from Protestant patriot, Wicklow gentry stock. As a young man, he was open-minded about Fenianism without knowing a great deal about Irish history. He joined the Home Government Association and the Home Rule League, lost as a Home Rule candidate for Dublin county in a by-election in 1874, but successfully contested a Meath by-election in 1875. When Parnell first arrived in the House of Commons, his Irish Party colleagues thought him a handsome but inarticulate young man. Butt, however, considered it quite a coup to have a Protestant landlord sitting on the Home Rule benches below the gangway. Parnell had no intention of remaining a backbencher. He conscientiously attended the House of Commons, spoke often, learned parliamentary procedures, and diligently reported back to his constituents.

Obstruction infuriated British politicians and journalists. Editorials and cartoons, particularly in *Punch*, portrayed Parnell and Biggar as simian Irish barbarians destroying that great assembly of British liberty, the House of Commons. Editors demanded changes in parliamentary procedures to muzzle these Irish hooligans. British politicians echoed journalists, but party leaders realized that rule changes would be a victory for Parnell, since any restrictions on debate would interfere with the traditional liberties of Liberal and Conservative M.P.s. Following the example of O'Connell, Parnell and Biggar were challenging and defeating the British at their own game and in their own forum. The louder the cries of anguish from Britain, the happier the shouts of joy in Ireland.

Finally in the House of Commons and in a letter to the *Freeman's Journal*, Butt censured Parnell and Biggar. He said that they antagonized moderate British and Irish opinion, creating doubts about the ability of the Irish people to manage their own affairs. Butt also charged that the two obstructionists divided the Irish Party. In reply, Parnell ridiculed Butt's contention that reason and good behavior in the House of Commons would impress British politicians with the justice of the Irish demand for self-government. He argued that parliamentary debates were not an instrument of reasonable discussion and decision, but a facade masking party politics committed to special interests. Parnell insisted that most British M.P.s shared the anti-Irish prejudices of their constituents and would remain deaf to Irish pleas for justice. To them, Ireland was a colony, not an equal partner.

According to Parnell there was only one way to persuade British politicians to give Ireland her own legislature: Force them to see that as long as Ireland was denied sovereignty, Britain would never have peace and security. Parnell said that Irish M.P.s must demonstrate that they considered the British Parliament only a temporary abode. They must come to Westminster as alien rebels rather than as obsequious second-class participants in the British political process. While there, they should retaliate for British misrule of their country by obstructing the government of Britain and the Empire. Though few in number, they could, if conscientious, disciplined, and determined on Irish independence, force a hearing in the House of Commons. Irish strength and detemination would coerce British Liberals and Conservatives to emancipate Ireland as an act of self-preservation.

As to Butt's charge that he and Biggar were disrupting the unity and discipline of the Irish Party, Parnell asked what unity and discipline? He pointed out that the Party was bound to only one issue, Home Rule, and that it had performed badly on that. Parnell suggested that the Party leader would do better to concentrate his criticisms on the absentees and opportunists rather than quarrel with the men attempting to carry out their obligations to Irish nationalism. He also insisted that his active policy was not merely obstruction. His amendments to British legislation were constructive alterations, and his motions for adjournment were made to insure the discussion of important issues at times when M.P.s were alert. Parnell accused British M.P.s of deliberating and voting in the wee hours of the morning after staggering in drunk from fashionable London parties. He told Butt that if Parliament was too burdened to give proper attention to important subjects, then Irish affairs should be delegated to a local assembly. Home Rule would free Britain from Irish distractions and Ireland from British incompetence.

As the Irish press, the Home Rule League, the Home Rule Confederation, and tenant-right clubs discussed the points of difference between Butt and Parnell, it became clear that Irish nationalist opinion leaned toward the latter. The Home Rule Confederation rejected Butt in 1877 and named Parnell President. Butt still controlled a majority of votes on the Executive Committee of the Home Rule League, though that organization now enjoyed little public support and was almost bankrupt. Parnell made no attempt to take over the tottering Home Rule League or the staggering Irish Party. Obviously, he preferred to wait until the fortunes of politics and another general election placed him in a position to command militant nationalists and a vital Irish Party.

In the late 1870's, a few members of the Irish Party joined Parnell and Biggar in their obstruction tactics; other respectable and conscientious Home Rule M.P.s, gauging the drift of nationalist sentiment, urged Butt to discipline Whiggish and apathetic Party members and to take a more energetic stance in Parliament. Instead of taking this advice, the Party Chairman continued his quarrel with Parnell. In an effort to impede the progress of Parnellism by enlisting the Catholic hierarchy, Butt accused his young opponent of appealing to the violent instincts of Fenianism. But the bishops and priests shrewdly remained neutral.

THE NEW DEPARTURE
AND THE ASCENDANCY OF PARNELL

Although the Clan na Gael condemned Home Rule as just another expression of constitutional nationalism that would ultimately betray the Irish people through collaboration with the British political system, a number of its leaders were impressed with the bold strategy of Parnell and Biggar in the House of Commons and its appeal to the Irish masses. They decided that perhaps they could construct an alliance between the Clan and the active wing of the Irish Party.

While Irish Republicanism projected a proletarian image, its economic and social consciousness was extremely limited. Revolutionary nationalists stayed clear of agrarian radicalism to avoid antagonizing Irish Protestants. Republicans liked to think that Irish independence automatically would solve class and sectarian conflict. Not all Irish American nationalists lived in that dream world. Patrick Ford in the *Irish World* and John Boyle O'Reilly in the *Boston Pilot* expressed the anger and frustration of the Irish working man in the United States and the Irish peasant in Ireland. They demanded changes in laws and institutions to control the excesses of American capitalism and Irish landlordism. Far more radical than O'Reilly, Ford declared total war on landlordism. And he warned the Clan na Gael to respond to the land question, or else Republicanism would never be a relevant force in Irish nationalism.

Ford's strategy was particularly appropriate to the Irish situation. In the late 1870's, inclement weather in Ireland, unemployment in urban Britain, and the impact of cheap American grain on the United Kingdom market all had resulted in bad harvests, potato famine, falling prices, the inability to pay rents, and evictions in rural Ireland. The eviction rate rose from 463 in 1877 to 980 in 1878 to 1,238 in 1879. And the 1873–1879 recession in the United States impeded the safety valve process of emigration, increasing the number of unemployed and raising the level of discontent in Ireland.

The economic crisis in Ireland presented Irish nationalism with an opportunity to establish contact with a new constituency. Previously, people in western Ireland were so involved with the basic problem of survival that they had little time or energy for agitations connected with social reform or political independence. In Connacht and west Ulster, peasants did not fully participate in the post-famine good times. The economy and the social system retained early nineteenth-century patterns: small farms, high population density, and a heavy reliance on the potato. As a result, the agrarian depression of the late 1870's was particularly hard on the people of these areas.

With the approach of the 1782 centenary, Irish-Americans planned a fitting celebration of Grattan's victory over British imperialism. Some of them, including John Boyle O'Reilly, thought that ingredients were available for a successful repetition of 1782. Discontent and agrarian violence were sweeping through rural Ireland. Disraeli's imperial ventures had polarized British politics and brought the United Kingdom to the brink of war with Russia. Perhaps "Britain's difficulty was Ireland's opportunity"? O'Reilly thought so. He predicted that a new generation of Irish volunteers would dictate terms to a beleaguered British government.

Moving from words to practical policy, John Devoy decided to integrate Ford's war on landlordism, Parnell's active parliamentary strategy, agrarian discontent in Ireland, and Anglo-Russian tensions into a New Departure strategy. He worked out the following timetable. Parnell and his colleagues would continue to articulate forcefully Irish grievances in the House of Commons, focusing British attention on constitutional Home Rule. Meanwhile, the clan would prepare the Irish people for revolution by mobilizing, radicalizing, and disciplining them around an agitation for tenant-right which would be a prelude to a demand for peasant proprietorship. When the agrarian masses were organized and ready for action, Parnell would demand Home Rule. If British politicians responded negatively, he and his associates would withdraw from Westminster and establish an Irish government in Dublin, which the Irish people would defend with guns, bullets, and leadership from Irish Americans. The Clan na Gael established 1882 as the target date for the culmination of the New Departure.

When Clan na Gael leaders contacted him and presented their terms for an alliance, Parnell faced a dilemma. He wanted and needed Irish American support in the campaign to become the leader of the Home Rule movement, but the Clan's offer had pitfalls. Parnell had no desire to become a cog

CHARLES STEWART PARNELL
1846–1891

As President of the National Land League and Chairman of the Irish Parliamentary Party, Charles Stewart Parnell made Home Rule and the Irish Question the dominant issue in British politics. His decline and fall led to a messiah myth and cult that inspired Irish literature and a new generation of intense nationalists. (Photo taken from R. Barry O'Brien, *The Life of Charles Stewart Parnell,* London, 1910.)

in a conspiratorial machine manipulated from New York, and he did not want to prove Butt's charge that he was an agent of physical force nationalism. He needed the Catholic bishops and priests as well as the Irish Americans. Parnell was polite to Clan envoys, but avoided making a commitment to the New Departure. He was, however, attracted by its agrarian program, especially by its spokesman, Michael Davitt.

Davitt, a released Fenian prisoner, became a New Departure disciple while visiting and lecturing in the United States. In 1879, he returned to his home county and launched the Land League of Mayo, which quickly evolved into the National Land League. As a foe of landlordism, the Land League attracted tenant farmers and absorbed the secret agrarian terrorist societies that had been revived in the late 1870's. Many of the grass roots leaders of the Land League were marginal middle-class people in the towns, petty bourgeosie threatened by the agrarian depression. Their experience as members of town councils and poor law boards of guardians gave them the political savvy that Davitt needed in his lieutenants.

First John O'Connor Power and then Parnell, Biggar, and other active Home Rule M.P.s began to appear on Land League platforms demanding "the land of Ireland for the people of Ireland." Other obstructionists began telling British audiences that it was time for the English and Scottish industrial proletariats to join with the Irish agrarian proletariat in a democratic alliance against the exploiters of the poor: British industrialists and Irish landlords.

In July, 1880, John Dillon, the son of John Blake Dillon, a Parnell lieutenant, militant Land Leaguer, and recently elected M.P. for East Mayo, advocated a general rent strike. He advised tenant farmers to join the Land League, to purchase arms for their defense, to march to meetings in military formation, and to refuse friendship to anyone cooperating with landlordism. Two months later in a speech in Ennis, County Clare, Parnell picked up Dillon's theme. He told his tenant farmer audience to shun the human instruments of landlordism. The Land League applied this suggestion to a Mayo estate managed by Captain Charles Cunningham Boycott. Irish agitators had added a new word to the English language and created a new radical tactic.

Parnell's influence over the Irish masses had a profound effect on Davitt, who realized that the parliamentarian had a charisma he lacked. To speed the pace and improve the prospects of the Land League, Davitt stepped aside and Parnell took his place as President of the organization. While Parnell was promoting the Land League, Butt was losing ground. His defense of Disraeli's imperialism in the Near East and negotiations with the Conservative government for scholarship aid to Catholic secondary schools—although successful—alienated Irish nationalist opinion. In May, 1879, he died a broken and rejected leader. Home Rule M.P.s selected William Shaw, a Protestant Cork banker, to succeed Butt as Party Chairman. When Disraeli called a general election in June, 1880, Parnell was in the United States soliciting funds for the Land League. He hurried home to contest and win three seats, finally deciding to sit for Cork. Following the election, a majority of the Irish Party elected him as Chairman. Shaw and about twenty of his followers refused to accept this decision. They sat as independent nationalists and collaborated with the Liberals.

As President of the National Land League, President of the Home Rule Confederation of Great Britain, and Chairman of the Irish Parliamentary

Party, Parnell commanded the attention, loyalty, and resources of the Irish in the United Kingdom and the United States. The Clan na Gael had set out to capture Parnell, and turn him into a tool of revolutionary nationalism. Now it was doing his bidding among the American Irish.

From 1880 to 1882, Parnell directed an agrarian movement bordering on insurrection. Not since the glorious days of Repeal in 1843 had any Irish agitation enlisted so much enthusiasm. Irish Americans contributed vast sums of money to aid evicted tenants and to purchase legal services for embattled farmers. Despite inflammatory rhetoric, Land League officials attempted to channel discontent into a constitutional, passive-resistance attack on landlordism. But it was a difficult task. Agrarian violence exploded in all parts of the country, but mostly in the West. Desperate and dangerous men maimed cattle, burned hay ricks, and assaulted landlord agents and those tenant farmers who dared occupy the farms of evictees. In the opinion of Irish landlords, British journalists, and Conservative politicians, anarchy ruled Ireland. Neither coercion bills nor the efforts of the Royal Irish Constabulary were able to intimidate the Land League.

As leader of the Irish Party, Parnell moved the land agitation into the halls of Parliament. Gladstone responded with a mixed policy of coercion and conciliation. The Liberal government outlawed the Land League and suspended habeus corpus in Ireland, imprisoning many League officials without formal charges. At the same time it passed remedial legislation. Although the Liberals stopped short of dismantling Irish landlordism, the Land Act of 1881 gave tenant farmers fixity of tenure at fair rents and compensation for improvements.

Conscious that Davitt and many other Land Leaguers wanted to destroy not reform landlordism, Parnell refused to acknowledge the Liberal proposal. He continued the agrarian agitation, insisting that tenants in arrears—one third of all the farmers in Ireland, two-thirds in Mayo—be restored to their holdings. Angered by Parnell's refusal to accept the Land Act as a final settlement, the government arrested him and a number of his lieutenants and placed them in Kilmainham prison, Dublin. Actually, Gladstone probably added to Parnell's strength. The Irish leader had exploited the land question to mobilize Irish opinion behind him as the leader of Irish nationalism. His strategy had worked and his confinement increased his popularity by making him a martyr. Now that the British government had conceded a significant measure of tenant-right, Parnell wanted to swing Irish agitation back in the direction of Home Rule. He was tired of keeping the Land League within the pale of constitutionalism. While Parnell pondered and brooded in Kilmainham, Gladstone crushed the Land League, eliminating a major problem for the Irish leader.

The surge of agrarian violence that followed the arrest of Parnell worried the Prime Minister. Against the advice of his law-and-order Chief Secretary for Ireland, W. E. Forster, who resigned over the issue, Gladstone decided to negotiate Parnell's release from Kilmainham. In exchange for Parnell's pledge to support the Irish policies of the Liberal government, Gladstone introduced an Arrears Act which guaranteed £800,000 in rent to restore 130,000 evicted tenants to their farms and to make them eligible for all the benefits of the Land Act. All in all, the Kilmainham Treaty was a considerable victory for Parnell. But much of the luster of this triumph was tarnished when, in May, 1882, the Invincibles, an IRB splinter group, assassinated the new Irish Chief Secretary, Lord Frederick Cavendish, and his Under-Secretary, T. H. Burke. In disgust, Parnell offered to retire from public life. Gladstone rejected this suggestion, but the pressures of British public opinion forced him to apply a tough coercion policy in Ireland.

THE LIBERAL ALLIANCE
AND THE FALL OF PARNELL

After 1882, Parnell concentrated on strengthening the forces of Home Rule in Ireland and at Westminster. He transferred funds from the suppressed Land League to the Irish Party, using this money and further contributions from Irish Americans to recruit sincere and talented young men as Home Rule candidates, to pay their election expenses, and to cover their living costs while they served their country at Westminster. The Ballot Act of 1872, which guaranteed secret voting, and the Third Reform Bill of 1884, which extended the franchise to the rural democracy, guaranteed the Irish Party at least eighty-five seats in the House of Commons.

Starting with the general election of 1880, the quality of nationalist M.P.s began to improve. Parnell insisted that they must conform to party discipline on all issues. He created the first efficient party to function in the House of Commons. Once he had a dependable body of men at his command, Parnell switched from the flashy but limited tactics of obstruction to a balance-of-power strategy designed to force one of the British parties to make a Home Rule commitment.

In Ireland, Parnell scrapped the dying Home Rule League, replacing it with the Irish National League. The Irish in Britain and America organized branches of the League. The main purpose of the National League and its local branches in Ireland was to gain constituency support for the Irish Party. The National Leagues in the United States and Britain collected and contributed funds to the Home Rule effort, and the latter organization worked to elect English and Scottish politicians friendly to Irish self-government. Irish Americans also applied pressure on Washington to prevent any Anglo-American entente until Ireland was independent.

During the 1880's, Parnell's control over the forces of Irish nationalism forced the Roman Catholic hierarchy to endorse his leadership over the Irish people. When Paul Cardinal Cullen died in 1878, he bequeathed a Catholic church in Ireland that was structurally, economically, and spiritually sound. But within a few years his achievements were in danger. Irish Catholicism became caught between an Irish nationalism energized by the Land League and the genius of Parnell, and Leo XIII's attempt to win British diplomatic recognition of the Vatican.

In his courtship of the British government, the Pope attempted to sever Irish bishops and priests from any connection with agrarian agitation or nationalism. Leo's pro-British policy infuriated Irish Catholics, threatening to destroy the Irish and Catholic twin identities. To prevent this calamity and to keep their flock in the Roman fold, and also to be true to their own patriotic convictions, Archbishops William J. Walsh (Dublin) and Thomas William Croke (Cashel) kept the hierarchy and clergy loyal to Irish nationalism and forced Rome to halt its policy of sacrificing Ireland to the papal quest for British recognition.

Under the guidance of Croke and Walsh, the bishops renewed the compact with Irish nationalism first negotiated by O'Connell and MacHale back in the 1840's. A majority of the hierarchy recognized the Irish Parliamentary Party's creation of a *de facto* Irish nation and endorsed its right to become a *de jure* state as long as the methods used to accomplish this goal were constitutional. In exchange, Parnell, like O'Connell, acknowledged the hierarchy's prerogative to control the spiritual life of the Catholic laity. This meant the Irish Party would work in Parliament for a state-financed Catholic educational system from the primary through the university levels.

From the beginnings of parliamentary nationalism in the 1830's, its leaders had arranged pragmatic alliances with the British left. In 1885, Parnell decided to stop this pattern in an effort to convince Gladstone of the power of the Irish Party in the House of Commons and the Irish vote in British urban constituencies. On his instructions, in June, Home Rule M.P.s voted with the Conservatives against the government, forcing Gladstone out of office and permitting the Marquess of Salisbury to construct a minority government. In order to retain the friendship of the Irish Party, the Conservative government abandoned coercion, appointed the Earl of Carnarvon, a friend of Home Rule, as Lord Lieutenant, and passed the Ashbourne Act which appropriated five million pounds for tenant land purchase at reasonable terms.

During the 1885 election campaign, Parnell had advised the Irish in Britain to vote Conservative. This advice was not capricious. Parnell had been convinced by Lord Randolph Churchill, the Conservative Party's bright young champion of Tory democracy, that a Conservative government would continue to pass valuable Irish reform legislation and would consider the merits of Home Rule. The Irish leader also knew that a Conservative government could get an Irish settlement involving self-government through the House of Lords, whereas Liberals would have a difficult time doing the same. Parnell's decision to help the Conservatives was popular with the Catholic hierarchy in Britain, who considered the Liberals the enemies of denominational education. And more important, the Chairman of the Irish Party wanted to reduce the Liberal majority in Britain to increase the influence of Home Rule M.P.s in the House of Commons. Irish voters in Britain may have been responsible for the victory of twenty-five or more Conservative candidates. But outside of Ireland the Liberals had an eighty-six seat majority. However, the Irish Party also won eighty-six seats and decided to permit Salisbury to continue as Prime Minister.

After the election was over, the Conservatives changed direction on their Irish policy. Perhaps they decided that since the Irish vote did not bring them a British majority, it was no longer necessary or in their best interests to court Parnell and his friends. Salisbury made it clear that despite Lord Carnarvon, Home Rule was out of the question. He announced his intention to restore coercion in Ireland. In response, the Irish joined with the Liberals and voted against the government on an amendment to the Address, forcing Salisbury to resign.

Gladstone once more was Prime Minister. Without consulting other Liberal leaders, he announced his conversion to Home Rule, commiting his party to the goals of Irish constitutional nationalism. Gladstone's embrace of Home Rule created the Irish-Liberal alliance, perhaps the most important event in British politics since Peel's Irish policy split the Conservatives in the 1840's. His decision to tie the future destinies of the Liberal and Irish Parties touched off cries of anguish among British Liberals, costing him considerable support in and out of Parliament, but it did help clarify the ideological position of British party politics.

When Gladstone introduced the first Home Rule Bill in 1886, many Whig aristocrats and Joseph Chamberlain and some of his Radical friends deserted the Prime Minister, which defeated the measure and destroyed the Liberal government. For a time, the defectors described themselves as independents or Liberal Unionists, but they eventually joined the Conservative Party. The Conservatives then changed their party name to Unionist to better exploit the impact of the Home Rule issue on no popery, anti-Irish, and pro-imperialist sections of British public opinion.

Whigs felt more at home in a party resisting demands for democracy and social reform, defending the House of Lords and the Protestant church, and demanding an expansion of empire, than they did taking directions from Gladstone who was always ready to place necessity ahead of dogma. Without the Whigs, Liberals were free to identify with the forces of change. As the two British parties competed for votes, the issue of Irish Home Rule defined left and right; it symbolized the forces of democracy, social justice, and colonial self-government engaged in a struggle against aristocracy, privilege, property, and aggressive imperialism.

The Conservative decision to tie their fortunes to the fate of the Union was a shrewd decision, consistent with the thinking of the British right wing throughout the nineteenth century. By opposing Home Rule they represented British nativism. Their slogan, "Home Rule is Rome Rule," was the accepted wisdom of the British majority. Conservatives were also able to exploit Irish sectarianism as a way to maintain the Union, the pivot of the Empire, and to frustrate the Irish-Liberal alliance. During the 1886 debate on Home Rule in the House of Commons, Lord Randolph Churchill, who negotiated with Parnell in the previous year, made a cynical bid for power within the Conservative Party. In an effort to embarrass the Liberals, he went to Belfast to "play the Orange card." While there, he incited Protestant hate and fanaticism by shouting "Ulster will fight and Ulster will be right."

By cultivating Ulster Protestant bigotry, British Conservatives were probing the Achilles' heel of Home Rule. Northeast Ulster was not part of the Irish Party constituency. Instead it was the core of resistance to Irish nationalism. The Belfast region was integrated into the industrial economy of the United Kingdom. Ulster Unionists feared that in addition to inflicting Rome Rule on them, Home Rule would destroy the commerce and industry of the North. Although Ulster Presbyterians were more anti-Catholic than Church of Irelanders in the South, and the Orange Order had more influence in the North than in other parts of the country, most Irish Protestants believed that Irish Catholics were inferior human beings who would use their majority position in an Irish Parliament to persecute their betters:

Underlying all Protestant attitudes—the very tap root of prejudice—was a belief that religion was the mould of character. Catholics were dirty, lazy, thriftless, unreliable and ignorant. They were taught that it was no sin to tell lies to a Protestant or to steal from a Protestant. They were kept in ignorance so that their priests could hold sway over them. Protestants according to this thesis were on top because they were better, and they were better because they were Protestant.[1]

Appealing to religious prejudice in Ireland was irresponsible politics, but Conservatives would do anything to protect the Empire by preserving the Union. They believed that once Britain surrendered to the pressures of Irish nationalism, she would no longer be able to resist independence moves in India or Africa. To the British, Irish Catholics were very similar to the brown and black savages in the outposts of Empire. Like other passionate, emotional, and irresponsible breeds, they too needed the guidance of British rule.

[1]Jack White, "The Cold Grey Light of Dawn," an extract from *Minority Report: the Anatomy of the Southern Irish Protestant*, Dublin: Gill and Macmillan, 1975, published in *The Irish Times*, October 9, 1975, p. 8.

After 1886, the independence of the Irish Party was limited by the exigencies of the Liberal alliance. In the House of Commons, Parnell had to soften the tone of Irish nationalism to please the ear of British Liberal opinion. His reluctance to endorse the Plan of Campaign was an example of the new caution in the Home Rule movement.

The agricultural depression did not end with the Land Act. Many tenant farmers still found it difficult to pay their rents. Some members of the Irish Party—John Dillon, William O'Brien, and Timothy Harrington— advised tenant farmers to ask for a further reduction of rents. If landlords refused this request, they suggested farmers withdraw the rents they were prepared to pay and put them in a fund to assist evicted tenants. This Plan of Campaign swept the country. The effort by the Unionist government to halt it by a policy of coercion, including the arrest of the radical Home Rule M.P.s, often provoked incidents of violence. Parnell, however, did not join the new war on landlordism, and grudgingly contributed Irish Party funds for the relief of evicted tenants. He refused to alienate British opinion, weaken the Liberal alliance, or divert constitutional nationalism from the path of Home Rule.

Parnell's lack of support for agrarian protest did not damage his reputation in Ireland. In fact, in 1889 his popularity reached new heights, when he was exonerated of a *Times'* (London) charge that he had encouraged the Phoenix Park assassinations in May, 1882. During cross examination, Parnell's attorney proved that the *Times'* accusation was based on evidence forged by Richard Pigott, a Dublin journalist. This triumph over an old enemy of Ireland brought British as well as Irish cheers. Many people in England, Scotland, and Wales believed that Parnell had been a victim of unprincipled and vindictive journalism. He received a standing ovation in the House of Commons.

Parnell's happiness was short-lived. In December, 1889, Captain William O'Shea sued his wife Katherine for divorce, naming Parnell as correspondent. Liberal leaders, Parnell's closest Irish Party associates, and even Captain O'Shea had known that Mrs. O'Shea had been Parnell's mistress for years. She was the mother of three of his children, two of whom survived infancy. O'Shea was a despicable man who had used his wife's charms to advance his own career. In return for his noninterference in her relationship with Parnell, O'Shea had accepted money from his wife and a Home Rule seat in Galway from Parnell. He never took the Party loyalty pledge. Parnell wanted to marry Mrs. O'Shea, but she hesitated to seek a divorce because the scandal might eliminate her from the will of a wealthy aunt, Mrs. Benjamin Wood. When Mrs. Wood died, Mrs. O'Shea agreed to buy a divorce from her husband for £20,000. When the estate got tangled up in legal proceedings, the impatient O'Shea began to doubt his wife's intentions. His revenge was a divorce suit.

When the announcement of the divorce trial first appeared in the newspapers, it had little impact on Irish nationalists. The Irish people seemed to think that the whole business was another dirty English trick to embarrass Parnell. He told Home Rule M.P.s that his honor would be vindicated in the court room. Later Parnell decided against contesting the divorce, because such action would postpone marriage to Mrs. O'Shea. As a result of this decision, in November, 1890, the judge handed down a verdict based on O'Shea's unchallenged testimony, evidence that Parnell was an unscrupulous fiend who had invaded the home of a friend and seduced his wife. O'Shea got the divorce and the custody of the children, including Parnell's.

Immediately after the judge's decision, the Irish Party and the National League pledged their loyalty to Parnell, but British Nonconformists, a powerful Liberal constituency, told Gladstone that either Parnell must resign as Chairman of the Irish Party or Liberals must cancel the Irish alliance. They warned that failure to heed this ultimatum would cost the Liberals dearly at subsequent elections. The rigidity and puritanism of the Nonconformist conscience compelled Gladstone to inform the Irish Party that either Parnell or the Liberal alliance must go. Parnell became a victim of the alliance he negotiated, a compact that restricted the independence of the Irish Party. Since Parnell was not as important as Home Rule, on December 6, 1890, after six days of acrimonious debate, a substantial majority of the Irish Party withdrew from Committee Room 15 of the House of Commons and in another place elected Justin McCarthy, historian and essayist, as their Chairman.

Parnell rejected this decision and appealed to the ultimate source of his strength, the Irish people. In a series of by-elections, he addressed the Irish nation. Parnell claimed that the independence of the Irish Party from Liberal dictation and not his leadership was the fundamental issue, and that his enemies were toadies of Gladstone. By taking his case to the Irish people, Parnell involved the Irish Catholic hierarchy and clergy in the dispute. When it came to sexual morality, they could not appear less demanding than British Protestants. They said that no public sinner, no adulterer, no defiler of the home was fit to lead the Irish people in their quest for freedom.

Fighting for his very political existence, Parnell appealed to the Fenian spirit. He suggested to the "hillside" men that if Home Rule did not accomplish quick results, he would lead the people in Republican passive resistance to British rule in Ireland. Parnell's struggle against British Liberalism and Catholic clericalism attracted significant IRB support, but as he traveled through the country he constantly confronted hostile mobs led by priests demanding that he retire from Irish politics. His candidates lost all three by-elections and Parnell ruined his health campaigning in the Irish cold and damp. On October 6, 1891, he died at forty-five years of age in Brighton, England, in the presence of his wife. After a massive Dublin funeral, managed by the IRB, Irish nationalists laid Parnell's body to rest in Glasnevin cemetery, close to O'Connell.

6

challenges
to home°rule

HOME RULE AND BRITISH PARTY POLITICS

In 1892, Gladstone formed his fourth and final administration. The next year, the House of Commons passed his Second Home Rule Bill, but the House of Lords rejected it. Gladstone wanted to take the subject of the Lord's veto power to the people in a general election, but most of his Cabinet colleagues thought it a risky issue, particularly when coupled with the Irish Question. The Prime Minister was at odds with his colleagues over another subject: he opposed increasing naval expenditures. Gladstone concluded that he no longer represented the will of his party and resigned as Prime Minister on March 1, 1894. His successor, Lord Rosebery, was a proponent of a strong defense establishment and a champion of Empire. He promptly announced that the Liberals would not offer another Home Rule bill to Parliament until they were convinced that a British majority favored Irish self-government. However, the Liberals were not long for office. In late 1895, divisions within the Cabinet, vetoes of government legislation in the House of Lords, and a slim Liberal majority in the House of Commons persuaded Rosebery to turn power over to the Unionists. A subsequent general election confirmed that the Liberals were out of public favor.

In opposition, the Liberals began to re-evaluate the Irish alliance. Rosebery was uncomfortable with Home Rule. He thought it raised barriers between the party and the British people. He wanted the Liberals to concentrate on social reform to woo working-class voters concerned about the poverty and unemployment resulting from a declining British economy. Rosebery sensed a militant nationalism in the British air as European countries armed to the teeth and competed for empires in Asia and Africa. He wanted to contest the jingoist vote with Unionists. And Irish nationalists offended Liberal imperialists. As the first victims of British colonialism, they ridiculed the humanitarian and religious cant that British politicians and journalists employed to rationalize imperialism. Irish Party sympathy for the Boers during the 1899–1902 South African War was considered unpatriotic. It infuriated majority opinion in Britain, driving many Liberals farther away from the Irish alliance.

John Morley, who best represented the Gladstone tradition of British Liberalism, insisted that Home Rule was a moral commitment. Most Liberals agreed with him that their party could not completely abandon the Irish alliance. They also supported Rosebery's contention that Liberalism should emphasize issues attractive to British middle and working-class voters, even if this meant postponing Home Rule until it was more popular in England, Scotland, and Wales.

Irish nationalists resented the Liberal retreat from Home Rule, but they were in no position to insist on compliance with the Irish-Liberal alliance. Since the fall of Parnell, Irish constitutional nationalism had been in a shambles. John Redmond, the leader of the Parnellites, had some constituency support in Ireland—much of it from segments of the IRB, but only a small number of M.P.s followed him in the House of Commons—nine were elected in 1892, eleven in 1895. The anti-Parnellite majority was split by personality and strategy differences and faced a shortage of funds. Without Parnell's leadership, his brilliant lieutenants—John Dillon, Tim Healy, and William O'Brien—took to feuding. Healy caused the most trouble. In a bid for clerical support, he suggested restructuring the Irish Party to give constituency organizations, where priests played a prominent role, more influence over policy. In 1895, John Dillon, a talented parliamentarian, succeeded Justin McCarthy as Chairman of the anti-Parnellite wing of the Irish Party. He managed to frustrate Healy's constituency strategy and his grasp for power. Although Dillon restored party discipline, he was unable to ease its financial burdens or to boost nationalist morale.

With the Liberals ambivalent toward Home Rule and Irish nationalism divided and demoralized, the Unionists had a favorable opportunity to experiment with the Irish Question. From 1886 to 1892 and then from 1895 to 1902, Lord Salisbury was Prime Minister. His nephew, Arthur J. Balfour, served as Irish Chief Secretary from 1887 to 1891 and then succeeded his uncle as Prime Minister in 1902. Balfour was the architect of the Unionist Irish policy. Both Salisbury and Balfour refused to entertain the possibility of an Irish Parliament. They thought the Irish were incapable of self-government, and they were convinced that Home Rule for Ireland would weaken Britain's defenses, unravel the fabric of Empire, and create an image of declining British power. They also felt a strong commitment to Irish Protestants and assured them that a Unionist government would never permit Catholic majority rule in Ireland.

Balfour decided that Unionist opposition to Home Rule did not exclude Irish reform. He convinced his uncle that the Irish Question demanded a solution to end turmoil and division within the United Kingdom, and the solution could stop short of Home Rule. Once Ireland was tranquil, British governments could concentrate on the pressing needs of Empire and national defense. In pondering the Irish situation, Balfour came to the same conclusions that Peel reached in the 1840's: Irish nationalism was a surface manifestation of deeper social, economic, and political discontent. He argued that if British politicians would address themselves to the problems underlying Irish protest, the issue of Home Rule would vanish into the mists and bogs of Ireland. Balfour assured other Unionists that they could "kill Home Rule with kindness."

In 1891, Balfour established the Congested Districts Board, which was empowered to found agricultural and technical schools, supply equipment to fishermen, and organize a cottage textile industry in the most underdeveloped areas of Ireland. The Unionist government also voted large sums of money for public works projects involving railroad construction, road improvement, and drainage schemes. The Congested Districts Board and the public works projects provided employment and invigorated the rural economy. Politically, the Unionists did make a significant concession to Irish demands for local control. The Local Government Act of 1898 stripped grand juries dominated by the Protestant gentry of fiscal and administrative authority over local government and transferred these powers to democratically elected urban, town, and county councils. In 1903, the Unionists capped their Irish reform policy with the Wyndham Land Act. This bill provided loans on very favorable terms to about 200,000 tenants for the full purchase price of their farms, which eventually replaced landlords with peasant proprietors.

Though they didn't grant Home Rule, by the time the Unionists left office in 1905, a variety of British governments had redressed all of the grievances that had melded into Irish nationalism, with the exception of university education. The Unionists, the party of aristocracy and property, had experimented with the welfare state in Ireland. But they underestimated the intensity of Irish nationalism. They did not realize that by the time their party got around to confronting social, political, and economic discontent in Ireland, nationalism had already assumed an identity independent of these issues. Peasant proprietorship, a higher standard of living, and control over local government encouraged rather than diminished a hunger for more dignity and freedom.

VARIETIES IN IRISH NATIONALISM

In 1900, after a decade of division, the Irish Party was reunited under the leadership of John Redmond. John Dillon graciously agreed to serve as Redmond's chief lieutenant. Under the new arrangement, the United Irish League replaced the Irish National League (Parnellite) and the Irish National Federation (anti-Parnellite) as the new constituency organization. William O'Brien had founded the United Irish League in 1898 to persuade the British government to divide and distribute the large grazing ranches in the West among Irish peasants as a means of checking emigration.

Not only did party reunification improve Home Rule prospects in the House of Commons, it also encouraged the Irish at home and abroad to open their purses to the Irish Party. To all visible appearances, Home Rule nationalism was in sound condition. Tim Healy and William O'Brien refused to conform to party discipline, but the vast majority of the Irish population continued to vote for the Irish Party at by-elections and general elections, and John Redmond commanded over eighty M.P.s in the House of Commons. But appearances were deceiving. There was a slowly expanding gap between the Home Rulers at Westminster and their constituents, particularly the younger generation.

Redmond, Dillon, and their Irish Party colleagues were politicians of talent and integrity, but they lacked Parnell's charisma. The trauma of Irish nationalism in the 1890's, with its feuds and splits, and the conviction of many that the Irish Party had betrayed Parnell to appease the Liberals, had renewed cynicism concerned the character of constitutional nationalism, an uneasy feeling that did not completely vanish with party unification. And after 1900, many problems continued to nag the Irish Party. Some critics said that Home Rule M.P.s were a clerical lobby at Westminster, others ridiculed them as pawns of the Liberal Party. Since Irish Party M.P.s had to insist that the Union was a failure and 'that only an Irish Parliament could do justice to Irish needs, they could not take credit for their substantial efforts and successes in the British Parliament. They could not dwell on the fact that the activities of Home Rule M.P.s at Westminster had forced British politicians to pass legislation that certainly improved the condition of the Irish people.

By 1900, the Irish Party had lost the bloom of youth and had become a familiar part of the nationalist landscape. The lessons of parliamentary experience and the restrictions of the Liberal alliance had transformed the energetic young firebrands, almost revolutionaries, who had arrived at

Westminster in the turbulent 1880's into cautious, prudent, sophisticated, practical, and pragmatic politicians. They never sold their convictions for place or profit or shirked their duty to Irish constituents, but over the years Home Rule M.P.s slowly, almost imperceptibly and unconsciously, became integrated into the British political system. They enjoyed the give and take of parliamentary debate, appreciated the corridors and vestibules of power, respected British institutions, and came to like and admire the British people. Westminster was a long way and a tedious journey from their Irish base of power. It was so easy for Home Rule leaders to lose touch with the nuances of Irish life. Redmond, an introvert, sometimes was insensitive to the undercurrents of Irish opinion. He and many of his colleagues did not understand the implications of a revived cultural nationalism or the depths of urban poverty and misery.

In many ways, the revival of Irish cultural nationalism was a response to Anglo-Saxon racism. In the eighteenth and early nineteenth centuries, anti-Irish prejudice in Britain mostly was based on religious differences. British and Irish Protestants believed that they were superior to Catholics who were caught in the authoritarian and superstitious clutches of popery. With the decline of religious enthusiasm among the British upper and middle classes, anti-Irish feelings began to assume a more racist garb. The contrast between Anglo-Saxons and Celts seemed a more scientific basis than that between Protestants and Catholics to explain British superiority and Irish inferiority. Racism was part of the evolving character of nationalism all over the Western world, and the "Cyclops" chapter of James Joyce's *Ulysses* reveals that it did not escape Ireland.

British intellectuals and scholars drew on Social Darwinism to create an apologia for Anglo-Saxon racism. Distinguished historians Edward A. Freeman, James A. Froude, William Stubbs, Goldwin Smith, and John R. Green claimed that the ancestors of the present inhabitants of Britain originated the concept of liberty in the forests of Germany and that this concept was enshrined in the British constitution. Scientists, social scientists, and pseudo-scientists measured skulls, jaw bones, and other parts of the human anatomy, and then ranked primates on a scale that placed Anglo-Saxons on top next to God, and the Irish, on the bottom, just above apes and blacks. Journalists simplified the "wisdom" of scholars and intellectuals and passed it on to their readers.

Anglo-Saxon racism erected another barrier to communication between the English and the Irish. Since the English considered the Irish intellectually and morally inferior, they refused to listen to Irish grievances and demands for independence. They discussed the Irish Question in a patronizing manner, viewing their responsibilities to the Irish as the same sort of duty that a man has toward women and children. To them, the Irish seemed feminine and childlike—emotional and dependent—needing the guidance of benevolent Anglo-Saxon masters to protect them from the consequences of their own weakness.

British politicians of all persuasions discussed the Irish Question in racist terms. Disraeli and Salisbury thought the Irish were savages, as incapable of self-government as the Hottentots. Advanced Liberals like Sir Charles Dilke and Fabians Sidney and Beatrice Webb considered the Irish an inferior race. In writing to a friend about a visit to Ireland, the Webbs also bracketed the Irish with the Hottentots:

> We will tell you about Ireland when we come back. The people are charming but we detest them, as we should the Hottentots—for their very virtues. Home Rule is an absolute necessity *in order to depopulate the country of this detestable race.*[1]

Freeman, the historian, also associated blacks and Irish. In 1881 he wrote from the United States:

> This would be a grand land if only every Irishman would kill a Negro, and be hanged for it. I find this sentiment generally approved—sometimes with the qualification that they want Irish and Negroes for servants, not being able to get any other. This looks like the ancient human weakness of craving for a subject race.[2]

Anglo-Irish racism encouraged the Irish to counter with Celtic racism. Although Young Ireland in the 1840's began to cultivate Celticism by insisting that the Irish were morally, intellectually, artistically, and spiritually superior to materialistic Anglo-Saxons, official Irish nationalism continued to reject sectarian or ethnic differences between various strains of the Irish population. And tenant-right, Land League, and Home Rule movements refused to exploit religious or cultural distinctions between the Anglo-Irish and the Catholic majority. But, after the fall of Parnell, Irish nationalism began to assume more racist tones.

Eliminating many bread-and-butter issues, Unionist reform measures contributed to the revival of Irish cultural nationalism by freeing Irish energies for intellectual concerns. In 1884, Michael Cusack, the Citizen in James Joyce's *Ulysses*, founded the Gaelic Athletic Association to discourage Irish participation in alien and effeminate English games. Hurling and Gaelic football became popular pastimes all over Ireland, particularly in small towns and villages. Those who continued to play cricket, rugby, or soccer were excluded or expelled from the Gaelic Athletic Association.

[1]Quoted from L. P. Curtis, Jr., *Anglo-Saxons and Celts: A Study of Anti-Irish Prejudice in Victorian England*, Bridgeport, Conn.: Conference on British Studies at the University of Bridgeport, 1968, p. 63. Reprinted by permission of the University of Bridgeport.
[2]Curtis, *Anglo-Saxons and Celts*, p. 81.

Priests encouraged enthusiasm for strenuous Gaelic games as a way of guarding the sexual purity of young people by distracting them from dangerous foreign cultural influences and by consuming their energies.

Middle-class urbanites were attracted by the Gaelic League, organized in 1893, largely through the efforts of its first Secretary, Eoin MacNeill. The League was dedicated to restoring Irish as the vernacular. League members visited Irish-speaking districts in Waterford, Cork, Kerry, Galway, Mayo, Donegal, and the Aran Islands to learn the native tongue from peasants uncorrupted by Anglo-Saxon culture. They sang songs in Irish, danced jigs and reels, started schools featuring instruction in the Irish language, and wrote plays, stories, and poems in Irish. Gaelic Leaguers were critical of those who were indifferent or hostile to an Irish-Ireland. They called them West Britons or Shoneens (little John Bulls).

The Gaelic League officially rejected sectarianism. Its first President was Douglas Hyde, an Anglo-Irish Protestant Celtic scholar. From the time of Sean O'Casey to the present, many Gaelic Leaguers have charged the Catholic hierarchy and clergy with anti-Irish language biases. This is a false accusation. A large number of priests realized that an Irish-Ireland would be a Catholic fortress against the assaults of English Protestant and secular cultures. Many of them joined the League and supported its demand that Irish should be taught in the schools, and that proficiency in Irish should be a qualification for admission to the new National University established by the Liberal government in 1908.

Celticism and the Irish-Ireland ideal inspired a literary movement of great distinction. The movement fostered the talents and genius of William Butler Yeats, Lady Augusta Gregory, A. E. (George Russell), John Millington Synge, James Joyce, and Sean O'Casey, artists who made Dublin a literary capital of the Western world. All but Joyce were Protestants, but their plays, poems, and stories reflected the search for a Celtic Irish cultural identity. Celtic mythology, themes, and values inspired their work. They praised Irish peasant simplicity, spirituality, and virtue as a continuation of the Celtic tradition, and scorned Anglo-Saxon industrialism, commercialism, materialism, and urbanization. In a way, the Irish Literary Renaissance was the last, brilliant gasp of the European Romantic Movement.

In contrast to their Young Ireland predecessors, the writers of the Literary Revival were essentially artists rather than propagandists. Because they wrote in English and were too dedicated to their art to hide the blemishes of their subject matter, many Irish-Irelanders attacked Anglo-Irish literature as "cosmopolitan" and "West British." When Synge's *Playboy of the Western World* was produced by the Abbey Theatre in 1907, the play touched off a riot. Many Irish and Catholic cultural nationalists (often it was

WILLIAM BUTLER YEATS
1865–1939

William Butler Yeats was the dominant personality in the Irish Literary Revival which perpetuated the cultural nationalism of Young Ireland and articulated it to a world opinion that pressured the British government into conceding Dominion status to twenty-six Irish counties. (Courtesy of the Bettman Archives)

hard to distinguish between the two) attacked Synge because he suggested that peasants did not spend all of their time saying the rosary; sometimes they could be bawdy and violent.

Although the Literary Revival occasionally scandalized and antagonized Irish-Irelanders, it made an important contribution to the momentum of Irish cultural nationalism. Audiences and critics disliked the pagan tones of Yeats' *Countess Cathleen,* but they loved his *Cathleen ni Houlihan* as the best theatrical representation of the spirit of Irish nationalism. Irish writers disproved the myths of Anglo-Saxon racism. Their work demonstrated to the world that the Irish possessed a unique and interesting cultural identity. And world opinion eventually helped persuade the British that the Irish genius deserved to develop in an environment of national independence.

Irish-Ireland cultural nationalism was a protest against parliamentary politics as well as Anglo-Saxonism. Like Young Irelanders before them, a new generation of Irish intellectuals and artists desired more than an Irish

Parliament in College Green. To them, freedom had intellectual and spiritual dimensions. They insisted that Ireland must be de-Anglicized. The people must think, speak, and act Irish.

This new emphasis on a multi-dimensional nationalism, and the generation gap between Irish Party M.P.s and young people caught up in the mystique of Parnell, the fallen Messiah, the rebel against British imperialism and Irish clericalism, and the beginnings of an urban social and economic radicalism did encourage political alternatives to Home Rule. In 1898 Arthur Griffith began to present the Sinn Fein ('ourselves alone') program in his paper, the *United Irishman.* The program synthesized (1) O'Connell's Repeal tactics, the arbitration courts and the proposed Council of Three Hundred; (2) Duffy's suggestion that Irish nationalist M.P.s should withdraw from Westminster and establish an Irish Parliament, an idea that the New Departure also recommended; (3) Griffith's interpretation of Austro-Hungarian history; (4) the protectionist theories of the German economist, Friedrich List; and (5) the values of Irish-Ireland.

Arthur Griffith preferred a Republican solution to the Irish Question, but he decided that the British would never concede complete separation and Ireland would never have the military strength to forceably break the British connection. He recommended his Sinn Fein program as a compromise between Republicanism and Home Rule. He proposed a Dual Monarchy arrangement as a reasonable conclusion to the long conflict between British imperialism and Irish nationalism. As a tactic to persuade Britain to concede a sovereign Irish Parliament, Griffith urged passive resistance to British authority rather than the submissiveness of parliamentarianism or the futility of revolutionary violence. For the future independent Ireland, Griffith proposed cultural and economic self-sufficiency involving the development of industrial and agricultural resources and protection against foreign competition.

Arthur Griffith was not an attractive personality. Like his hero, John Mitchel, he put Irish nationalism in a provincial context. He had no compassion for other people suffering oppression. Griffith was anti-black and anti-semitic. The economic and cultural dimensions of his program also were narrow. He insisted that the writers of the Literary Revival should be patriots first and artists second, and in his emphasis on the need for Irish industrial development, committed Sinn Fein to a pro-capitalist, anti-labor position.

Except for arranging patriotic funerals, the Irish Republican Brotherhood had been an ineffective force in Irish politics after the rise of Home Rule. Without the prodding and the financial contributions of the Clan na Gael, the IRB might have vanished from the scene. But after the turn of the century, new leaders gave the Republican movement a sudden burst of energy. Thomas J. Clarke, a veteran of English prisons and a close friend of John Devoy, returned to Dublin from America and opened a tobacco shop that became a center of conspiracy. Bulmer Hobson and Denis McCullough from Belfast and Sean MacDermott were the young men who began to energize and discipline the IRB. Although there were only around 1,500 IRB members, Republicans infiltrated the Gaelic League, the Gaelic Athletic Association, and Sinn Fein when it became an organization in 1905. IRB people persuaded Griffith to abandon Dual Monarchy and to keep his options open.

Throughout the nineteenth century, Irish nationalism had been concerned with the economic and social grievances of tenant farmers, but it had ignored the needs of the urban poor, who suffered far worse conditions in Ireland than in Britain. Most city working-class people lived in overcrowded tenements that lacked even the most primitive sanitation facilities. Their diet of tea, jam, and bread resulted in malnutrition. Tuberculosis decimated many Irish families and the infant mortality rate was appalling. In a country with little industry, few natural resources, and a low level of capital investment, the working class suffered from unemployment or partial employment and low wages. Poverty, hunger, disease, and filth bred prostitution and alcoholism. Rooted in the tradition of agrarian protest and dependent on Catholic middle-class funds, the Irish Party could neither understand nor respond to urban problems. The Irish working class had no alternative but to turn for help to militant labor unions inspired by socialism.

In 1908, James Larkin, a Liverpool-born Irishman with Syndicalist leanings, organized the Irish Transport Workers Union. His chief lieutenant, James Connolly, an Ulster-born Catholic raised in Scotland, also believed in Syndicalist socialism. Ultimately, Larkin unionized about 10,000 workers, and through a series of strikes won significant concessions from Dublin employers. But in 1913, led by William Martin Murphy, a close associate of Tim Healy and the wealthiest man in Ireland with extensive economic interests in the United Kingdom and throughout the Empire, the employers combined in a no-surrender war against Larkin. When the Transport Workers Union struck Murphy's United Tramway Company, the combined employers retaliated by locking out 25,000 workers. After four months of hunger, police brutality, and the opposition of the Catholic hierarchy, Larkin had to surrender. Workers returned to work on the bosses' terms.

The general lockout revealed the frustrations and poverty of Irish urban life, exposed the limitations of the Irish Party as representative of working class interests, and indicated that nationalism in Ireland and Britain was a more powerful force than socialism or class solidarity. During the strike and lockout, Home Rule M.P.s sat on their hands. Their sympathies were pro-business and they feared Larkin's radicalism, but they despised

Murphy because he encouraged Healy's attacks on the Irish Party. As the strike dragged on, the support of the British Trade Union Congress grew lukewarm, suggesting that the British working class and its leaders shared the establishment's anti-Irish prejudices. As a result of the strike's failure and the inadequate backing of the British Trades Union Congress, the working-class movement in Ireland tended to become more nationalist and less socialist.

At the conclusion of the strike, Larkin went to the United States to raise money for the depleted union treasury. He remained there for a number of years, organizing American labor, promoting the Communist Party, and encouraging anti-British activities during World War I. In his absence, Connolly took charge of the Irish trade union movement. He created a Citizen Army to protect workers against further incidents of police brutality. More of a nationalist than Larkin, Connolly committed the Irish labor and socialist movements to the revolutionary goal of a worker's republic.

Irish-Ireland cultural nationalism, Sinn Fein, and socialist Republicanism were straws in the Irish wind. While attractive to young idealists, they were not yet a challenge or in some instances even a contradiction to Home Rule. Most Gaelic Leaguers, members of the Gaelic Athletic Association, and Irish writers considered themselves as part of the Irish Party constituency. While more bland than in the days of Parnell, the Irish Party still enjoyed the electoral support of the vast majority of the Irish people. It was safe as long as it continued to win victories at Westminster. The Liberal alliance remained both the strength and weakness of Irish constitutional nationalism.

THE CLIMAX OF HOME RULE

The human and financial costs of the Boer War, the steady decline of the British commercial and industrial economies, and the fear that the Unionists might further injure British trade and industry by applying protective tariffs resulted in a decisive Liberal victory in the general election of 1906. British voters gave the Liberals a 224 seat majority in the House of Commons. Free from the pressures of Irish nationalism, aware of the divisive nature of the Irish Question in Britain, less than enthusiastic about the Irish alliance, and eager to cater to the social and economic reform demands of the British electorate, Liberal leaders decided to keep Home Rule low on their list of priorities. They did, however, offer one concession to Irish nationalism. In 1907, the Prime Minister, Sir Henry Campbell-Bannerman, presented the Irish Party with a devolution proposal as a prelude to Home Rule. His scheme called for an Irish Council of eighty-two elected and twenty-nine appointed representatives, financed by a generous government subsidy, to assume the tasks of existing administrative agencies and boards. Campbell-Bannerman told Home Rule M.P.s that the Irish Council would give the Irish people an opportunity to convince the British that they were capable of self-government.

At first, Redmond was receptive to devolution, but finally, on the instructions of a National Convention, he rejected the government's offer. Convention delegates decided that devolution might prove a substitute for rather than a precursor to Home Rule. Some Catholic bishops also asked the Irish Party to reject the Irish Council Bill because it could result in lay interference in Catholic education. At the conclusion of the National Convention, Redmond told Campbell-Bannerman that Irish nationalists would accept nothing less than Home Rule as the Liberal obligation to the Irish alliance.

Defeated in their effort to compromise and postpone Home Rule, Liberals turned to less volatile Irish subjects. In 1908, they satisfied the Catholic education lobby by creating the National University of Ireland. It included the Queen's Colleges campuses in Cork and Galway and a new University College in Dublin built on the academic foundations of the Catholic University. Trinity College, Dublin, and Queen's University, Belfast, remained to serve the education needs of Protestants and Nonconformists. The next year, the Liberals smoothed out some of the wrinkles in the Wyndham Land Act and increased the money available for land purchase, speeding the process of peasant proprietorship.

Compared to their British reform legislation, the Liberal's Irish policy paled in significance. During their first three years in office, Liberal ministers concentrated on solving British social and economic problems which followed in the wake of a declining industrial economy that featured unimaginative leadership, static technology, increasing foreign competition, and an unfavorable balance of trade. Since many members of the upper and middle classes still enjoyed incomes from overseas investments, the urban working class bore most of the burden of a faltering economy. Proletarian insecurity and discontent fostered militant, syndicalist trade unionism and encouraged constituency support for the new Labour Party, which managed to win twenty-nine seats at the general election in 1906.

To calm urban unrest and forestall a mass working-class defection to socialism, the Liberal government introduced legislation laying down the foundations of the British welfare state—old age pensions, health insurance, unemployment compensation, employer's liability, and labor exchanges. This comprehensive program strained a budget committed to heavy defense spending to match German naval expenditures. The Chancellor of the Exchequer, David Lloyd George, once a Welsh Home Ruler, decided to make the rich pay for both the welfare state and national defense. In his search for new sources of tax revenue, he borrowed ideas from Fabian socialism. The government imposed substantial duties on the unearned profits from land and high income taxes on the wealthy. Inheritance taxes were also increased. Lloyd George satisfied the puritan, Nonconformist Liberal constituency by punishing vice with heavy taxes on liquor and tobacco.

With the exception of their views on denominational education, Home Rule M.P.s generally agreed with the Liberal line. They approved of the welfare-state direction of Liberal policy, winning some modifications for agrarian Ireland, but objected to increased liquor taxes. Though puritan in sexual matters, Irish Catholicism has been extremely tolerant concerning the consumption of alcohol. More important, distilling and brewing were important Irish industries, and both made generous contributions to the Irish Party. Redmond and Dillon protested the liquor taxes to Henry Herbert Asquith, Campbell-Bannerman's successor as Prime Minister, but they finally gave in since they had to support the budget to preserve the Liberal alliance with its hope for Home Rule.

During the late nineteenth century, British Conservatism had become quite reckless, often irresponsible, in its efforts to defeat the Irish-Liberal alliance and reform in Britain. During the 1880's, Lord Randolph Churchill encouraged Irish Protestant violence against Home Rule. In the 1890's, Conservatives flying a Unionist Party banner employed the veto power of the House of Lords to defeat the Second Home Rule Bill and to frustrate the efforts of a small Liberal majority in the House of Commons. Following their massive defeat in 1906, they returned to the House of Lords' veto strategy to prevent the welfare state. Considering the overwhelming mandate that the British electorate had given the Liberals at the polls, this was a risky tactic which placed the aristocracy in the path of an advancing democracy.

In 1909, the House of Lords violated centuries of constitutional tradition by vetoing the budget. The Liberals took the issue of the Lords to the country in January and December, 1910 general elections. The January election reduced the Liberal margin over the Unionists to two seats in the House of Commons; the December election left the two major parties at even strength, each with 273 seats. This situation placed the Liberals under obligation to the Irish and Labour Parties, who controlled the balance of power.

Obviously, the House of Lords was more popular with British voters than the Liberals had suspected, but there were other issues that influenced the closeness of the general elections. Many traditional middle-class Liberal electors were far from happy about the soak the rich, welfare-state philosophy of their party. And since the Labour Party grew to forty members in the House of Commons, it seemed apparent that middle of the road Liberalism was no more attractive to working-class radicals than it was to middle-class property owners. And a large number of working-class people resented Nonconformist, middle-class Liberals taxing the simple pleasures of the poor, a pint and a smoke. No doubt, many Britons were apprehensive concerning German military and naval strength and arrogance on the international diplomatic frontier. Perhaps they thought that the Unionists, the party of imperialism and the military establishment, would conduct a more aggressive foreign policy and modernize the British army and navy.

Home Rule was also an important issue in the 1910 general elections. Throughout the campaigns, Unionist politicians and journalists emphasized that Home Rule would follow a successful Liberal attempt to muzzle the House of Lords. Before the December election, Asquith went to Dublin and promised that Home Rule would result from a curbing of the Lord's veto power. There can be little doubt that traditional anti-Irish British nativism damaged the Liberals at the polls, but the Unionist charge that the two general elections did not produce a Home Rule British majority in the House of commons is untrue. The Labour Party was in favor of Irish self-government and its forty-two M.P.s (a gain of two seats in the December election) gave Home Rule 315 British votes in the House of Commons, compared to 254 against (seventeen of the 273 Unionist M.P.s were Ulster Protestants, and two represented Trinity College, Dublin). Altogether, in December, 1910, Home Rule had a 126 majority in the House of Commons, and since Irish self-government was a major issue in both 1910 elections, this majority was a considerable accomplishment for Irish nationalism.

When Asquith seemed reluctant to move against the House of Lords, Redmond warned him that the Irish Party would not vote for the budget unless the Liberals carried out their pledge to reform the House of Lords. Responding to this Irish threat, the government in February, 1911, introduced and passed the Parliament Act in the House of Commons, limiting the veto power of the House of Lords to three consecutive sessions or two years. When the Unionist majority in the House of Lords balked at passing the Parliament Act, King George V warned them that he would have to pack the peerage with Liberals to carry out the nation's wishes. The King's threat persuaded the Unionist majority to abandon the House of Lord's absolute veto. Thanks to Irish nationalism, Britain in 1911 took a major step toward democracy.

The Parliament Act removed the last constitutional obstacle to Home Rule. In the spring of 1912, Asquith presented the Third Home Rule Bill to the House of Commons; a mild proposal establishing an Irish Parliament with a popularly elected lower house and an appointed Senate. A small delegation of Irish M.P.s were to remain at Westminster to represent and defend Ireland's interest in the Empire. The British government retained jurisdiction over the Royal Irish Constabulary. And there were other restrictions on Irish sovereignty. The Irish Parliament could not impose tariffs, conduct an independent foreign policy, or legislate in areas of religion. This last limitation indicated that Britain would continue to protect the interests of the Protestant minority in Ireland. Irish Protestants received another bonus. The Home Rule Bill gave northeast Ulster over-representation in the lower house of Parliament, and it was expected that Crown appointments to the Senate would include a disproportionately high number of Protestants.

Despite its limitations, John Redmond accepted the Home Rule Bill as a satisfactory British answer to the Irish self-government demand. His response seemed to be an accurate reflection of Irish nationalist opinion. Even Sinn Feiners and Irish cultural nationalists said they were happy with the Home Rule Bill. In the spring of 1912, the Irish Party could take pride in its victory. Home Rule M.P.s had completed the work of O'Connell and Parnell, within the framework and rules of the British constitutional system.

But as soon as Redmond sat down, Sir Edward Carson and Sir James Craig, speaking for Protestant Ulster, said no to Home Rule. They insisted that their constituents would always remain loyal to the Union and the British Protestant constitution. Carson and Craig described Home Rule as a knife pointed at the heart of Ulster. It would destroy the economy and the liberties of Protestant people by submitting them to the rule of Catholic politicians interested in the agrarian economy of Leinster, Munster, and Connacht.

To prove that they were not bluffing, Carson and Craig went from Westminster to Ulster where they obtained the signatures of 471,000 anti-Catholic zealots for a Solemn League and Covenant to use "all means which may be found necessary to defeat the present conspiracy to set up a Home Rule Parliament in Ireland. And in the event of such a Parliament being forced upon us we further solemnly and mutually pledge ourselves to refuse to recognize its authority." Carson then created an Ulster Provisional Government, which was to go into operation in the event Home Rule became law, and he raised an Ulster Volunteer Army to resist the enforcement of Home Rule in the North. Craig announced that Ulster Protestants, if necessary, were prepared to swear allegiance to the German Kaiser to save themselves from the jurisdiction of an Irish Parliament.

British Conservatives decided to take political advantage of Ulster fanaticism. In their effort to destroy the Liberal government, defeat Irish nationalism, and preserve the Empire, they attached their political fortunes to the paranoid personality of Protestant Ulster. Andrew Bonar Law, Balfour's successor as Unionist Party leader, a man with an Ulster Presbyterian heritage, promised Ulster Protestants that he would support their resistance to Home Rule and the British constitution, even if the result was civil war. He said that

They would be justified in resisting by all means in their power, including force. .... I can imagine no length of resistance to which Ulster can go in which I should not be

prepared to support them, and in which, in my belief, they would not be supported by
the overwhelming majority of the British people.[3]

Seconding Bonar Law, the *Times* (London), an old enemy of Irish
nationalism and Irish Catholicism, assured Ulster Protestants that they had
the approval "of the whole force of the Conservative and Unionist Party."

In the past, British governments had jailed or transported Irish
nationalists for saying and doing less than Carson, Bonar Law, or the Editor
of the *Times*. However, Asquith was reluctant to prosecute British and Ulster Unionist leaders because he realized that British public opinion was
deeply divided on Home Rule. The Prime Minister did not want to encourage civil strife over the issue in the United Kingdom when Europe was on
the brink of war. And Redmond assured Asquith that Carson and Craig were
only bluffing. He said that government prosecutions would only strengthen
their position in Ulster by making them appear as martyrs. The leader of the
Irish Party told his nationalist followers to remain calm and not to be disturbed by the Ulster situation. He promised them that "the ship of Home
Rule would sail safely into port, borne on the tide of British Liberal opinion."
Rationality, calmness, and decency turned out to be Redmond's fatal flaws.
He never really comprehended the lunatic quality of Unionist Party strategy
or the vacillating mentality of British Liberals.

As the Home Rule Bill proceeded on its three-session, two-year journey through the House of Commons, violence became more probable and
plausible. British Conservatives were so angry with Liberals who imposed
the welfare state, curbed the powers of the House of Lords, and jeopardized
the Empire with Home Rule that their support of Ulster Protestants became
more aggressive. Lord Milner, a Pro-Consul of the British Empire, pleaded
with Carson to start the shooting. He also persuaded two million people to
sign a British Solemn League and Covenant in support of Ulster Protestants.
F. E. Smith, the future Lord Birkenhead, was even more vocally militant
than Bonar Law when he assured Carson and his friends that British Conservatives would come to their aid if the Home Rule crisis reached the stage of
civil war. Treason seemed to be in fashion. A. V. Dicey, the distinguished
Oxford professor of constitutional law, intellectualized Ulster defiance of the
constitution; Geoffrey Dawson, Editor of the *Times*, promoted the Ulster
Unionist cause; Rudyard Kipling wrote emotional poems praising "loyal Ulster"; and Waldorf Astor and Lord Rothschild contributed large sums of
money to the Ulster Volunteers.

Army generals also joined the conspiracy against constitutional government. Lord Roberts, Chief of Staff, recommended Lieutenant General
George Richardson to Carson for the position of Commander of the Ulster

[3]The *Times* (London), July 29, 1912. Reproduced from The Times (London) by permission.

Volunteers. Orangeman Sir Henry Wilson, Director of Military Operations, passed on confidential information to Bonar Law and Carson, and he advised them to resist Home Rule by blocking military appropriation bills in the House of Commons. In March, 1914, British officers stationed at the Curragh, County Kildare, Ireland, loyal to their class and party backgrounds, announced that they would resign their commissions rather than participate in a military effort to impose Home Rule on Ulster. Officers quartered in Britain expressed similar sentiments; some of them threatened to offer their services to the Ulster Volunteers.

Weighing the significance of a divided British opinion on Home Rule, recurring crises in Europe, disloyalty in the army, and a possible insurrection in Ulster, some Cabinet members began to flinch. Lord Loreburn, a prominent Liberal and a consistent supporter of Irish Home Rule, and Winston Churchill, Secretary of the Admiralty, suggested excluding Protestant Ulster from a Home Rule settlement on the premise "that Orange bitters and Irish whiskey will not mix." Redmond responded to the partition suggestion with a counter-proposal: Irish nationalists were prepared to offer Ulster a great deal of autonomy within a Home Rule Ireland, but they would never accept a divided Ireland. Carson also rejected partition. He said that Ulster Protestants were not selfish people. They could not accept partition since they were trying to save all of Ireland from the political and economic perils of Home Rule.

Finally, some nationalists in the South realized that Ulster and British Unionist militancy had unnerved British Liberals, dimming the prospects for a united Home Rule Ireland. They decided to adopt Orange tactics and demonstrate to British politicians that Irish nationalists were as ready to fight for an Irish nation as Ulster Unionists were to fight against it. In November, 1913, members of the Irish Republican Brotherhood took the lead in creating the Irish Volunteers. To mask their role, the IRB people selected Eoin MacNeill, a founding father of the Gaelic League and a Celtic studies scholar at University College, Dublin, as President of the Irish Volunteers.

At first Redmond opposed the Volunteers because he feared their existence would irritate a tense situation. But when he saw the Liberals bending in the direction of a partition compromise, the Home Rule leader first endorsed, and then in July, 1914, took command of the Irish Volunteers. Redmond's association with the Volunteers meant more prestige and funds for the organization. Volunteer membership increased from 10,000 in January, 1914, to 180,000 by September of that year. With three unofficial armies in existence—the Ulster and Irish Volunteers and the Transport Worker's Citizen Army—confrontation seemed imminent.

By 1914, Asquith, always a luke-warm Home Ruler, and a Cabinet majority were committed to partition. Suddenly aware of the possible consequences of his irresponsible words and reckless conduct, Bonar Law also was ready to settle the Home Rule question through Ulster exclusion. Even Carson retreated from an all or nothing at all position. He said that he would accept a divided Ireland if all nine Ulster counties remained under the jurisdiction of Westminster. This was a most unreasonable demand. Five of the nine counties had Catholic majorities and in 1914 Ulster's representation in the House of Commons was divided between seventeen nationalist and sixteen Unionist M.P.s (the Unionists lost a seat in a 1912 by-election).

For obvious reasons, Redmond could not consent to partition. At the same time, he was not in a position to repudiate the Liberal alliance and expel Asquith and his colleagues from office. A general election might produce a Unionist majority in the House of Commons or lead to some kind of coalition government, hostile to Home Rule and independent of Irish influence. And it might be a long time before nationalist M.P.s would again be in a balance of power position to influence government policy. With the consent of his Irish Party colleagues and the Ulster Catholic bishops, Redmond finally offered his own partition compromise: Ulster counties could decide by separate plebescites to remain outside the jurisdiction of the Home Rule Parliament for a period of six years. In addition, he insisted on and got the Liberals to agree to plebescites for two Ulster cities, Newry in south Down and Derry, both with large Catholic majorities on the fringes of counties that would probably vote for exclusion. While this plan gave partition the appearance of a temporary arrangement, a sop to nationalists, Redmond knew that a general election would take place before the expiration of the six year period, and that a probable Unionist majority in the House of Commons would transform a temporary arrangement into a permanent settlement. The result would be a twenty-eight county—plus Newry and Derry—Home Rule Ireland and a truncated four county Protestant Ulster within the United Kingdom. This was not a pleasing prospect to any nationalist, but it was much better than a twenty-three county Home Rule Ireland, and a considerable improvement on what did emerge, a twenty-six county Free State.

Carson chose to ignore the reality of Redmond's concession. He continued to insist on the exclusion of all nine Ulster counties, obviously still hoping to nullify Home Rule for any part of Ireland. In July, 1914, at the request of King George, Redmond, Dillon, Asquith, Lloyd George, Bonar Law, Lord Lansdowne, Carson, and Craig met at Buckingham Palace, but they failed to agree on the boundaries or time limits for partition. The government then introduced an Amending Bill in the House of Lords, which called for the temporary exclusion of the four Protestant counties, minus Newry and Derry, from the Home Rule settlement. But the Unionist majority altered the Bill to exclude all of Ulster on a permanent basis and sent it to the House of Commons. Asquith scheduled a discussion of the Amending Bill and the Lords' alterations for July 27, but discussion was delayed since by that time tensions in Ireland had exploded into violence.

As a deterrent to civil war, the government in December, 1913, banned the importation of arms into Ireland. Four months later the Ulster Volunteers defied this ban by smuggling a large shipment of military hardware from Germany, including 20,000 rifles and 2,000,000 rounds of ammunition. Not only did this bold gesture embarrass the government, it made the Ulster Volunteers a much more formidable obstacle to Home Rule. Impressed by the success of the Ulster Volunteers smuggling operation, and determined on balancing the forces of intimidation, Irish Volunteers on July 26, 1914, landed 900 rifles and 125,000 rounds of ammunition at Howth, a short distance from Dublin, and on August 1, 600 rifles and 20,000 rounds of ammunition at Kilcoole, County Wicklow. Both these shipments were purchased in Germany. Alerted by police, British soldiers—the King's Own Scottish Borderers—marched out to disarm the Volunteers who had unloaded the yacht at Howth harbor. When the Borderers met the Volunteers on the Howth Road, the front ranks of the latter held off the former with rifle butts while their comrades disappeared into the fields and byways with the guns and ammunition.

When the frustrated soldiers marched back into Dublin, a crowd in Bachelor's Walk taunted them, and a few people threw stones at the Borderers. Tired by the long, futile summer march, irritated by the jeers of Dublin civilians, and angered by the stone throwers, a few soldiers lost control and began firing into the crowd, killing three and wounding thirty-six. The next day, Redmond, in the House of Commons, asked the government why Ulster Volunteers could openly march with loaded guns while British soldiers attempted to disarm Irish Volunteers? Redmond's question forced an official inquiry into the Bachelor's Walk incident and delayed discussion of the Amending Bill. The inquiry led to a censure of the Assistant Commissioner of the Dublin police and the commanding officer of the Borderers.

Before the House of Commons could return to Home Rule, Austria had declared war on Serbia, Russia had mobilized, and Germany had declared war on Russia and France and issued an ultimatum to Belgium demanding the passage of troops through that small, neutral nation. Perhaps German boldness was partially based on a conviction that the divisiveness of the Irish Question would prevent British intervention on the Continent. But on August 3, Sir Edward Grey, the Foreign Secretary, informed the House of Commons that Britain would honor her obligation to defend Belgium's neutrality. Redmond then rose and said that the government could withdraw all troops from Ireland while the Irish Volunteers joined with the Ulster Volunteers to defend their common homeland. Unionists and Liberals stood and cheered the patriotism and generosity of the Home Rule leader.

Following Britain's entry into World War I, the Liberals attempted to settle the Home Rule issue without disturbing national unity. To please Irish nationalists, the government placed Home Rule on the statute books; to appease Ulster Unionists, it added a Suspensory Bill postponing Irish self-government for the duration of the war.

World War I might have saved Britian and her constitutional system from the destructive forces of civil war. But British politicians had evaded rather than solved the Ulster dimension of the Home Rule issue. In 1914, Liberal, Conservative, Home Rule, and Ulster Unionist M.P.s failed to appreciate the nuances of the crisis they had just passed through. When British Conservatives encouraged and cooperated with Ulster defiance of constitutional government and British Liberals surrendered to intimidation, they destroyed the credibility of Irish constitutional nationalism, thus unleashing the forces of violence that still haunt Anglo-Irish relations. In refusing to award the Irish Parliamentary Party the trophy of Home Rule, which it had fairly won in the game of parliamentary politics, British politicians proved the thesis of Irish revolutionary nationalism. They publicly announced that the Union was a farce, that the constitution did not apply to Ireland, and that they would only concede Irish freedom to physical force. Ulster Protestants, British no-popery, anti-Irish public opinion, and Liberal and Conservative M.P.s had created an Irish revolutionary situation. After 1914, the decision on Irish freedom moved from the halls of Westminster to the hills, glens, and streets of Ireland. Now it would be guns and grenades and not parliamentary roll calls that would determine the outcome, and perhaps the long-term future of Britain and her Empire.

7

Wars of liberation

EASTER WEEK

John Redmond sincerely believed that World War I was a confrontation between good and evil. To him, Germany represented authoritarianism, militarism, irresponsible imperialism, an attack on Western civilization, and a menace to the rights of small nations. He told Irish nationalists that they had a moral responsibility to help France and Britain preserve liberal democracy and the sovereignty of small nations like Belgium. He said that an Irish sacrifice for international justice would persuade Britain to concede Home Rule on an all-Ireland basis once the war was over. Sinn Feiners, Irish-Irelanders, and Republicans did not agree with Redmond. To them, Britain, the oppressor of Ireland, was not a fit champion of democracy or small nations. They pleaded with Irishmen not to risk their lives for the glory and power of the British Empire.

In August, 1914, approximately 12,000 out of the 180,000 Volunteers refused to accept Redmond's position on the war. The majority wing took the name National Volunteers, while the dissenters continued to call themselves the Irish Volunteers. Many National Volunteers enlisted in the British army. Eoin MacNeill commanded the Irish Volunteers, but he continued as a front man for the Irish Republican Brotherhood, which controlled many important positions on the Executive Committee. MacNeill knew that the IRB was a major component of the Volunteers but did not completely understand his puppet role. Patrick Pearse, IRB Director of Organization, barrister by profession, poet by inclination, and Master of St. Enda's, a school featuring instruction in Irish, was the main link between the Republican Military Council and the Irish Volunteers.

Pearse, who had shifted his allegiance from Home Rule to Republicanism, and two other poet friends, Joseph Mary Plunkett and Thomas MacDonagh, developed a nationalist ideology colored by the atonement theme of Christianity. They argued for revolution as redemption rather than victory. They insisted that Ireland needed a blood sacrifice to wash away the corruptions of parliamentary politics and Anglo-Saxon culture. British soldiers would slaughter Irish rebels, but victory would emerge from defeat. The Irish soul would be cleansed by the revolutionary experience and a new, stronger, purer generation of Irish nationalists would eventually drive the British out of Ireland and de-Anglicize the country.

Soon after Britain entered World War I, Republican leaders in Ireland, cooperating with the Clan na Gael in the United States, began preparations for revolution. They decided to fight before the war on the Continent concluded so that Ireland could demand a place at the peace conference. John Devoy contacted the German Ambassador in Washington who promised that his government would aid an Irish rebellion. Sir Roger Casement, an Ulster Protestant knighted for his humanitarian efforts as a member of the British Consular Service in Africa and South America, went to Germany via the United States to recruit an Irish brigade from prisoners of war. Neither the German government nor the vast majority of Irish POWs took Casement very seriously. Other Republican envoys did, however, impress the Germans and returned to Ireland with solid offers of arms and ammunition.

James Connolly also was planning a revolution. He was not a romantic, blood sacrifice propagandist. Connolly believed that victory was possible. Although there were only about 200 recruits in the Citizen Army, he was convinced that a rising in Dublin would spark the whole country. According to Connolly's strategy, the British, caught by surprise in Ireland, tied down on the Western Front, and reluctant to destroy property by suppressing Irish insurrection, would evacuate Ireland, leaving the path clear for a socialist republic. To avoid competitive planning and split allegiances, the IRB at the end of 1915 concluded an alliance with Connolly, and he joined the Military Council of IRB.

From August, 1914, to April, 1916, companies of Irish Volunteers and members of the Citizen Army drilled in the Dublin and Wicklow mountains and held public reviews in the streets of Dublin. At the same time, Republicans and Sinn Feiners conducted a campaign against recruiting. Their orators and newspapers told young Irishmen not to become involved in a contest among European imperialist nations. They urged them to stay at home and get ready for the struggle for Irish freedom. Attempting to avoid another violent incident like Bachelor's Walk, British authorities in Ireland ignored the parades and maneuvers of the Volunteers and the Citizen Army, but they did jail or deport leaders of the anti-recruiting campaign. They also shut down extremist nationalist newspapers, most of which quickly reappeared under new names.

For a while Redmond's support of the war effort did not seriously diminish his position in Ireland, but his popularity gradually was eroded by the conduct of British military and political leaders. Lord Horatio Herbert Kitchener at the War Office permitted the Ulster Volunteers to enter the British army as a separate division with their own officers and insignia, the Red Hand of Ulster, but denied a similar privilege to the National Volunteers. Kitchener's Unionist prejudices, and heavy Irish casualties in Gallipoli and on the Western Front, widened the anti-war circle in Ireland and discouraged Irish enlistments in the British armed forces.

British deaths and failures on the Western Front provoked extensive political and newspaper criticism of government policy. In reply, Asquith created a Coalition Cabinet to broaden public support for the government. He invited Unionists, Labourites, and Irish nationalists to join the Coalition. Consistent with the principles of the Irish Party, Redmond refused to participate in a British government, but the enemies of Home Rule—Carson, Bonar Law, and F. E. Smith—did join the Cabinet. The composition of the Coalition made it difficult for Irish nationalists to trust the intentions or the integrity of the British government.

Meanwhile, the Military Council of the IRB in consultation with the Clan na Gael set a date for revolution, Easter Sunday (April 23), 1916, and Germany promised to furnish them with rifles and ammunition. Patrick Pearse persuaded an unknowing MacNeill to summon a general review of all Volunteer units with full equipment on April 23. Joseph Mary Plunkett and some of his friends forged and distributed a British government document purporting to be plans by the authorities to raid the headquarters of the Irish Volunteers, the Citizen Army, Sinn Fein, and the Gaelic League, and to arrest the leaders of those organizations. This forgery, which actually may have represented British intentions, was used by the IRB as a method of convincing MacNeill and the Volunteers that they were fighting a defensive war rather than starting a revolution.

On Holy Thursday, Bulmer Hobson found out about the plans of the Military Council and informed MacNeill. Both men tried to stop the revolution because they believed it a futile gesture that would result in the slaughter of Irish nationalists. MacNeill insisted that a rising would contradict the purpose of the Volunteers. They existed to demonstrate the will for self-determination of the Irish people and to serve as an army of liberation if Britain refused Home Rule after the war. He argued that a revolution without determining British intentions or without a reasonable expectation of success would be "immoral." Hobson protested that Pearse and his friends were violating the IRB constitution of 1873, which declared that only a majority of the Irish people could decide the time and appropriateness of an Irish revolution. He said that the Military Council was a junto that did not represent either the Irish people or the IRB.

Since Hobson was a stubborn and powerful personality who could influence other IRB people, Sean MacDermott pulled a revolver on his old friend and colleague and had him detained until the revolution was underway. Pearse and Thomas MacDonagh told MacNeill that it was too late to withdraw from insurrection; a German ship was on the way with arms and ammunition. This information persuaded MacNeill to turn the direction of the Volunteers over to the Military Council of the IRB. But the next day, the authorities captured Casement on the Kerry coast after he came ashore from a German submarine to tell Irish nationalists that German assistance would be inadequate and to advise them not to rebel. Also on Good Friday, a German ship, the *Aud*, arrived off the Munster coast with the promised arms and ammunition. A confusion of orders and plain inefficiency prevented the Volunteers from coming to unload the cargo, and while the *Aud* waited, a British naval vessel intercepted her. In order to avoid the disgrace of capture, the Captain of the *Aud* scuttled his ship, sending the cargo of obsolete Russian armaments, captured on the Eastern Front, to the bottom of the Atlantic.

On Holy Saturday, when MacNeill learned of the capture of Casement in Kerry and the fate of the *Aud*, he changed his mind and canceled orders for Easter Sunday maneuvers. Pearse and his associates knew that there would be little support from the rest of the country, but they were determined on a blood sacrifice that would redeem the Irish nation. They proceeded with the insurrection. Even Connolly, who once thought victory possible, must have realized the mission was suicidal, but Pearse seemed to have persuaded him that Irish blood could nourish Irish freedom:

> But deep in the heart of Ireland has sunk the sense of degradation wrought upon its people—so deep and so humiliating that no agency less powerful than the red tide of war on Irish soil will ever be able to enable the Irish race to recover its self-respect. . . . Without the slightest trace of irreverance but in all due humility and awe, we recognize that of us, as of mankind before Calvary, it may be truly be said "without the shedding of blood there is no Redemption."[1]

On Easter Monday morning, while most Dubliners were still off work enjoying the holiday season, a force of 1,528 rebels, including twenty-seven

[1]C. D. Greaves, *The Life and Times of James Connolly*, London: Laurence & Wishart, 1961, pp. 318–319. Also quoted in F. S. L. Lyons, *Ireland since the Famine*, New York: Charles Scribner's Sons, 1971, f.n.p. 347. Reprinted by permission of International Publishers.

women, quietly marched through the streets of the city and seized the General Post Office and other strategic buildings. They almost took Dublin Castle. Rebels hoisted a Republican tricolor—green, white, and orange—to the top of the Post Office while from the balcony Pearse read a declaration of independence.[2] This Proclamation established an Irish Republic committed to social reform and full civil rights for all inhabitants of the nation. It read in part

> We declare the right of the people of Ireland to the ownership of Ireland, and to the unfettered control of Irish destinies, to be sovereign an indefeasable. . . . Standing on that fundamental right and again asserting it in arms in the face of the world, we hereby proclaim the Irish Republic as a Sovereign Independent State, and we pledge our lives and the lives of our comrades-in-arms to the cause of its freedom, of its welfare, and of its exaltation among the nations.
>
> The Irish Republic is entitled to, and hereby claims, the allegiance of every Irishman and Irishwoman. The Republic guarantees religious and civil liberty, equal rights and equal opportunities to all its citizens, and declares its resolve to pursue the happiness and prosperity of the whole nation and of all its parts, cherishing all the children of the nation equally, and oblivious of the differences carefully fostered by an alien government which have divided a minority from the majority in the past.

If Pearse indoctrinated Connolly with his own version of redemptive theology, Connolly instructed Pearse in socialist ideology. The declaration of "the right of the people of Ireland to the ownership of Ireland" pointed out the influence of both Connolly and James Fintan Lalor on Pearse. It is ironic that while Connolly has lived in the memory and song of Irish nationalism—he even has a railway station named after him—his socialism has had little impact on post-revolutionary Irish thought or action.

For six days the Citizen Army and the Volunteers fought the Royal Irish Constabulary, the Dublin Metropolitan Police, and the British army, quickly re-enforced with men and equipment. During the fighting 508 people were killed (300 civilians, 132 soldiers and policemen, and 76 rebels) and 2,520 were injured (2,000 civilians, 400 soldiers and policemen, and 120 freedom fighters).[3] The Volunteers and the Citizen Army fought with courage, but the cause was hopeless. The enemy had superior forces and equipment. And Connolly was mistaken: "Britannia's sons with their long range guns" did not hesitate to bombard the city with fire and shell.

Since most Irish people had relatives or friends fighting with the British army in France, they were hostile to the Easter Week rebels. They

---

[2]Green represented the Catholic tradition, Orange the Protestant tradition, white the bond of love between the two traditions.

[3]These figures are taken from Ruth Dudley Edwards, *An Atlas of Irish History*, London: Methuen and Co., 1973, p. 75.

considered them cowardly backstabbers. When Connolly, Pearse, and their comrades surrendered on April 29, and British soldiers herded them off to jail, Dubliners cursed, jeered, and even spit on them. In the House of Commons, Redmond denounced the insurrection, describing its participants as German dupes. He reaffirmed Irish support for the war effort.

Brutalized, terrorized, and insensitized from twenty months of violence and defeat in France, British officials decided not to imprison Irish rebels as misguided fools, but to turn them over to military courts for trial and punishment. Over a ten-day period, under the supervision of General Sir John Maxwell, firing squads executed fifteen Irish nationalists, including the seven signers of the Republican Proclamation.[4] Although he was wounded in defending the Post Office, British soldiers strapped Connolly in a chair and shot him. In addition to the execution, British soldiers angrily assaulted citizens in the Dublin streets, and an officer murdered F. Sheehy Skeffington, a prominent pacifist with no connection to the rising. And British authorities seized and transported over 2,000 Sinn Feiners and Republicans, many of them completely innocent of revolutionary conspiracy, to British prisons, often without trial.

Although understandable, British reactions to an Irish rebellion while the United Kingdom was engaged in a war of survival on the Continent were seriously mistaken when considered in the historical context of Anglo-Irish relations. They presented an image of revenge rather than justice, which resulted in an Irish public opinion re-evaluating Easter Week. The "backstabbers," "dirty bowsers," and "hooligans" became martyred heroes. People read and quoted the poems of Pearse, Plunkett, and MacDonagh. Pictures of the martyrs appeared in Irish homes. As William Butler Yeats described it in his "Easter, 1916" poem, blood sacrifice had transformed Ireland: "all changed, changed utterly: a terrible beauty is born."

This shift in Irish opinion forced a belated glimmer of reason in Britain's Irish policy. She needed more Irish canon fodder on the Western front and help from the United States to defeat Germany. But the Irish vote was an important factor in American politics, particularly with a Democratic administration. Asquith called on Lloyd George, soon to take his place as Prime Minister, to pacify Ireland. The "Welsh Wizard" offered Redmond immediate Home Rule with the exclusion of six Ulster counties—Antrim,

---

[4]The seven signatories, members of the Provisional Government of the Irish Republic, were Thomas J. Clarke, Sean MacDiarmada (MacDermott), James Connolly, Patrick Pearse, Thomas MacDonagh, Eamonn Ceannt (Kent), and Joseph Plunkett. Pearse's brother, William, also was shot. On August 3, Casement was executed in England. During his treason trial, the government released the contents of a diary indicating that Casement was a promiscuous homosexual. This was designed to influence opinion, particularly in the United States, against Irish nationalism.

Armagh, Derry, Down, Fermanagh, and Tyrone until a permanent boundry of partition could be determined after the war. The Irish leader was willing to accept these terms until he discovered that Lloyd George had promised Carson that this arrangement would be permanent.

When Ulster Protestant obstinancy and Lloyd George's duplicity wrecked the possibility of immediate Home Rule, the government attempted to appease a restless Irish nationalist opinion by releasing the internees. When they returned to Ireland, they came back as heroes, particularly Eamon de Valera, the only Easter Week commandant who survived the British execution. De Valera was born in New York of an Irish mother and a Spanish-Cuban father. He was raised and educated in Ireland, became an ardent Gaelic Leaguer, taught mathematics in a Dublin secondary school and in a teacher's training college, temporarily joined the IRB, enlisted in the Volunteers, and rose to the rank of commandant. On Easter Monday, he and his men occupied Boland's flour mill and for the duration of the rising successfully prevented British reinforcements who landed at Bray from reaching Dublin.[5]

THE ANGLO-IRISH WAR

In 1917, Volunteer leaders took command of Arthur Griffith's Sinn Fein organization and used it as a political front to frustrate British recruiting and to defeat the Irish Parliamentary Party. By the end of the war, Sinn Feiners had defeated Home Rulers in six by-elections and then refused to take their seats in the British House of Commons. This turn-about in Irish politics should have warned the British government that the Irish Party no longer represented majority Irish nationalist opinion, and that the next general election would alter completely the situation in Ireland.

After the American entry into World War I in April, 1917, the United States government informed the British that the enthusiasm of its contribution would be somewhat determined by the Irish Question. As Prime Minister, Lloyd George resumed his effort to satisfy Irish nationalists. He again approached Redmond, offering immediate Home Rule with the permanent exclusion of the six Ulster counties. The Irish leader said no! The most that he was prepared to concede was the 1914 compromise: temporary exclusion of Ulster counties and Newry and Derry if those territories indicated by plebescites that they were unwilling to accept the jurisdiction of an Irish Parliament. But this concession was unsatisfactory to Carson and his British

---

[5]Some historians have said that de Valera's technical American citizenship saved his life in 1916. But his survival owed more to the British realization that terror had become counter-productive than to his birth in the United States.

Unionist associates. In a stalemate situation, Redmond suggested to Lloyd George an Irish convention of interested parties—Home Rulers, Unionists, and Sinn Feiners—to work out mutually acceptable terms for Home Rule. The British Prime Minister agreed to Redmond's proposal.

The Irish Convention met in Dublin from July, 1917, to April, 1918, but Sinn Fein refused an invitation to participate. Ulster unionist delegates obstructed rather than contributed to an atmosphere of conciliation. Accepting the inevitability of some form of Home Rule, Southern Protestant unionists were more open minded, but they insisted that the Westminster Parliament must retain control over Irish customs, excises, and defenses. Anxious to placate these men, Redmond consented to their terms. In doing so, he alienated a significant portion of the nationalist community, particularly the Catholic bishops.

A month before the Convention dispersed in failure, Redmond died after a routine gall stone operation. Perhaps he was too exhausted and disillusioned to summon the spirit or the energy to live. At least he did not have to witness the destruction of the party he served for so long and so well. John Dillon took his place as Chairman of the Irish Party. He had the impossible task of attempting to save Home Rule nationalism in the wake of Easter Week.

At the close of 1917, Russia was out of the war and Germany had concentrated her troop strength on the Western Front. There was no way of determining how long it would take the United States to mobilize and send a significant number of men to help the British and French. British politicians felt they must apply conscription to Ireland. In April, 1918, when Parliament authorized the draft of Irish manpower, John Dillon led the Irish Party out of the House of Commons, returned to Ireland, and joined Sinn Feiners, trade unionists, and Catholic bishops in a united front against conscription. The anti-draft campaign increased the respectability of the Republican movement, speeded up the rebuilding of the Volunteer companies, and goaded Britain into more coercion. British officials deported some Sinn Feiners, arrested others on the flimsiest of charges (including de Valera), and suppressed a number of Republican newspapers. But when the war ended in November, 1918, the government had not as yet applied conscription to Ireland.

The post-Armistice, December, 1918, general election provided Lloyd George's Conservative-dominated National Coaliation government with a substantial parliamentary majority over Labour and the Asquith Liberals. But in Ireland Sinn Fein won seventy-three seats to six for the Irish Party and twenty-six for the Unionists. Except for the Trinity College constituency, all of the Unionists victories were in Ulster. Only two Irish Party candidates—Captain William Redmond, the son of the former leader, and Joseph Devlin from Belfast—won in direct contests with Sinn Fein. In East

Mayo, de Valera defeated Dillon by an almost two to one majority. Sinn Fein victories owed much to an increase in the Irish electorate. By extending the vote to all men over twenty-one and women over thirty, the 1918 Representation of the People Act expanded the number of Irish voters from 701,475 in 1910 to 1,936,673. Since the election results show that the Irish Party actually increased its vote since 1910 in those constituencies it contested, it is reasonable to assume that older voters and their wives remained loyal to Home Rule while younger people declared for Sinn Fein.

Victorious Sinn Fein candidates refused to take their seats at Westminster. Instead, they assembled in Dublin and constituted themselves as Dáil Éireann and began to rule Ireland in the name of the Irish Republic. The Dáil established Arbitration Courts to replace the British system, an Industrial Disputes Board to mediate labor-management conflicts, a Land Bank to offer land purchase loans, and it sent delegates to the Versailles Peace Conference to obtain international recognition of the Irish Republic. They made little impression on the Anglophile American President, Woodrow Wilson, who said that Ireland did not qualify for his interpretation of national self-determination.

In February, 1919, two members of the Sinn Fein Executive Committee, Michael Collins, the dominant personality of the IRB, and his close friend, Harry Boland, arranged de Valera's escape from Lincoln gaol in England. On his return to Ireland, the members of the Dáil elected de Valera their President. But in June, 1919, he left for the United States to collect money for the Irish Republic and to recruit American support for the Irish cause. Arthur Griffith, who in 1917 stepped down as Sinn Fein President in favor of de Valera, served as Acting President of the Dáil in his absence. Although he managed to collect a large sum of money, de Valera did not persuade Republican or Democratic politicians to add planks to their national convention platforms recognizing the Irish Republic. And de Valera's personality conflicted with the equally strong-minded Clan na Gael leaders, John Devoy and Judge Daniel Cohalan. Many members of the Clan were more interested in preserving Irish power in American politics than in liberating Ireland, and Devoy and Cohalan thought that de Valera's attitude toward England was too mild. They resented his willingness to have Ireland take a subordinate position in relationship to England similar to the one Cuba had with the United States.

While de Valera was having his troubles in the United States, Collins emerged as the strong man of the Sinn Fein Executive Committee. He was Minister of Finance, but his real power evolved from his roles as leader of the IRB and Adjutant General and Director of Operations for the Volunteers. Collins resisted Dáil control over the IRB, which he kept independent of the Volunteers. Cathal Brugha, Minister of Defense and Volunteer Chief of Staff, resented the existence of a secret army outside the control or juris-

EAMON DE VALERA
1882–1976

Eamon de Valera was the dominant personality in post-Treaty Ireland. During his many years as Taoiseach he altered the Treaty and led Ireland on the road from Free State to Republic. His neutrality policy during World War II was the ultimate test of Irish independence. (Courtesy of the National Library of Ireland)

diction of the elected representatives of the Irish people. No doubt jealousy figured in the frequent clashes between Collins and Brugha. Collins' handsome looks and dashing personality, his brilliant intelligence network and operations, and his daring evasions of capture made him the Scarlet Pimpernel of Irish nationalism. Collins' glamour overshadowed Brugha's solid but less colorful contributions.

The issue of the connection between the Dáil and the military forces of the Republic became more critical after January, 1919 when the passive resistance of Sinn Fein evolved into a shooting war of liberation with the

British government. Members of the Irish Republican Army, the new name for the Volunteers, practiced guerrilla tactics. Dressed as civilians, they ambushed military lorries, captured arms, assasinated suspected spies and informers, and shot soldiers and policemen. The IRA concentrated its attacks on the para-military Royal Irish Constabulary (RIC), destroying barracks, seizing weapons, and killing constables. Even before the Anglo-Irish War began, the RIC was a demoralized body that was losing its personnel at a rapid rate. The IRA completed the destruction of what once had been an excellent police force. Many Constables resigned from either fear or a reluctance to wage war against their own flesh and blood. The collapse of the RIC permitted the IRA to take control over large sections of the country. Lloyd George and other members of the British government described IRA tactics as murder, but guerilla warfare was the only practical strategy for a small nation fighting a powerful one.

British politicians decided to meet terrorism with terrorism, recruiting ex-servicemen, who often were sadists bored with civilian life, and sent them to Ireland to reinforce the now depleted RIC. Their dark green caps and khaki pants earned them the name Black and Tans. Later the government enlisted ex-army officers to serve as RIC auxilliaries. Tans and Auxilliaries often tortured and sometimes murdered IRA prisoners, and they looted and burned towns, demolishing a large section of Cork. But compared to the conduct of some other twentieth-century armies of occupation, British atrocities were relatively restricted. Even the Tans were reluctant to molest women.

In attempting to respond to the Irish situation, British politicians were confounded by their own World War I propaganda concerning the rights of small nations and national self-determination. In co-authoring the 1919 peace treaties, the British had participated in the dismemberment of the Austro-Hungarian and Turkish empires by recognizing the sovereignty claims of Arabs and Slavs. During the Anglo-Irish War, many people throughout the world asked if the British Empire was more sacred than those of the defeated powers. Was its discontented Irish population less deserving of independence than Arabs, Czechs, Slovaks, Croats, Serbs, or Poles?

Since the British government refused to accept the Sinn Fein election victory as a mandate for an Irish Republic, British leaders insisted that they were not engaged in a "war" in Ireland, but a police action to suppress illegal terror and restore law and order. This distinction tied British hands, preventing them from waging a war of annihilation. They were trying to contain rather than destroy Republicans, hoping to force them into a negotiated settlement that would result in something less than an Irish Republic.

While the IRA was a courageous and troublesome foe, British and world opinion was an even more difficult challenge for the British government. When it came to propaganda, the Irish were more persuasive than the

British. They successfully exploited anti-imperialism attitudes in the post-war period. Influential leaders all over the world regarded Ireland as a gallant little nation standing up to a bully. Black and Tan and Auxilliary terror tactics damaged Britain's reputation as a civilized nation, even shocking a large and important section of British opinion. During the early stages of the Anglo-Irish War, most Britons seemed indifferent to violence in Ireland. But Irish propagandists and British journalists changed this apathy into concern. Labour, Liberal, and some Conservative M.P.s; Anglican, Catholic, and Nonconformist clergymen; writers in newspapers and periodicals; trade union leaders; businessmen; university professors; distinguished authors; and even members of the peerage criticized government policy in Ireland. Many of them joined The Peace With Ireland Council, which agitated an end to barbarism by British forces in Ireland and an accomodation with Irish nationalism. They argued that while concessions to the Irish might weaken the Empire and the fabric of the Commonwealth, the risk was preferable to the erosion of Britain's image as a civilized force in the world.

By 1920, most British opposition to Home Rule had vanished. As early as March, 1919, the *Times* said that "We are all Home Rulers today." Unfortunately, British politicians and their constituents did not comprehend that the failure to award the Irish Parliamentary Party its properly earned constitutional victory in 1914 had escalated Irish nationalism beyond federalism. But in 1920, Lloyd George returned to Home Rule as a solution to the Irish crisis and as a response to world opinion. The Coalition government introduced and Parliament passed a Better Government of Ireland Bill, which created a Home Rule Parliament for the six Ulster counties of Antrim, Armagh, Derry, Down, Fermanagh, and Tyrone, and another for the remaining twenty-six. It also included a Council of Ireland to administer services of mutual interests to both Irish governments and to function as a bridge of reconciliation and eventual unity between North and South. The Bill retained both nationalist and unionist M.P.s at Westminster.

Lloyd George's Home Rule formula did not satisfy nationalist aspirations, but it did officially partition Ireland. In the South, Sinn Fein took advantage of the elections for the Home Rule Parliament to demonstrate to Britain and the world that Irish public opinion was behind the Republic. Although Ulster unionists never asked for self-government, they accepted the Better Government of Ireland Bill as an opportunity to create a "Protestant nation for a Protestant people." So the Anglo-Irish War continued with its ambushes, assasinations, burnings, lootings, torture, night raids, curfews, and general atmosphere of violence and terror. Anti-British world opinion intensified and became more vocal, forcing Lloyd George to accept the Sinn Fein reality and to negotiate with its leaders. In July, 1921, the British government concluded a truce with Irish rebels preliminary to treaty negotiations.

In mid-July, 1921, de Valera and Lloyd George discussed peace terms in London. In these conversations and a subsequent correspondence, the British Prime Minister offered Ireland Dominion status with the following reservations: Irish nationalists would have to accept a permanent partition of their island, maintain free trade with Britain, contribute to the British war debt, limit the size of their army in conformity with the British military establishment, permit the continued presence of British air and naval bases in their country, and allow the British armed forces to recruit Irish manpower. Lloyd George warned de Valera that if he rejected this offer, there would be all out war. Ignoring the threat, the Irish leader rejected Dominion status with its reservations as unacceptable. De Valera did, however, indicate that he was no doctrinaire Republican and said that he would submit the British proposal to the Dáil for discussion.

Although the Dáil agreed with de Valera that conditional Dominion status was an inadequate British concession, Lloyd George kept open the channels of communication and scheduled a treaty conference for London. In a still puzzling and controversial decision, de Valera decided not to attend the London talks. Perhaps he thought that other Sinn Feiners might have more success in communicating with the British Prime Minister? Perhaps he decided that he would be more useful in Dublin than in London? In Dublin, de Valera could restrain hot-headed doctrinaire Republicans, and he could control the tempo of the London negotiations. The Irish envoys would have to refer all offers back to Dublin for discussion. This would prevent them from caving in to the pressures of operating in enemy territory. Whatever his reasons, de Valera stayed behind while Collins, Griffith, George Gavan Duffy, Eamon Duggan, and Robert Barton went to London as the representatives of the Irish Republic. Barton's cousin, English-born Erskin Childers, accompanied the delegation as Secretary. Author of a classic spy novel, *The Riddle of the Sands*, Childers smuggled guns into Howth on his yacht in late July, 1914. He then became a British hero in World War I. As a dedicated Republican, Childers was de Valera's watchdog in London. The Irish envoys arrived in London with vague instructions. As plenipotentiaries, they had the authority to negotiate and to conclude a treaty with the British government, but at the same time they carried orders not to sign anything without first consulting the Dáil.

In London, unsophisticated Sinn Feiners negotiated with Lloyd George, Austen Chamberlain, Lord Birkenhead, and Winston Churchill, tough and tested politicians skilled in all of the nuances of pressure diplomacy. And they found themselves caught between the problems of British party politics and Republican fanaticism back in Ireland. Lloyd George's Coalition government was dominated by an anti-Irish Conservative majority. It would not permit the Prime Minister to make too generous an offer to Irish nationalists.

Lloyd George resubmitted his plan for conditional Dominion status and Irish delegates objected to taking an Oath of Allegiance to a British monarch and the partition of their country. They made a serious tactical blunder by concentrating on the rather abstract, almost metaphysical, argument against the Oath rather than emphasizing the divided Ireland issue, and Lloyd George took advantage of their mistake. Conservatives in the Coalition were loyal to Northern Ireland Protestants, but British public opinion would not have tolerated a renewal of the Anglo-Irish War over the question of partition. On the other hand, Britons were as passionately committed to the symbols of monarchy and Empire as Sinn Feiners were to the tokens of Republicanism. They insisted that Ireland must remain in association with Britain by pledging allegiance to the Crown. If the Irish delegation immediately would have accepted Dominion status on the condition that it involved a united Ireland, Lloyd George would have been in a quandary.

When the British told the Irish that an Oath of Allegiance to the Crown would have to be part of an Irish constitution, they responded with an alternative arrangement, External Association. According to this plan developed by de Valera, an Irish Republic would recognize the Crown as head of an association of states comprising the British Commonwealth. After World War II, Britain accepted the principle of External Association in regard to India and Pakistan, but in 1921 it was too *avant garde* for her leaders. Instead of a flat no to de Valera, the British made another concession by offering an oath of allegiance that would place primary loyalty to an Irish government rather than the Crown.

Frustrated by the frozen state of negotiations, Lloyd George decided on a two-pronged blitz on the weary Irish delegation. He split the Ulster and Oath of Allegiance issues, first concentrating on the former where his position was the weakest. He told Irish envoys that he could not persuade Ulster Protestants or his British Conservative allies to accept a united Ireland, and that any effort to do so would return Anglo-Irish relations to a 1912–1914 setting. Lloyd George then got Griffith to agree to a post-Treaty Boundary Commission that would redefine the border between Northern Ireland and the new Dominion on the basis of population preferences. He suggested that the findings of the Boundary Commission would shrink Northern Ireland to a small enclave around Belfast. And he predicated that the unviability of the reconstructed Northern Ireland and heavy British taxes would result in a united Ireland.

Once the British Prime Minister evaded the shoals of the Ulster problem, he concentrated on Dominion status. In early December, 1921, the Irish envoys returned to Dublin and presented Lloyd George's offer to the Dáil. Led by Cathal Brugha and Austin Stack, Republican extremists refused to accept an Oath of Allegiance to the Crown. De Valera instructed the envoys to return to London and negotiate on the principle of External Association. When they arrived, Lloyd George bluntly told them either to accept Dominion status or prepare for war against the might of the British Empire. Griffith found Dominion status compatible with his original Sinn Fein Dual Monarchy proposal. Collins knew that just previous to the truce, the IRA had reached the point of exhaustion, and that the cessation of hostilities had further eroded the Irish will to return to the hardship and inconveniences of war. Since he believed that Ireland could not resist unrestrained British military power, and was convinced that Dominion status was a major British concession and a firm foundation upon which to expand Irish sovereignty, Collins joined Griffith in accepting Lloyd George's offer. Together they persuaded their colleagues to accept British terms. With little enthusiasm, weary minds and bodies, depressed spirits, and many doubts, the Irish envoys on December 6, 1921, signed the Treaty which established a twenty-six county Irish Free State as a Dominion within the British Commonwealth of Nations.

In early January, 1922, the Dáil debated the Treaty in the Mansion House, Dublin. De Valera led the opposition. He insisted that Dominion status betrayed the Republic and perpetuated British tyranny and influence in Ireland. Collins replied that Dominion status was a considerable improvement on Home Rule. He said that the Irish people could build on Dominion status; it was a beginning not an end. After long and increasingly bitter debate—the partition issue was almost completely ignored—the Dáil ratified the Treaty sixty-four to fifty-seven votes. Following this decision, de Valera resigned as President of the Dáil. The pro-Treaty majority elected Griffith as his successor. Within a few weeks, British officials began to turn over the instruments of government to the Free State and to depart from their oldest colony, a country they had occupied for almost eight-hundred years.

From the distance of over a half-century, and with knowledge of the contemporary crisis in Northern Ireland, some historians and Irish politicians have made a case that the results of the Anglo-Irish War did not justify the human sacrifice. They also argue that the cult of the gunman is a legacy of the 1916–1922 period, one that endangers the principles and institutions of liberal democracy. These revisionists admit that Sinn Fein did achieve a degree of freedom beyond the demands made by O'Connell, Young Ireland, Butt, Parnell or Redmond, but they point out that the Treaty left a divided Ireland. Critics of the Sinn Fein tradition seem convinced that if the Irish would have continued to express their desire for independence, a post-World War I British public opinion, committed to principles of national self-determination, combined with world opinion would have forced the British government to concede Home Rule. They maintain that given the changing nature of British opinion and of the structure of the Empire, there was no reason why Home Rule could not have evolved into Dominion status or even a Republic if that is what the Irish people wanted.[6]

Assuming that Home Rule might have evolved into Dominion status or even a Republic, the revisionist argument makes sense, but it ignores the importance of myth and legend in history. An intelligent case can be presented against the necessity of the American Revolution, including the charge that the war against the British contributed to the cult of guns and violence in the United States. But like the American Revolution, Easter Week and the Anglo-Irish War provided heroes and examples of sacrifice and courage that helped sustain and inspire a new nation in her times of difficulty. Because people did die for Irish independence, it became more precious to the citizens of the Irish state that their blood sacrifice created.

Controversy between revisionists and the defenders of the Sinn Fein tradition is really a discussion of *ifs* and *might-have-beens*. There was an Easter Week, an Anglo-Irish War, and a Treaty creating the Free State. These events altered Irish, British, and, to a certain extent, world history. Ireland was the first victim of imperialism and colonialism to wage a successful twentieth-century guerrilla war of liberation. Her example inspired similar efforts in other places. After 1921, Ireland continued to be a relevant testing ground. Britain and the world watched to see if the Irish had the patience, the fortitude, and the skills to translate their nationalist tradition into a workable, stable political community.

[6]Another group of revisionists have suggested that if Sinn Fein would have followed Griffith's prescription of withdrawing from Parliament and then confronting British rule with passive resistance, an Irish state might have come into existence without violence.

8

post-treaty
Ireland

ESTABLISHING THE FREE STATE

The Free State faced the challenges of independence and parliamentary government with an apparent shortage of political talent. Irish voters had repudiated the veterans of the Irish Parliamentary Party, the only men in Ireland with years of legislative experience. Although the new leaders of the Irish people had more training in the ideological rigidity of a revolutionary situation than in the compromise of parliamentary politics, thanks to the Unionist Party's Irish Local Government Act, many of them had acquired a political education. And the commitment to liberal democracy and the respect for the principles of British constitutionalism that O'Connell instilled in Irish nationalism managed to survive the violence and fanaticism of revolution.

Survival was the first test for the Free State government. A June, 1922, general election gave the Free State an endorsement from a substantial majority of the Irish public. But the more than twenty percent anti-Treaty vote was too large, denying the Free State a healthy consensus.[1] Many

[1]Anti-Treaty Sinn Feiners won thirty-five out of the 128 Dáil seats in the 1922 election. The ninety-three pro-Treaty seats were divided as follows: pro-Treaty Sinn Fein, 58; Labour 17; Independents, 7; Farmer Party, 7; Dublin University, 4. Altogether, 620,283 people voted: 239,193 for the pro-Treaty panel; 133,864 for the anti-Treaty panel. Labour, Independents, and Farmer Party candidates divided 247,266 votes. They should be considered pro-Treaty candidates since they were prepared to participate in the politics of the Free State.

opponents of the Treaty wanted to wipe out its parliamentary majority with the gun. They insisted that the fate of the Irish Republic could not depend on compromising parliamentarians elected by fickle voters. They said that the Republic founded by Pearse and Connolly on Easter Monday, 1916, was inviolate; promising to defend it against cowardice and treason since majorities could not decide right and wrong, truth and error. The Republic was both true and right.

More moderate than most of his associates, de Valera preferred persuasion to violence, although his words and conduct incited the latter. On St. Patrick's Day, 1922, he warned the Irish people that the Treaty would lead to a civil war with Irishmen killing Irishmen. Although Republicans considered de Valera the legitimate President of the Irish Republic, and Griffith and Collins the pawns of British imperialism, IRA generals pushed politicians like de Valera into the background and took charge of the campaign against the Treaty.

In April, 1922, Rory O'Connor, a prominent IRA leader, seized the Four Courts in Dublin. For three months Collins permitted him to occupy the hub of the Irish judicial system, hoping to settle differences with Republicans through negotiations. Collins was under pressure from the British government, which expressed doubts concerning the ability of the Irish to rule themselves in a constitutional manner. Realizing the fate of the new nation was at stake, on June 26, 1922, he ordered Free State troops to shell the Four Courts. The Civil War had begun. It lasted until May, 1923.

Most of the guerrilla war heroes of the Anglo-Irish conflict joined the anti-Treaty forces, men like Rory O'Connor, Liam Mellows, Ernie O'Malley, Sean Russell, Tom Barry, Harry Boland, Erskine Childers, Cathal Brugha, and Eamon de Valera. Republican women were even more hostile to the treaty than the men. All of the women in the Dáil had voted against the Treaty, and their organization, Cumann na mBan, rallied behind the anti-Treaty war effort. But the Free State army had superior numbers and weapons, and it enjoyed the backing of majority opinion. Most Irish people were tired of violence and rejected the metaphysical, almost theological, theories of Republicans. They wanted to get on with the job of constructing a viable nation state, and thought that the Free State offered such an opportunity. Prominent trade union leaders and the Labour Party denounced Republican violence. And the Roman Catholic hierarchy blessed the Free State and condemned using physical force to destroy it.

The costs of the Civil War were high. Over six hundred people lost their lives and three thousand were wounded. The government spent about £17,000,000 to put down the rebels, funds that could have been invested in agriculture, industry, and social services. In addition, violence took a heavy toll on Irish leadership. On August 12, 1922, Arthur Griffith, President of the Provisional Free State government, died of a heart attack. Ten days later Michael Collins was killed in a Republican ambush in County Cork. On the

Republican side, Harry Boland, once Collins' best friend, and Cathal Brugha, his most passionate opponent, both were killed by Free State bullets. A Free State firing squad executed Erskine Childers for carrying a concealed weapon.

Childers' execution was part of a policy that finally defeated the Republicans and brought an end to the Civil War. William T. Cosgrave succeeded Griffith and Kevin O'Higgins, Minister for Home Affairs, replaced Collins as the strong man in the Cabinet. O'Higgins was determined that majority rule would prevail against minority violence. He and his colleagues decided that harsh measures were necessary to preserve liberal democracy. To demonstrate its determination not to submit to intimidation, the Free State government executed seventy-eight Republican prisoners, including Childers and O'Connor. In less than a year, Free State authorities executed far more Irish rebels than the British did throughout the course of the Anglo-Irish War (seventy-seven to twenty-four).[2]

Free State terror and the hostility of majority Irish opinion and the Irish Catholic clergy demoralized Republicans. De Valera re-emerged from the shadows. He finally convinced IRA leaders that they could not defeat the Treaty by violence. In May, 1923, they ordered their men to dump arms, and without officially surrendering, members of the Republican army merged into the ordinary activities of Irish life without abandoning their principles.

The Civil War left a legacy of hatred that continued to factionalize Irish politics. Despite pressing economic and social problems, support for or opposition against the Treaty defined Irish politics during the 1920's, 1930's, 1940's, and 1950's. Reflections on the past distracted attention from problems of the present and future. And pro- and anti-Treaty controversy sometimes spilled over into violent acts. On July 10, 1927, gunmen murdered Kevin O'Higgins as he walked home from Sunday Mass.[3]

For the most part, the continuing Treaty debate took place within the narrow confines of political nationalism. In this context, Free Staters appeared to be reasonable men pragmatically trying to create a functioning political community while Republicans seemed to be simple-minded fanatics without regard for political necessity or reality. There were, however, Treaty opponents who embraced Republicanism as a protest against conservative Free State social policies. To them, the Free State represented an aborted revolution, a change of establishments rather than a transformation of soci-

---

[2]These figures come from Dorothy MacArdle, *The Irish Republic*, Dublin: Irish Press, 1951, pp. 983–985. And if you include in the 1916 "martyrs" the number of men executed by the British from 1916 through 1921 was forty.

[3]Three men fired the shots, but no one was ever apprehended for the murder of O'Higgins. His assassins were probably Republicans, but he did have other enemies, particularly in reference to his role in suppressing a 1924 mutiny among officers in the Free State Army.

ety. They viewed the Catholic clerical, landowner, shopkeeper, Protestant Unionist support of the Free State as a counter-revolutionary effort to preserve vested interests. A socialist minority continued to play a significant role in the Republican movement, at times exerting an influence disproportionate to its numbers.

Attempts to analyze the distinctions between Free Staters and Republicans in nonpolitical ideological terms can distort the essence of the conflict. Personal loyalty, always an important consideration in Irish politics, often decided where a man stood. Many people were either loyal to Collins or to de Valera and trusted the judgment of their leaders. Although Arthur Griffith was extremely conservative on social and economic issues, bishops, businessmen, large farmers, and wealthy Protestants did not necessarily endorse the Free State because they found its leaders congenial defenders of status, property, investments, or organized religion. They wanted law and order and that is what the Free State offered. However, the support that the church and the prosperous classes gave the Free State certainly nudged it in a conservative direction. The pro-Treaty Sinn Feiners became the conservative political party in post-revolutionary Irish politics.

As an issue, partition had played a minor role during the Dáil debate on the Treaty. However, during the Civil War, Republicans made divided Ireland a major issue. Protestant oppression of Catholic nationalists in Northern Ireland gave an additional emphasis to the partition question. From 1920 through 1935, Protestant violence in the Six Counties killed hundreds of people and wounded thousands, almost all of them Catholic. After the Civil War, Republicans continued to point to partition and the existence of Northern Ireland as visible signs of British imperialism in Ireland, and as the unfinished business of Irish nationalism.

Although Lloyd George assured Griffith and Collins that the Boundary Commission would shrink the size of Northern Ireland and eventually unify the country, he was not in office when the Commission met in 1924. Chaired by Justice R. Feetham of South Africa, the Boundary Commission proceeded on the instructions of Article XII of the Treaty: to "determine, in accordance with the wishes of the inhabitants so far as it may be compatible with economic and geographic conditions, the boundaries between Northern Ireland and the rest of Ireland." The specific wording of Article XII is quite different from Lloyd George's verbal promise. The limiting phrase "compatible with economic and geographical conditions" provided a loophole to destroy the expectations of a United Ireland.

In early November, 1925, a newspaper leak predicted that the Boundary Commission was going to expand the territory of Northern Ireland by attaching to it portions of Donegal. Eoin MacNeill's resignation as the Free State representative on the Boundary Commission confirmed the rumor. In order to prevent the publication of the Boundary Commission report, which according to the Judicial Committee of the Privy Council would give it the force of law, the Free State government entered into negotiations with Britain and Northern Ireland. In December, 1925, the Free State accepted the existing frontier. In return, Britain absolved both the Dublin and Stormont governments of their obligations to the British debt, and Free State and Northern Ireland officials agreed to negotiate problems of mutual concern. This tripartite agreement eliminated the Council of Ireland, the intended bridge of Irish unity. Since the Council of Ireland had never functioned, direct negotiations between the two Irelands was probably a more realistic approach to future relations between nationalists in the South and unionists in the North. But the deep hatred and suspicions between the two communities did not suggest the probability of constructive dialogue.

Free State politicians seemed to think that they had salvaged something in this arrangement with Britain and Northern Ireland. But Republicans argued that the tripartite agreement gave a permanent sanction to partition. They accused Free Staters of selling out a united Ireland for a mess of pottage. From 1925 on, the North and partition became the principle topics in Republican criticism of the Free State and the targets of IRA violence against the British.

The end of the Civil War gave the Free State government an opportunity to consolidate its position and to establish permanent administrative and political institutions. Examples of Republican violence—arson and armed robbery—convinced Free State politicians to make some exceptions to normal judicial methods. From 1923 to the present day, Public Safety Acts directed against the real and potential dangers of IRA terrorism have been a feature of Irish law. Frequently, Irish governments have arrested and interned members of the IRA without the usual police and court room procedures.

Once survival of the state seemed assured, the government turned to the economy. The Free State began its existence as an under-developed nation, lacking mineral and other important natural resources. Partition had deprived the Free State of the only industrially developed portion of the country. And, as previously discussed, the Civil War had directed government funds into unproductive channels and further undermined the economy by chaos.

Arthur Griffith's Sinn Fein program had projected a self-sufficient Ireland to be achieved by protective tariffs and subsidies to agriculture and industry, but Free State politicians had to adapt theory to the reality of Dominion status. Geography and history had integrated Ireland into the British economy. After the Anglo-Irish War, she had little choice but to remain part of the British economic complex. Britain was the natural market for Irish agriculture. Over ninety percent of Irish trade was with the United Kingdom, and Ireland remained in the sterling block. Free State leaders feared that policies protecting Irish industry could lead to British reprisals against Irish agriculture. Therefore, they adopted a cautious program, encouraging a few industries to manufacture for local consumption while subsidizing agriculture development to produce food for export.

Despite hopes and encouragement, Irish agriculture remained in a static condition. No doubt the residues of the landlord system debilitated the energies of Irish farmers. In the late nineteenth and early twentieth centuries, when the application of technology to agriculture in other parts of the Western world significantly increased food production, the volume of output from Irish farms improved only marginally. Under the Free State, larger farms, subsidies, and increasing prices for food raised the rural standard of living, but production levels remained constant as farmers continued to resist experimentation.

While agriculture floundered in inertia, domestic industries often were inefficient. During the 1920's, about six percent of the work force was unemployed, and there was a high level of temporary and partial employment. Average family incomes were substantially lower than those in the United Kingdom, although the cost of living was almost the same. People in rural Ireland often fled to the cities, and emigration persisted as a depressing and demoralizing factor in Irish life, with the United Kingdom as the main recipient of the surplus Irish population. From 1926 to 1946, the rural population declined by 85,400 and from 1922 to 1927 the annual emigration rate averaged about 27,000. In 1911, the population of the twenty-six Free State counties was about 3,100,000. Fifteen years later it was near 2,970,000. While emigration continued to function as a safety valve, draining off social, economic, and political discontent, it also deprived the country of much youth, talent, intelligence, ambition, and energy.

In post-Treaty Ireland, Catholicism continued as the dominant influence over Irish mores, values, and culture. Its association with the state has been the subject for much comment and criticism. Many commentators have described Ireland as a theocracy. Most of the important Irish writers have characterized Catholicism as a negative force in Irish life. Unlike the upper-class Anglo-Irish Protestants of the Literary Revival, the majority of post-revolutionary Irish writers were from working or lower middle class Catholic families. They had participated in cultural and revolutionary nationalist movements. Sean O'Casey, a Dublin proletarian Protestant, had belonged to the Gaelic League and the Citizen Army. Sean O'Faolain and Frank O'Connor learned their nationalism in Cork city from Daniel Corkery, a talented writer, brilliant teacher, and Irish-Ireland propagandist. Both of them joined the Republican forces during the Civil War. Literary Revival writers attempted to isolate and inoculate Ireland from the urban materialism of the outside world. Theirs was a romantic, backward look with little or no concern for the social and economic problems of twentieth-century

Ireland. While the new generation of Irish writers respected their elders, they participated in nationalism to modernize and reform as well as liberate Ireland.

Disillusionment was a dominant theme of post-revolutionary Irish literature. The writers observed and evaluated the Ireland of the 1920's, 1930's, 1940's and early 1950's. They saw its stagnant economy, poverty and emigration; the inertia of the people who remained at home; the power and profit motives of priests, politicians, and businessmen and their resistance to social and economic progress; and the censorship laws. They decided that the shift from British to Irish rule had changed little for the better and some things perhaps for the worse.

Writers blamed the Catholic church for the failed revolution. They said that the bishops and priests were the nucleus of a conservative coalition that prevented Ireland from confronting the social and economic problems demoralizing the nation or from adjusting to the modern world. Sean O'Casey referred to the Catholic seminary at Maynooth as "the brain, the body, the

SEAN O'FAOLAIN
1900–

Sean O'Faolain has been the most important intellectual force in post-Treaty Ireland. As novelist, short story writer, literary critic, biographer, political commentator, and editor he has served as the liberal conscience of Irish nationalism. (Courtesy of Radio Telefis Eireann)

nerve and the tissue of the land, controlling two-thirds of the country, influencing it all." Sean O'Faolain also complained about clerical power independent of the pressures of democratic opinion. He argued that bishops exploited their influence over a devout laity to dictate political, social, and economic policy to the politicians in Dublin.[4] Irish writers also insisted that Catholic authoritarianism, anti-intellectualism, and puritanism had enslaved the Irish imagination and intellect. Since Irish literature continued to impress a sophisticated world audience, the writers view of post-Treaty Ireland and the Catholic church's role in the community became a widely accepted portrait of Irish society.

As the writers have insisted, Catholic power is a reality in Ireland. The historical connection between the Irish and the Catholic identities; the leadership roles of bishops and priests in the agitations for Catholic Emancipation, Repeal, tenant right, and Home Rule; the alliances between Irish nationalism and Catholicism which conceded the control of education to the clergy; and the deep piety of the ninety-five percent Catholic majority in the Irish state has given the Catholic hierarchy and clergy prestige and respect among the people. They have exercised their special position and their virtual monopoly over the education system to affect the laws of the land. Irish politicians have legislated Catholic morality on such minor subjects as drinking hours and dance-hall licenses and on such major issues as divorce and family planning. Certainly, the Irish legal and political systems have not left much room for private conscience and morality.

The rather sketchy dimensions of Irish nationalism and its Irish-Ireland expression both contributed to the thrust of Catholic power. Since the ideology of Irish nationalism tried to avoid conflict with Anglo-Irish Protestant interests by de-emphasizing the economic and social aspect of the Irish Question, Irish Catholicism filled the vacuum. With the support of pious laymen, bishops and priests have insisted that the message of papal encyclicals and the theses of neo-Thomist philosophers and moral theologians must determine the conscience of Catholic Ireland. Cultural nationalists, in their effort to de-Anglicize Ireland, have insisted on an Irish-Ireland. Catholic spokesmen twisted this nationalist hope for a unique, intellectual, Gaelic Ireland into a demand for a unique, holy, Catholic Ireland. They turned the Irish-Ireland condemnation of shallow, materialistic, and alien West Britonism into a campaign against secularism, liberalism, and socialism.

If the links between the Irish and Catholic identities have made it difficult for nationalism to develop social and economic programs essential to the needs of twentieth century society, they have also limited the responses of the church to the contemporary world. Throughout the twentieth century,

[4]Sean O'Casey, *Innisfallen Fare Thee Well*, New York: MacMillan, 1949, pp. 320–321; Sean O'Faolain, "The Dáil and the Bishops," *The Bell*, Vol. 17, no. 3 (June, 1951), 5–13.

Irish Catholicism has been more conservative in theology, philosophy, liturgy, and sociology than Catholicism in most other parts of the Western world. It is very difficult for the Irish church to change her image because innovations in religious thought or worship might disturb the national self-concept which many citizens still associate with Catholic pietism and puritanism.

Despite priestly power, theocracy is a harsh and inaccurate description of post-Treaty Ireland. A Catholic confessional state is more accurate. Irish nationalism embraces a liberal democratic as well as a Catholic tradition. Catholic influence is only effective when it harmonizes with the climate and goals of nationalist opinion. Frequently since 1922 bishops and priests have suffered defeat or have had to retreat when their ambitions irritated the liberal democratic spirit of Irish nationalism. In post-Treaty Ireland, Anglo-Irish Protestants have retained their civil rights. They own much of the property of the country and they are still prominent in cultural and political affairs. In fact, they have furnished the country with two Presidents. Although Irish constitutions have insisted on the separation of church and state, it is a principle easier to define in theory than practice, particularly in a nation of deeply religious people. Most important matters of legislation involve moral as well as political, social, and economic considerations. Both the friends and the enemies of divorce, birth control, and abortion surely would admit that these issues have moral implications. Laws in Ireland against practices popular in other places are more representative of democratic public opinion than clericalism.

The Gaelic has never been as controversial as the Catholic component in Irish nationalism, but it has provoked considerable discussion and criticism. Irish-Ireland ideology contributed enthusiasm, dedication, and a sense of purpose to the liberation movement. In his autobiography, *Vive Moi*, Sean O'Faolain described how Irish-Ireland idealism created a sense of community among young idealists:

> Irish became our runic language. It made us comrades in a secret society. We sought and made friendships, some of them to last forever, like conspirators in a state of high exaltation, merely by using Irish words.[5]

Leaders of post-Treaty Ireland implemented Pearse's intention to make "Ireland Gaelic as well as free." They have spent a considerable amount of money to preserve the Gaeltacht—the Irish speaking districts of Waterford, Cork, Kerry, Galway, Mayo, and Donegal—as an inspiration and source of instruction to the rest of the country. Although only about seventeen percent of the population could speak Irish in 1922, the Free State constitution established it as the "national language." In order to make that

[5]Sean O'Faolain, *Vive Moi*, Boston: Little, Brown and Co., 1963, p. 135.

claim more than an empty aspiration, the government required civil servants and members of the army and police force (Garda Siochana) to be proficient in the language. It also recognized Irish as an official language for Dáil debates and legal proceedings, and it required elementary and secondary schools to instruct their pupils in Irish. Recruiting a sufficient number of teachers competent in Irish hampered early efforts to revive the language, but government-sponsored prizes, bonuses, and scholarships helped remedy this shortage. Until 1973, Irish language requirements increased in the schools, and it was necessary for students to earn a pass in the language to be eligible for the leaving certificate.

Despite these efforts, English remains the spoken language and the means of communication for most Irish citizens, and people continue to leave the Gaeltacht and settle in English-speaking places in Ireland and the United Kingdom. Still, the Irish-Ireland movement remains a powerful lobby. Its members insist that Irish independence requires cultural integrity as well as political sovereignty. And although the Irish people have continued to resist using the language, a majority of them have continued to piously conform to the Irish-Ireland ideal.

Some critics of the language movement have protested that compulsory Irish has lowered the quality of education below the standards of the old national schools. They say that the time and money invested in teaching Irish would be better spent on improving English language skills and in promoting vocational education. Parents of potential emigrants want their children prepared to survive and advance in Britain, Canada, Australia, or the United States. Others insist that the language movement promotes a kind of elitism. They point out that while the government has poured money into the Gaeltacht, other impoverished areas like Leitrim, Monaghan, and Cavan have received little official concern or attention. And they complain that the preference shown to speakers and readers of Irish in civil service appointments discriminates against other well qualified people.

Many intellectuals, including those friendly to the language movement, have argued that the insistence on an Irish-Ireland has reinforced the partition that divides Catholics in the South from Protestants in the North because the latter group continues to identify with the British historical and cultural tradition. They insist that Irish-Ireland represents an exclusive, Catholic, provincial, puritanical, and culturally anti-intellectual and isolationist perspective. While Sean O'Faolain paid tribute to the contribution that Irish-Ireland idealism made to the freedom struggle, he has also admitted that it no longer expresses the hopes or values of the nation:

> The language that once spoke to teeming life, and which is already speaking to fewer and fewer, will then only speak to ghosts, the language of the dead. Already, by 1958, a Swiss philologist could write in a publication of the Dublin Institute of Advanced Studies, "We are dealing with the ruins of a language," and report that Irish was the

vernacular only in pockets of coastal Mayo, of Connemara, of Dingle, and of Donegal. English was infiltrating even into the Aran Islands. The Great Blasket Island was depopulated. Seven years earlier the Institute reported that there were then (1951) not more than three thousand people in Ireland who could not speak English, and not more than thirty-five thousand in all who used Irish as their ordinary medium of speech. So the old life dies, the old symbols wither away, and I and my like who warmed our hands at the fires of the past are torn in two as we stand on the side of the bridge and look back in anguish at the doomed Ireland beyond it.[6]

FROM FREE STATE TO REPUBLIC

Makers of the 1922 Free State Constitution had to harmonize their obligations to Commonwealth membership with the sovereignty aspirations of the Irish people. A Governor General represented the British Crown. The President of the Executive Committee, equivalent to the British Cabinet, functioned as Prime Minister. The Oireachtas (Parliament) contained two houses: the Dáil and Seanad Eireann. Ultimate power rested in the former. Irish voters elected their T.D.s (the 153 Dáil Deputies) through a system of proportional representation.[7] The President of the Executive Committee selected half of the sixty Senators, the Dáil chose the rest. In selecting the first Senate, the President and the Dáil made an effort to convince Protestants that they were full-fledged members of the new nation. There were twenty-four Protestants in the first Senate, including the poet, William Butler Yeats; sixteen of them were former unionists. Senators could suspend legislation for nine months, suggest amendments to bills, and initiate legislation in certain areas.

Despite obvious similarities to the British parliamentary system, the Free State did attempt to make some original contributions to liberal democracy. In addition to proportional representation, the constitution contained a Bill of Rights, Initiative and Referendum, and Extern-Ministers chosen for their skills in political, economic, and cultural matters. Authors of the constitution believed that proportional representation would defeat the corruption, vested interest, and anti-democratic tendencies associated with traditional party politics.

Proportional representation did encourage a variety of political organizations and the election of independent T.D.s, but the Treaty controversy and the Civil War polarized Irish politics around two major factions. Consequently, party considerations dominated the Irish parliamentary process as they did throughout the English-speaking world. Party strength in the Dáil determined who would be President and who would compose the Executive Committee. In time, Initiative and Referendum retreated before the

[6]O'Faolain, *Vive Moi*, p. 142.
[7]T.D. means Teachta Dála or Dáil Deputy.

power of parliamentary majorities and the Executive Committee no longer recruited the talents of Extern Ministers.

From 1922 until 1932, William T. Cosgrave, leader of the pro-Treaty party, Cumann na nGaedheal (Community of Irishmen) served as President of the Executive Committee. Elected anti-Treaty Republicans refused to take their seats in the Dáil, insisting that it was an illegitimate body. While not a charismatic personality, Cosgrave was an intelligent and efficient administrator, who deserves a large share of the credit for placing the Irish nation state on firm political and institutional foundations. His government suppressed rebellion, organized an efficient system of local government, created a police force, recruited a civil service, and in 1924 put down an incipient mutiny in the Free State army, firmly subordinating the armed forces to civilian authority.

Cumann na nGaedheal did little to improve social services or to reduce the rates of unemployment or the flow of emigration, but it did not raise taxes and it did stabilize the economy. International bankers and financiers judged the Irish economy as sound and firm. While Cosgrave's conservative economic program reflected a pro-treaty constituency of businessmen and large farmers, he and his colleagues did innovate with government intervention in economic areas too risky or too expensive to attract private investments. Beginning with the Electricity Supply Board (1927), which developed water power and turf (peat) as energy sources, and consolidated all electrical production in the country into one national supply, the government established a number of state-sponsored bodies combining government and private funds and initiative. At present there are fifty-nine of them in Ireland, covering such varied activities as tourism, air travel, ground transportation, shipping, agriculture, sugar production, and banking.

The biggest successes won by Cumann na nGaedheal were in foreign and Commonwealth relations. In 1923, the Free State joined the League of Nations, where its representative articulated a foreign policy independent of Britain and the other Dominions. Ireland appointed ambassadors to the United States, Canada, France, and Italy, and issued her own passports. During Commonwealth conferences, the Irish joined with Canadians and South Africans in demanding maximum sovereignty for the Dominions. They were opposed by Australians and New Zealanders who, isolated in the Pacific and nervous about the "yellow peril," wanted to retain close cultural, economic, political, and military ties with Britain.

Captained by Kevin O'Higgins and Desmond Fitzgerald, the Irish were the best briefed, most diligent, and most articulate delegates attending Commonwealth conferences. Their leadership of the Dominion sovereignty block resulted in significant changes in the concept and operation of the Commonwealth. Governor Generals became representatives of the Crown rather than the British government, the British Parliament completely abandoned any claim to legislate for the Dominions, and members of the Commonwealth no longer had to abide by treaties or agreements that Britain negotiated with foreign powers. In 1931, the Statute of Westminster codified the work of Commonwealth conferences during the 1920's by defining Dominion status as a free association of sovereign and equal states united in common allegiance to the same monarch. The definition came very close to de Valera's proposal for External Association.

Unimpressed with the successes of Free State diplomats, Republicans continued to concentrate on the symbols of British influence in Ireland rather than the reality of Irish sovereignty. They still insisted that they were the legitimate government of the Irish Republic, the voice of the one, true nationalist faith, describing Free Staters as heretics, traitors, and usurpers. Republican extremists dismissed Irish majority opinion as irrelevant: the people had "no right to surrender their independence at the ballot box . . . no right to do wrong." De Valera, a complex blend of pragmatist and ideologue, depending on the circumstances, finally decided that Republican theology and metaphysics was a political dead end. Facing reality, in 1925 he organized a new anti-Treaty party, Fianna Fáil (Soldiers of Destiny) to challenge Cumann na nGaedheal. Sinn Fein, the IRA, and its women's auxiliary, Cumann na mBan, excommunicated de Valera from the pure Republican fold.

De Valera wanted to enter the Dáil but did not want to take the required Oath of Allegiance. He feared that such an act would damage his credibility. In 1927, after the assassination of O'Higgins, Cosgrave forced his hand by pushing through an Electoral Amendment Act that required all political candidates to take the Oath to qualify for the ballot. Realizing that he must adjust his principles or remain in the wilderness, de Valera led his followers to Leinster House, took the Oath, and entered the Dáil. Sensitive to criticism that he lacked principle, de Valera later insisted that he never really subscribed to the Oath of Allegiance to the Crown:

> . . . I have here a written document in pencil, in Irish—the statement I made to the officer who was supposed to administer the oath. I said:—"I am not prepared to take the oath. I am not going to take it. I am prepared to put my name down here in this book in order to get permission to get into the Dáil, and it has no other significance." There was a Testament on the table, and in order that there might be no misunderstanding, I went over, took the Testament, put it away, and said—"You must remember I am not taking any oath."[8]

Whether de Valera did or did not actually take the Oath was a matter for his own conscience and the faith of his supporters, but Fianna Fáils' entry into

---

[8]DeValera made this statement in the Dáil in 1932 while urging the repeal of the Oath of Allegiance. Sean O'Faolain, *DeValera*, Harmondsworth, Middlesex, England: Penguin Books, 1939, p. 122.

the Dáil was a major gain for Irish constitutional politics. Differences between the friends and enemies of the Treaty could now be discussed in a parliamentary context.

The results of the 1927 general election justified de Valera's gamble, proving that constitutional Republicanism could command the respect of voters. De Valera's charisma and the unpopularity of Cosgrave's conservative economic policies strengthened Fianna Fáil in the Dáil. Cumann na nGaedheal still controlled 67 seats, but Fianna Fáil offered strong opposition with 57. Since no single party held a majority, the Cosgrave government survived on the goodwill of independent and Farmer Party T.D.s.

From 1929 to 1932, Cosgrave, like other leaders in the Western democracies, had to cope with a depression. Holding fast to orthodox capitalist theories and practices, he preferred retrenchment to government spending, deciding to reduce the salaries of teachers, civil servants, and policemen, and to cut back on pensions and other social welfare programs. Austerity and a tough policy in regard to an outbreak of IRA violence and robberies antagonized many Irish citizens. In 1931, the government outlawed the IRA and many of its auxilliary organizations, and introduced a Public Safety Act that gave a five man military tribunal the power to intern or execute political criminals with appeal only to the Executive Committee.

In its 1932 election campaign, Fianna Fáil promised a united, free and Gaelic Ireland, an extensive social welfare program, economic self-sufficiency, land for the rural proletariat, and an alteration in Anglo-Irish relations toward a Republican solution. De Valera said that Irish farmers had more than compensated their former oppressors, and that an Irish government should stop paying land purchase annuities to Britain. General election results gave Fianna Fáil more votes than any other party and a plurality of seats in the Dáil—72 to 57 for Cumann na nGaedheal. Labour Party support permitted de Valera to form a government.

Once in office, de Valera set out to redeem his election pledges. Fianna Fáil appropriated large sums of money for rural and urban housing, increased the size and number of old age pensions, provided welfare benefits for widows, orphans, and the unemployed, imposed tariffs on foreign imports, and enlarged and expanded subsidies to agriculture and industry. During the election campaign, some farmers assumed that a de Valera victory would mean that they would no longer have to pay their land purchase annuities. Fianna Fáil did reduce annuity payments, collected them, but did not send the funds to Britain. De Valera applied the money to social services.

The Fianna Fáil government repealed the Public Safety Act and released IRA internees. Republicans responded to this conciliatory gesture by increasing their intimidation of the constitutional process. Their tactics provoked a right-wing response. Back in 1931, Dr. T. F. O'Higgins, Kevin's brother, organized an Army Comrades Association to protect Cumann na nGaedheal meetings from extremist Republican disruptions. In 1933, when the IRA renewed its thuggery, O'Higgins revived the Army Comrades Association, changed its name to the National Guard, and turned the leadership over to General Eoin O'Duffy. De Valera had dismissed O'Duffy, who had been a close friend of Collins, from his position as Commissioner of Police. Under O'Duffy's instructions, members of the National Guard wore blue shirt uniforms and gave fascist salutes. Professors James Hogan, University College, Cork, and Michael Tierney, University College, Dublin, and other right-wing Irish intellectuals pointed to Saor Eire, a leftist IRA faction under the guidance of Peadar O'Donnell, Donegal writer, as evidence of a dangerous communist menace in Ireland. Tierney and Hogan authored a Blue Shirt social and economic policy which borrowed ideas from Pius XI's *Quadragesimo Anno* and Benito Mussolini's fascist corporate state.

Violent clashes between the IRA and the Blue Shirts endangered Irish liberal democracy. Still hoping to conciliate the Republican left, de Valera outlawed the National Guard and recruited from the IRA for a Garda Special Branch to cope with political extremism. Frustrated by Fianna Fáil's growing popularity among Irish voters, Cumann na nGaedheal leaders decided to form a coalition with the Blue Shirts and the Centre Party, which had considerable support among large farmers. This coalition produced a new right of center party, Fine Gael (United Ireland), with O'Duffy as its Chairman.

O'Duffy's extravagant and irresponsible ideas and behavior, de Valera's firmness, Irish individualism, and the common sense of moderate Cumann na nGaedheal and Centre Party politicians defeated the fascist threat in Ireland. James Dillon, son of the last Chairman of the Irish Party, and Frank MacDermot from Leitrim, who represented Centre Party interests in the new Fine Gael Party, could not stand O'Duffy's addiction to fascist symbols, rhetoric, liturgy, and ideas. They forced him to resign as party Chairman.[9] Cosgrave took his place.

In addition to de Valera's welfare program and economic self-sufficiency policies, he bid for Republican support by altering the Free State Constitution. In 1933, he removed the Oath of Allegiance and reduced the role of the Governor General. Two years later, the Fianna Fáil government abolished the right of appeal from Irish courts to the Judicial Committee of the British Privy Council. A year later, Britain's constitutional crisis, involving the abdication of Edward VIII and the accession of George VI, presented de Valera with another opportunity to expand Irish sovereignty. He com-

[9]O'Duffy and the IRA fought on different sides during the Spanish Civil War. O'Duffy took a Blue Shirt Brigade to Spain to fight for Franco. An IRA contingent was part of the International Brigade defending the Spanish Republic. The Blue Shirts saw little action and many returned to Ireland thoroughly disillusioned. The IRA people suffered heavy casualties.

pletely eliminated the office of Governor General and removed the Crown from the Irish constitution except for purposes of External Relations.

In 1937, de Valera gave the Irish people a new constitution incorporating changes in Anglo-Irish relations. It defined Ireland (Eire) as "a sovereign, independent, democratic state" with all powers derived "under God, from the people," made the green, white, and orange tricolor the official flag of the nation, and elevated Irish to the first language of the state.

Under the new constitution, a popularly elected President replaced the Governor General as Head of State. He could only serve two terms and his role was mainly but not completely symbolic. As Chairman of the Executive Committee (Cabinet), the Taoiseach (Prime Minister) was actually functioning chief executive, and the Dáil remained as the expression of popular sovereignty. With the new constitution, de Valera restored the Senate, which he had abolished the year before as a nest of unionist conservatism, but he gave it a vocational rather than a political representation. Despite the vocational ideal, in practice Senators were often party hacks compensated for their loyal years of service after they were defeated in Dáil elections. The new constitution reduced the Senate's power to suspend legislation from nine to six months.

Vocationalism was a tribute to the corporate state theories of papal encyclicals. Catholic values also appeared in other portions of the constitution. The state recognized "the family as the natural primary and fundamental unit group of society, and a moral institution possessing inalienable and imprescribable rights antecedent and superior to all positive law." Article 44 acknowledged "the special position" of the Catholic church as the religious expression of the majority of citizens, but also recognized other Christian and the Jewish congregations in Ireland. The state promised financial support to religious schools of all denominations as well as to secular educational institutions.

De Valera submitted the new constitution to a national referendum. The vote was closer than he expected. 685,105 (thirty-nine percent) voted yes, 526,945 (thirty percent) voted no, and thirty-one percent did not express an opinion. With the new constitution de Valera had taken advantages of the liberties of Dominion status, extended by Free State diplomats, to create an Ireland that was a Republic in fact if not in name. He refrained from declaring a Republic because he feared that a complete break with the Commonwealth would strengthen partition. The constitution claimed jurisdiction over a united, thirty-two county nation, but temporarily suspended application in Northern Ireland.

When the Irish government refused to transfer the land annuities, Britain retaliated with tariffs on Irish imports. Since most of Ireland's commerce was with Britain, the trade war hurt her economy more than Britain's. Hardest hit by the Anglo-Irish economic conflict, large Irish farmers, particularly cattlemen, became enthusiastic supporters of Fine Gael. De Valera never wanted an affluent Ireland. His goal was frugal comfort: an austere, virtuous, self-reliant Irish-Ireland, isolated from the secularism and materialism of the outside world. He viewed the hardship of the trade war as a stimulus for Ireland to develop her small industries and progress toward self-sufficiency.

When Neville Chamberlain became British Prime Minister in 1937, he decided to achieve an alliance of friendship and common interest with Ireland. He made it clear that partition was outside the scope of compromise, but said that he was prepared to negotiate the land annuities, the trade war, and British naval bases in Ireland. After conversations in London during the spring of 1938, Ireland and Britain signed agreements eliminating British tariffs on Irish imports, compensating Britain for the land annuities with a final Irish payment of £10,000,000, and transferring the Treaty ports to Irish jurisdiction. The London settlement also involved a reciprocal trade pact providing duty-free access of each country's goods to the other's markets. British critics condemned Chamberlain for risking British security by surrendering ports in Ireland at a time when Germany was girding for war. Irish public opinion received de Valera as a hero. In a June, 1938, general election, voters gave Fianna Fáil a sixteen-seat majority in the Dáil.

World tensions and crises during the 1930's posed a foreign policy challenge to de Valera's leadership. In 1932, as President of the Council of the League of Nations, he urged collective security, warning the big powers that they must subdue their egos in the cause of world peace. He advised them not to let their own selfish interests destroy the freedom or integrity of small nations. In response to Italy's aggression against Ethiopia, de Valera pleaded with the League of Nations to invoke sanctions against the offending party. His futile efforts to protect the rights of small nations were in opposition to French and British appeasement of fascism.

When World War II began in September, 1939, de Valera concluded that Ireland had no interest in a war that was the result of big power refusal to protect collective security in the League of Nations, and he insisted that Ireland could not collaborate with Britain while she occupied the Six Counties in Ulster. During the war, many British and American leaders criticized Irish neutrality as a betrayal of liberal democracy. This criticism was both unfair and hypocritical. Switzerland and Sweden, two other Western democracies, remained neutral. Britain and France had appeased fascist aggression from 1934 to 1939 and only reluctantly went to war. And the United States, the cradle of liberty, had to be bombed at Pearl Harbor before entering into the anti-totalitarian crusade.

Neutrality was a real test of Irish sovereignty and the mettle of the Irish people. They supported de Valera's foreign policy and they were pulled together in adversity by the hostility of American and British opinion plus the wartime shortages and poverty. This spirit of unity produced national pride and energy, which were expressed in a brief but interesting Second Literary Revival. In 1941, Sean O'Faolain started to publish *The Bell*, an excellent journal devoted to creative writing, literary criticism, and political comment. In addition to O'Faolain, during the early 1940's, Frank O'Connor, Francis MacManus, Liam O'Flaherty, Denis Johnston, Austin Clarke, Patrick Kavanagh, Donagh MacDonagh, Peadar O'Donnell, Denis Devlin, and Mervyn Wall were among the writers who contributed to the body of Irish literature.

Irish neutrality was biased toward Western democracy. About 60,000 Irish citizens enlisted in the British armed forces, a higher number than the figures from Nothern Ireland. Hundreds of thousands of Irish men and women worked in British defense plants. And Irish farmers supplied badly needed food to hungry mouths in Britain. When German pilots force landed in Ireland, the government interned them, but when British and American flyers mistakenly touched down on the wrong side of the border, they were allowed to cross to Northern Ireland and rejoin their units. Many members of the IRA participated in sabotage efforts against the British war effort and tried to manipulate Ireland into the war on the Axis side. They labored under the foolish notion that a German victory would lead to a United Ireland. De Valera interned many IRA activists through the war years.

Although the North Atlantic Treaty Organization offered a variety of economic aid projects, de Valera and his successors as Taoiseach maintained a policy of Irish neutrality following World War II. Not many other small nations had the moral courage or restraint to resist the lure of American dollars.

THE URBANIZATION AND INDUSTRIALIZATION
OF IRISH SOCIETY

With the war over, Irish political opinion became restless. A long period of Fianna Fáil rule, continuing shortages, inflation, unemployment, inadequate housing and medical services for the poor, and emigration encouraged a desire for change. A new political party, Clann na Poblachta (Republican Family) represented a demand for new leadership and polices. Sean MacBride was the leader of the Clann. He was the son of the 1916 "martyr" and the beautiful Maude Gonne, Yeats' lost love. MacBride fought on the Republican side during the Civil War, kept in touch with the IRA, and defended Republicans in the law courts as a prominent barrister. His party, the latest group defection from IRA violence, moved from the revolutionary into the parliamentary arena demanding a united Ireland and radical social changes.

Following the 1948 general election, 10 Clann na Poblachta T.D.'s joined with 31 from Fine Gael, 19 from Labour, 7 from Clann na Talmhan (Farmer's Party), and James Dillon, independent, in a coalition which ousted Fianna Fáil with 68 Dáil seats from office. John Costello, Chairman of Fine Gael, became Taoiseach. Most Cabinet members came from Fine Gael, but the other parties in the Coalition were also represented.

Shortly after taking office, while visiting in Canada, Costello declared an official end to the Free State and the beginning of the Irish Republic. To many, this seemed a surprising move from the leader of the political party most associated with the Treaty and Free State. But Fine Gael decided that it was prudent policy to raid Fianna Fáil's Republican constituency, appease its Clann na Poblachta allies, and bring to a logical conclusion Ireland's constitutional development. Britain's Labour government reacted to the Irish Republic with a pledge to sustain Northern Ireland as long as it had the support of a majority of its citizens. But Ireland's withdrawal from the Commonwealth did not substantially alter Anglo-Irish relations. Britain still recognized Irish people resident in Britain as British subjects, and the most favored trade arrangements between the two countries remained in force.

Despite Coalition social and economic programs involving land reclamation, housing construction, home improvements, and the encouragement of exports, the rate of economic growth remained slow and unemployment and emigration high. The government attempted to improve the quantity and quality of health care and to bring social and welfare benefits closer to the prevailing United Kingdom standard. A comprehensive program of X-ray diagnosis, increased and improved sanitarium facilities, and finally vaccinations in the schools virtually eliminated tuberculosis as a recurrent Irish plague. Dr. Noel Browne, Clann na Poblachta Minister of Health and a former TB victim, played a major role in the successful war on the disease. He was also interested in lowering the high infant mortality rate in Ireland.

In 1951, the Coalition presented to the Dáil a Browne authored pre- and post-natal health program. Immediately, the Irish Medical Association labeled the Mother and Child Bill as socialistic, interfering with doctor-patient relationships. Catholic bishops joined the medical profession in attacking the Bill. Both criticized the absence of a means test and warned that government medicine could result in sex education contrary to the teachings of the Catholic church.

Browne defended the Mother and Child Bill against the powerful medical and clerical lobbies, but Costello and MacBride, Minister for External Affairs, abandoned their Cabinet colleague. This split within the Coalition and its Clann na Poblachta component destroyed the government. The conflict over the Mother and Child Bill was an example of Catholic clericalism confronting the liberal democratic dimension of Irish nationalism. Public opinion resented the intrusion of the bishops and priests in what they considered an essentially secular matter. Fianna Fáil returned to power and, with its mandate from the people, enacted the substance of Browne's health proposal.

Except for two other experiments in Coalition government, 1954–1957 and 1973–1977, Fianna Fáil has been in office for most of the time since 1951. But in 1959, de Valera stepped down as Taoiseach to become his party's successful candidate for President of the Republic. Sean Lemass became the new parliamentary leader of Fianna Fáil and Taoiseach. He came to power at a time when a new generation of voters obviously were bored with the old quarrels between the veterans of the Treaty debate and Civil War. They wanted to join the main stream of Western culture and to enjoy the comforts and luxuries that result from modern technology.

Lemass responded to these new aspirations. He created a new Fianna Fáil economic program based upon the recommendations of a committee that the Coalition government appointed and that Dr. T. K. Whitaker, an economist, chaired. Abandoning the self-reliance of Sinn Fein economic nationalism and de Valera's frugal comfort idealism, the government, through offers of tax exemptions, and land and financial grants for factory location and construction, and by emphasizing the availability of cheap labor, tried to lure foreign investment into the Irish economy. Many companies and firms from all over the Western world and from Japan accepted the advantageous Irish offer, setting up factories, employing many men and women, and thus stemming the tide of emigration.

This mini-Industrial Revolution has changed the profile of the country. From 1962 to 1972 Irish exports rose 271 percent, and in 1973 another 31 percent with all segments of the economy profiting. Ireland has developed export industries that virtually did not exist in the 1950's. They include synthetic textiles, electrical machinery, ship and boat building, scientific equipment, chemicals, drugs, and lead, copper, and zinc ore. Industrialism has shifted population and changed vocations. From 1961 to 1971, agricultural employment declined from 371,000 to 274,000, a drop of 25 percent. In contrast, the number of people involved in industrial production increased by about 25 percent, 187,000 to 233,000. During this period industry created 15,000 new jobs.

Signs of affluence are everywhere. Well dressed young men carrying briefcases discuss stocks and bonds over lunch in restaurants or drinks in lounge bars. They dance in discotheques to rock music with fashionably dressed, attractive young women. Automobiles crowd narrow country roads and city streets, polluting the air with exhaust fumes. Inflation drives up the cost of living and sex mores are changing. The new Irish life style has challenged traditional Catholic values and authority. There have been relaxations in book and cinema censorship. Liberated men and women demand a greater secularization of Irish society. A public opinion majority favors birth control and many people want the state to recognize divorce and cut back clerical control over education.

Contemporary Irish literature both reflects and attacks the new Ireland. Irish writers appreciate the recent openness and cosmopolitanism of a changing Ireland. They seem less nationalist, more interested in identifying with the trends and themes of international literature. They dismiss as irrelevant the old conflict between the artist and Catholic puritanism and narrow-minded nationalism. In his poem "The Seige of Mullingar," John Montague announced that

Puritan Ireland's dead and gone,
A myth of O'Connor and O'Faolain. [10]

At the same time, many Irish writers are immersed in the history and traditions of their people, retaining the values of Irish cultural nationalism. They are worried that industrialism and the market place might tarnish the Irish soul.

All that glitters is not gold. Much of the new prosperity is superficial. Agriculture still has a production growth much lower than expected. Some foreign investors have been disappointed by the lack of energy and initiative among members of the Irish labor force and have shut down their factories. There is always the danger that a large scale recession or depression in other countries could lead to a withdrawal of foreign capital from the Irish economy. And prosperity for some has brought hardship for others. That is the other aspect of Irish industrialism: while the new economy has expanded and fattened the middle class, the poor suffer from inflation with price increases far exceeding the rise in wages. Inflation has also wounded tourism, which emerged in the 1950's and 1960's as Ireland's second most important economic industry, next to agriculture. In the 1970's, many Britons and Americans found the cost of living higher in Ireland than in their own countries, and decided not to vacation there.

Irish foreign policy has accommodated to shifting economic, cultural, and social climates. After the Soviet Union withdrew its objections, Ireland became a member of the United Nations in 1956. In New York, intelligent and articulate Irish diplomats condemned imperialism and spoke as representatives of Third World victims of colonialism. They said that their nation's history fitted them for such a role. Their conduct at the United Nations often infuriated Catholic bishops in Ireland and the United States, particularly

---

[10]Puritan Ireland was no myth when O'Faolain and O'Connor wrote about it. John Montague, "The Seige of Mulingar" in *A Chosen Light*, (Chicago, The Swallow Press, Inc. 1970). Reprinted by permission of The Swallow Press, Inc. and MacGibbon; Kee and John Montague, *The Golden Stone*, 25, Grattan Hill, Cork, Ireland.

their open-minded position in regard to the admission of Red China into the international organization.

On January 1, 1973, following a referendum, Ireland joined the Common Market. Since Britain, her leading customer, also planned to participate, she had little choice in the matter. The Common Market offers many advantages: high food prices for Irish farmers, funds for Irish industrial development, and consumers for Irish goods. With her entry into the Common Market, Ireland's foreign policy stance has shifted from Third World to European, with attention directed more to Brussels than to the United Nations in New York. Perhaps this new perspective is actually more provincial than cosmopolitan. But Third World or Europe, Ireland since 1958 has certainly turned her back on Irish-Ireland and/or Catholic Ireland isolationism.

9

the northern
specter

By any reasonable standard of measurement, post-Treaty Ireland has been a success story. But almost a decade of Ulster violence has tempered optimism in the Republic. The crisis in the Six Counties is more than a dark cloud on a relatively bright Irish horizon; it is an ominous presence that irritates Anglo-Irish relations, bewilders the British people and tests their patience, and threatens to reverse over sixty years of progress in the Republic.

From its beginning, Northern Ireland made little sense as a geographic entity or as a cultural community. During the 1912–1914 Home Rule crisis, British politicians decided that they must partition Ireland under pressure from armed Ulster fanatics. They concluded that it would be unjust and unfair to place a twenty-five percent Protestant minority in a state controlled by a seventy-five percent Catholic majority. So in 1920, they placed a thirty-three percent Catholic minority under the domination of a sixty-six percent Protestant majority. Two of the Six counties, Fermanagh and Tyrone, have small Catholic majorities. And South Down, South Armagh, and West Derry are predominantly Catholic. The Catholic minority in Northern Ireland was committed to the values and destiny of Irish nationalism, and it could not accept exclusion from the long awaited Irish nation or a permanent inclusion in a remnant of the United Kingdom.

Northern Ireland's first constitution was unique. It provided self-government while Northern Ireland remained an integral part of the United

Kingdom. Six County voters sent twelve M.P.s to Westminster, but the Parliament at Stormont managed local affairs. Ulster Unionists never asked for Home Rule, only accepting it as preferable to a united Ireland, but they quickly took advantages of its possibilities. Lord Craigavon (Sir James Craig), the first Prime Minister, announced that Northern Ireland would be a Protestant nation for a Protestant people. He sought and gained British permission to scrap the proportional representation features of the Better Government of Ireland Bill. His successor, Sir Basil Brooke, once advised Protestants not to employ Catholics so as to drive them out of the Six Counties. The Northern Ireland constitution relegated Catholics to second-class citizenship. While Westminster and Stormont franchises were based on democratic British election practices, gerrymandering, a household suffrage, and plural votes for business property denied Catholics fair representation in local government. Even in places where Catholics were a majority, they did not always control county, town, or urban councils. In Derry, Catholics made up two-thirds of the population, but there were twelve Protestants to eight Catholics on the city council. This absence of local influence was even more damaging to Catholic interests than their minority position at Stormont, because local government authorities allocated jobs, housing, and social welfare.

Since politics in Northern Ireland have been rooted in sectarian distinctions rather than attitudes toward social and economic issues, democracy as majority rule cannot work there. Since 1920 Northern Ireland has functioned as a one-party state. The vast majority of Protestants have been uncritically and unreservedly loyal to a Unionist Party under the dictation of the Orange Lodges. In its economic development programs, the Stormont government has ignored the Catholic districts west of the Bann river with a result of chronic Catholic unemployment of close to forty percent in some sections of that area.

Six County Catholics have had good reason to believe that they are victims of an authoritarian system. In addition to the over-whelmingly Protestant Royal Ulster Constabulary, the Stormont government created the armed and exclusively Protestant B-Special force to supplement the regular police. To Catholics, oppressed by B-Special arrogance, brutality, and bigotry, they were the gestapo of the Orange police state. The work of the RUC and the B-Specials was made easier by a Special Powers Act that permitted authorities to arrest and imprison suspected nationalist enemies of the state without ordinary legal procedures and to detain them in jail for an indefinite period without trial.

Inferior educational opportunities plus government and employer discrimination policies have meant that Catholics have experienced the greatest poverty in the Six Counties, although it is not an exclusively Catholic condition. In rural Northern Ireland, Protestants own most of the best lowland

ATLANTIC
OCEAN

North Channel

Lough Foyle

Derry
(Londonderry)

U L S T E R

Lough
Neagh

Belfast

Donegal
Bay

Dundalk

LOUTH

Irish

Drogheda

Sea

C O N N A U G H T

Dublin

L E I N S T E R

Wicklow

R. Shannon

ARAN IS.

Limerick

Wexford

Waterford

M U N S T E R

Cork

Youghal

Dingle Bay

St. George's Channel

54°

52°

Bantry Bay

I R E L A N D

```
0        25       50       75      100
         MILES
```

— NORTHERN IRELAND (U.K.)
····· — REPUBLIC OF IRELAND

Over 50% of the population
is Catholic

Between 25% and 50% of
the population is Catholic

Less than 25% of the
population is Catholic

The Republic of Ireland
where 95% of the popula-
tion is Catholic

CATHOLIC POPULATION CENTERS IN NORTHERN IRELAND

farms, while Catholics grub out a hazardous existence in rocky hill country, but most Protestant farmers are not exactly affluent. And a post-World War II decline in the ship building and linen industries has made Northern Ireland the most economically depressed portion of the United Kingdom, with a unemployment rate that victimizes Catholics and Protestant alike. For many years Northern Ireland has been a mendicant state living off the British dole.

Irish Republicans with socialist leanings have described Northern Ireland as an example of capitalist divide and conquer tactics. They say that men of wealth and property have encouraged and manipulated sectarian rivalries to prevent working-class solidarity, leaving the wealthy in control of the economic and political structures. This is a plausible interpretation of the situation. Sectarian conflict has helped preserve poverty-ridden Northern Ireland as the most conservative portion of the United Kingdom. Protestant farmers and urban workers follow and support the leadership of the ultra-right Unionist Party, and the issue of no-popery has made it possible for politicians to distract the Protestant proletariat from its pressing economic and social problems. It is an interesting paradox: British welfare state policies have eased the political burdens of reactionary Ulster Unionism.

Despite the rationalism of the socialist perspective, bigotry in the North defies reasonable explanations. The loyalty of the Protestant masses is more than the product of capitalist manipulation. As do poor whites who despise poor blacks in the United States, Ulster Protestants receive a psychological lift in believing that they are superior to Catholics. And poor Protestants appear to be much more bigoted than their upper- and middle-class co-religionists.

Protestant xenophobia is often expressed in racist rhetoric. They refer to Catholics as "Pope heads," "Teagues," "bloody Micks," and "Fenians." Many Protestants warn their children against associating with Catholics because they are inherently treacherous, violent, dirty, and lazy. They say that Catholics breed like rabbits on orders from their priests so that they will outnumber Protestants at the polls. Some of the ultra-militant Protestants insist that there will never be peace or harmony in Northern Ireland as long as Catholics live there, and they want to drive them completely out of the Six Counties.

Anti-Catholicism in Ulster reflects insecurity and fear as much as ignorance. After almost four centuries in Ireland, Protestants still feel like strangers in the land, convinced that the native, Catholic Irish are determined on revenge. They really have little confidence in the staying power of the British when things get tough. They have translated their fear of Catholic vengeance and doubts about British fortitude into over forty years of brutal oppression, which Catholics have recently answered with determined resistance.

Protestant anxieties are not completely unfounded. The reality of

Catholic power in the South and the institutionalization of Irish-Ireland nationalism in the constitutions of both the Free State and the Republic have contributed to the cultural and religious dimensions of partition. World War II played a significant part in defining the separate identities of North and South. To nationalists in the Twenty-Six Counties, the neutrality of their country was a statement of sovereignty, a tangible proof of independence. Going it alone from 1939 to 1945 gave Irish nationalists a psychological lift and confidence in the durability of the state they had created. To Ulster unionists, the neutrality of nationalists was an unconscionable tribute to the forces of totalitarianism that threatened the survival of the United Kingdom. World War II divided the historical experiences of the two Irelands, emphasizing the Irishness of the South, accentuating the Britishness of the North.

Many critics of Northern Ireland Catholics point out that they must share some of the responsibility for their status in the Six Counties. From the beginning they were hostile to the state and never really participated in the political system. They could have had more positions in the Royal Ulster Constabulary if they would have applied for them. Since one-third of the population refused to accept the legitimacy of the government, the other two-thirds had no choice but to exclude them from the benfits of complete citizenship. On the other hand, there is no convincing evidence that the Protestant Ascendancy in the North ever intended to include Catholics on equal terms in its community. Stormont apartheid policies certainly did not promise Catholics much hope of improving their situation. Instead, they forced them to retreat further and further into their ghetto way of life. Segregation between Catholics and Protestants in the Six Counties became more complete than separation between races in the United States. Catholics attend their own religious schools, which emphasize Irish history, culture, language, and games. They carry the tricolor in their processions. Protestants attend schools that feature British history and culture.

Northern Ireland Protestants cling to a no-popery nativism out of fashion in Britain and the nationalism of Catholics is more intense than in the South. Ulster Catholics treasure myths, legends, and memories of revolutionary heroes that are fading in Common Market, European Ireland. Since there always has been a close connection between Irish nationalism and the literary muse, the Northern troubles have inspired much writing talent, energy, and production in the Ulster Catholic community, perhaps more than in the Republic. Seamus Heaney, John Montague, Brian Moore, Patrick Boyle, Benedict Kiely, Seamus Deane, and Brian Friel are some outstanding examples of the Northern Catholic genius. Surprisingly, for all of its advantages in education, wealth, and opportunity, the Northern Ireland Protestant community has not come close to matching the literary contribution of the people it considers inferior. One Protestant writer describes his own kind as "An ugly race . . . No poet will ever sing for them—of them."[1]

More Catholics have expressed frustration through violence than through literature by joining the Irish Republican Army in terrorist attacks on symbols of British authority. Some Northern Irish Catholics were so bitter about their condition and partition that they hoped and prayed for a German victory in World War II as a prelude to a united Ireland. In Brian Moore's *The Emperor of Ice Cream,* Burke, a middle-class Catholic solicitor in Belfast, tells his son "when it comes to grinding down minorities, the German jackboot isn't half as hard as the heel of John Bull."[2] And Gallagher, the working-class Catholic from the Fall's Road, and his neighbors "considered it a point of honor to leave a light shining in their upstairs window at night in case any German bombers might come over the city." Gallagher once had been a member of the IRA but lost confidence in it: "He put his money on Hitler. When Hitler won the war, Ireland would be whole again, thirty-two counties, free and clear."[3] Burke and Gallagher did not change their minds about the Nazis until a bombing raid on Belfast destroyed the home of the former and the family of the latter.

After World War II, many Catholics realized that neither the oratory of politicians in the Republic nor IRA terrorism would unite the two Irelands. They also understood that the British Labour government's welfare-state program could improve the condition of their existence. A 1947 British education act introduced free secondary education and led to an extraordinary rise in the number of Catholics in Northern Ireland attending university. An increasing segment of Catholic opinion, particularly among the expanding middle class, decided that first-class citizenship in Northern Ireland was a more practical objective than a united Ireland. This shift in attitude, and the work of police forces on both sides of the border, resulted in the failure of an IRA 1956–1962 terrorist campaign, forcing militant Republicans to re-evaluate their strategy. For all practical purposes, the IRA ceased to function in the Six Counties after 1962.

Richard Rose's *Governing Without Consensus: An Irish Perspective* (1971), a public opinion study, revealed that in the late 1960s a large portion of Northern Ireland's Catholic community was eager to participate as first-class citizens in the affairs of the general community, and that Catholics had a more tolerant view of Protestants than Protestants had of Catholics. Despite majority Protestant determination not to give an inch to Catholic demands, a few intelligent and realistic Unionist politicians began to compre-

---

[1]Maurice Leitch, *Poor Lazarus,* London: Panther Books, 1970, p. 186.
[2]Brian Moore, *The Emperor of Ice Cream,* London: Mayflower Books, 1967, p. 28.
[3]Moore, *The Emperor of Ice Cream,* p. 47.

hend that continued apartheid policies endangered the future of Northern Ireland.

In the Republic, the ascendancy of Lemass heralded a more accommodating approach to the partition question. During the 1960's, united Ireland became a mute issue as attention focused on economic expansion. Even the IRA, operating under a Sinn Fein banner, abandoned the gun for socialist politics, protesting foreign influence over the Irish economy and demanding decent housing and more social services for the poor. When citizens of the Republic paused to think about the North, they assumed things were improving on the other side of the border. At least leaders of the two Irelands were communicating. In January and February, 1965, the Prime Ministers, Terence O'Neill and Sean Lemass, exchanged visits. These courtesy calls were followed by discussions between the two governments on economic and other matters of mutual concern.

These friendly contacts and talks between Northern and Southern politicians suggested that the Ulster Question was moving from hate-provoking rhetoric and violence toward negotiation and conciliation. In *Ireland Since the Rising*, Timothy Patrick Coogan, an influential Irish journalist, predicted that while there were still serious problems of sectarian discrimination in the Six Counties, conversations between Northern and Southern leaders would "have healthy repercussions on the relationships of Protestants and Catholics on both sides of the border ... the new spirit discernible in so many quarters is more representative of the future character of the North than the present evidence of gerrymandering and discrimination."[4]

The process of slow but gradual change in Northern Ireland came to an abrupt halt in 1968. Civil rights agitations in other parts of the world, particularly in the United States, inspired Northern Ireland Catholics. In 1967, the Northern Ireland Civil Rights Association started as a coalition effort to achieve equal citizenship, rights, and opportunities for all residents of the Six Counties. Catholic middle-class moderates joined with socialists, Republicans, socialist republicans, Protestant liberals, and the People's Democracy, a radical student's group from Queen's University. They marched through the streets singing the songs of the American civil rights movement, mainly "We Shall Overcome." The Royal Ulster Constabulary, B-Specials, and Protestant mobs harrassed and beat them. Television cameras brought life behind the Orange Curtain to the attention of British and world opinion, creating a wave of international sympathy for the oppressed Catholic minority in Northern Ireland.

Encouraged by the Labour government in Britain, O'Neill, cautiously

---

[4]Timothy Patrick Coogan, *Ireland Since the Rising*, New York: Praeger, 1966, pp. 327, 328. Reprinted by permission of Praeger Pub., Inc., a Division of Holt, Rinehart and Winston.

weighed the situation and decided to take a few small steps in the direction of civil rights and social justice. But fanatics in the Orange Order, among them Reverend Ian Paisley, the leading no-popery demagogue, and ambitious politicians like William Craig, shouted "No Surrender." Frightened by the frenzy of majority Protestant opinion, O'Neill lost his nerve, equivocated, procrastinated, and finally resigned office. His successor, James Chichester-Clark, promised reform. After moving too slow for the Green and too fast for the Orange, he also resigned, turning power over to Brian Faulkner, a somewhat flexible Unionist.

Since 1969, the older issues of partition and a united Ireland have emerged from the shadows to reduce the importance of civil rights. Orange extremists with their rhetoric of hate and taunting sectarian parades; the Royal Ulster Constabulary and B-Specials (before they were abolished in October, 1969), acting as partisan Protestant armies rather than police forces; timid Stormont and Westminster politicians; and impatient Catholic radicals, socialists, and Republicans combined to transform confrontation protest tactics into a condition of civil war. Encouraged by police apathy, and sometimes support, Protestant mobs forced Derry and Belfast Catholics to retreat into barricaded ghettos. During the civil rights phase of the Ulster crisis, the IRA kept a low profile, promoting civil liberties as a strategy to mobilize and radicalize Catholic ghetto communities. In 1969, Protestant violence revived the IRA as a Catholic defense force, and Catholics welcomed IRA protection. The Irish in Britain and America supplied the Republicans with money to purchase weapons.

At the same time that the IRA revived, it split into Official and Provisional wings.[5] Officials interpret the Northern Ireland situation within a Marxist context. They project an all Ireland socialist republic as the ultimate solution to conflict. Until a truce with the British army in 1974, Officials directed their violence against British authority, carefully avoiding attacks on Irish Protestants. Provisionals who are less discriminating in their terrorism, killing Protestant civilians as well as British soldiers, also claim to be socialists but not Marxists. Despite their workers' republican slogans, Provisionals represent the traditional Republican thesis that the British presence is the essence of the Ulster Question and violence is the only way to persuade the British to evacuate Northern Ireland and to unite the country. They say that a nine-county Ulster regional legislature subordinate to an all Ireland Parliament would satisfactorily compromise Catholic nationalist

---

[5]Leaders of the Official IRA claim that some Fianna Fáil politicians encouraged the split in the Republican movement, using the Provisionals to distract the IRA from socialist agitation and activity in the Republic. In *Northern Ireland: A Report on the Conflict*, New York: Vintage Books, 1972, p. 87 ff., The *London Sunday Times* Insight Team supported the claim of the Officials, but there always have been tensions in the IRA between socialist ideologists and the more traditional and simple-minded brand of Republicanism.

hopes for a united Ireland and Ulster Protestant unionist demands for regional autonomy.

In August, 1969, after weeks of violence in Derry and Belfast, the British government sent troops to Northern Ireland to keep the peace. At first, Catholics welcomed them as protectors, but within a few months the IRA and the soldiers were at war. Permanent good relations between the Catholic community and the British army were almost impossible to sustain. Since the army was a law-and-order extension of the Protestant Unionist state, it could not function as a neutral agency. Soldiers disarmed Catholics, while permitting Protestant extremists to keep their weapons. The presence and the conduct of the army supported IRA propaganda that the conflict in the North was a renewal of the Anglo-Irish War.

On August 9, 1971, acting on the orders of the Faulkner regime, the army aided the police in seizing and interning 342 people who were supposed to be members of or sympathizers with the Provisional and Official IRAs. Those Protestant extremists who first instigated violence in the Six Counties were spared internment at the time. By mid-December, the authorities had apprehended over fifteen hundred suspects (934 were quickly released), virtually all of them Catholic. Instead of calming the situation, internment intensified minority bitterness, consolidating the ghettos behind the IRA. While Republicans vigorously protested the existence of Long Kesh and other internment camps, and the torture that went on in them, in reality, they were a blessing to the IRA cause, providing evidence of British injustice and cruelty in Ireland.[6] After internment Catholic opinion lost all interest in coming to terms with Stormont: extremists demanded a united Ireland; moderates would accept nothing less than the end of Northern Ireland as established in 1920.

On Sunday, January 30, 1972, British paratroopers killed fourteen Derry Catholics who were participating in a protest demonstration. Thirteen were killed immediately but one died later in a hospital. "Bloody Sunday" further fanaticized Catholic nationalist opinion and dealt a death blow to Stormont. In March, 1972, the British Conservative government suspended the authority of the Northern Ireland government for a year and placed the Six Counties under direct Westminster rule. It promised a quick and satisfactory solution to the Northern Ireland crisis. William Whitelaw, who went to Belfast as Secretary of State for Northern Ireland, seemed to have a feel for the Irish milieu and was able to communicate with both Protestant and Catholic camps.[7]

---

[6]In 1976, Northern Ireland Catholic charges, supported by the Dublin government, concerning the brutality of the British army in Northern Ireland were upheld by the European Commission on Human Rights. British soldiers did torture Catholic internees.

[7]Merlyn Rees and Roy Mason (both Labourites) have followed Whitelaw and Francis Pym (Conservatives) as Secretaries of State for Northern Ireland.

When the blood soaked streets of Derry and Belfast shattered Southern optimism concerning the situation in Northern Ireland, politicians in the Republic expressed sympathy and concern for Six County Catholics, and traditional nationalist commitments to a united Ireland. The Fianna Fáil government sent frequent protests to Westminster concerning the harsh treatment of Northern Ireland Catholics, unsuccessfully tried to get the United Nations to mediate the crisis, and established refugee camps and hostels for Catholics who had fled Protestant violence in the North. Official Irish government response to the Northern situation went beyond protest when it said that the Republic could not stand by idly if the Stormont regime or Protestant mobs continued to menace the Catholic minority with acts of brutality.

In the early years of the Northern conflict, the Fianna Fáil government was often negligent in preventing revolutionary activity in the South directed against Stormont. Army personnel instructed some Six County Catholics in the use of weapons. Important Fianna Fáil politicians encouraged Provisional IRA guerrilla war tactics north of the border and some of them were indicted for involvement in a plot to smuggle arms into Northern Ireland. This 1970 gun-running scandal made Irish leaders realize that violence in the North was contagious and could effect the South. Jack Lynch, the Taoiseach, dismissed Neil Blaney and Charles Haughey from the Cabinet for their alleged role in the arms smuggling scheme—a court acquitted them—and in 1972, after bomb blasts in Dublin, rushed emergency anti-terrorist legislation through the Dáil providing for special courts without jury trials that accepted the validity of hearsay evidence and placed the burden of proving innocence on the defendants.

The more serious 1974 bombings in Dublin and Monaghan, the November, 1975, explosions at the Dublin airport, pub and hotel bombings, and the assassination in 1976 of the British Ambassador to Ireland, Christopher Ewart-Biggs, have increased apprehensions that the Northern madness has swept South. After the assassination, the Dáil and Senate passed resolutions declaring a State of National Emergency. The Fien Gael-Labour Coalition government, with Liam Cosgrave as Taoiseach, then introduced and passed an Emergency Powers' Bill giving the state and the courts more power to apprehend and intern suspected terrorists. Since 1972, a large number of IRA members have been in prisons south of the border.

When people discuss Northern Ireland in their homes and in pubs in the Irish Republic, many express sympathy for the IRA as the heirs of Easter Week and the Anglo-Irish War. However, except for reactions to "Bloody Sunday," including the IRA provoked burning of the British Embassy in Merrion Square, Dublin, Irish opinion has been calm and ambiguous on events in the Six Counties. Only about three percent of the voters support Sinn Fein candidates in elections. And as expressed in Conor Cruise O'Brien's *States of Ireland* (1973), many are deeply concerned that the virus of

Northern violence could destroy liberal democracy in the Republic. Many members of the business community are frightened that the turbulence in Northern Ireland could discourage potential investors in Irish industry, and they are sure that it has scared off likely British and American tourists. Frequently, citizens of the Republic will admit frankly that they do not understand or even like Ulster people, Protestant or Catholic. They consider them a separate breed with their own regional personality, presenting difficult if not insurmountable religious, economic, and cultural problems of assimilation for a united Ireland.

Many Irish people of a liberal disposition—politicians, intellectuals, writers, and journalists—have seized on the Ulster Question to agitate social reform and a toning down of the Catholic and Gaelic features of Irish life. They argue that the Irish Republic must prove to Ulster Protestant unionists and world opinion that a united Ireland would not be a Catholic state and that people from Northern Ireland would not diminish their British standard of living as citizens of a unified country. In response to this kind of pressure, a 1972 national referendum has removed the special status of the Catholic church from the constitution (Article 44), the government has raised most Irish welfare benefits to compare favorably with those in the United Kingdom, Irish is no longer a requirement for the secondary-school leaving certificate or for all civil service appointments, the Dáil is discussing the demand for civil divorce and the right to practice birth control, and in 1973, the Supreme Court ruled that prohibitions on the sale of birth control devices were unconstitutional, leaving Irish politicians with the problem of public morality and private conscience in a liberal democracy where the Catholic church plays an important historic role.

In March, 1973, the British government presented its solution to the Northern Irish problem in a White Paper, *Northern Ireland Constitutional Proposals*. The White Paper rejected majority rule for power sharing. It proposed an eighty-member Assembly elected by proportional representation and an Executive Committee with Catholic participation relative to numbers. Britain refused to give the new government Stormont authority or stature, reserving police and judicial powers for Westminster. In addition to establishing new power-sharing political institutions, the White Paper guaranteed Catholic civil rights in voting, local government, jobs, housing, and education. It also constructed a bridge to Irish unity by suggesting a Council of Ireland composed of British, Irish, and Northern Irish representatives to discuss problems of mutual interest and concern. Britain had finally acquiesced to the principle of a united Ireland and its desirability, if accomplished through negotiations and the consent of the people on both sides of the border.

Led by Paisley and Craig, extreme unionists denounced the White Paper as a betrayal of Ulster Protestants and a major step in the direction of a united, Catholic Ireland. Paisley said that he would prefer complete integration into the United Kingdom to the existence of a power-sharing, puppet legislature. The IRA also rejected the White Paper, arguing that it perpetuated the British presence in Ulster. Ignoring these dissenting expressions, Whitelaw commenced implementing the White Paper. Faulkner's moderate Unionists; the Social Democratic and Labour Party, a socialist, nationalist, parliamentary movement with more support in the Catholic community than the IRA; and the Alliance Party, a non-sectarian coalition of moderates, all agreed to give the British proposal an opportunity to work.

June, 1973 elections for the Northern Ireland Assembly gave Faulkner's Unionists 23 seats; SDLP 19; Unofficial Unionists, 10; Democratic Unionists, 9; Alliance, 8; Vanguard, 6; West Belfast Loyalists, 2; and Northern Ireland Labour, 1. Five months later a Coalition formed an Executive Committee of six Faulkner Unionists, four SDLP, and one Alliance. Faulkner was Chairman and Gerry Fitt, the SDLP leader, his deputy.

In December, 1973, representatives of the British, Irish, and Northern Ireland governments met at Sunningdale in England. After four days of discussion they agreed to establish a Council of Ireland with a fourteen-member Ministry, equally divided between representatives of the Irish Republic and Northern Ireland, and a Consultative Assembly elected by citizens of both Irelands on a basis on proportional representation. The Sunningdale Conference also recommended that the Irish Republic recognize British sovereignty over Northern Ireland as long as a Six County majority preferred to remain in the United Kingdom, and it urged the British government to agree to implement Irish unity as soon as that objective represented a Northern Ireland consensus. In March, 1974, the Taoiseach of the Republic, Liam Cosgrave, responded to the Sunningdale recommendation by recognizing Northern Ireland as British territory until its citizens in a democratic election indicated another preference.

Public opinion in Britain and in the Irish Republic was confident that the White Paper and Sunningdale would pacify Northern Ireland and bring Ireland closer to national unity. But the new arrangement was doomed from the start. Consensus, not documents, produces stability and the White Paper and the Sunningdale agreements did not represent the will of the Six County majority. While most Catholics were ready to compromise their grievances and aspirations, the vast majority of Protestants disliked power-sharing and hated the Council of Ireland.

While politicians talked in the Assembly, bombings, murders, assassinations, and burnings terrorized Northern Ireland, with a variety of Protestant para-military organizations competing with the Provisional IRA as instruments of violence. By the spring of 1974, over one thousand people had died from shootings, bombings, and fires in the Six Counties; three years later the figure approached 1,500. Protestant terror gangs assassinated

Catholics in all sections of Northern Ireland and carried their campaign of intimidation into the South. On Friday, May 17, 1974, bombs killed five people in Monaghan and twenty-three in Dublin and wounded hundreds of others. And in 1975, the IRA transported terror to Britain in the forms of arson, bombing, and assassination in an effort to coerce British withdrawal from Ulster.

In the spring of 1974, Protestant extremists opened a determined and coordinated offensive against the White Paper program, concentrating first on the Council of Ireland. On May 15, the Protestant Ulster Workers Council, with the support of ultra-Unionist politicians and para-military terrorist groups like Vanguard and the Ulster Defense Association, began a general strike, insisting on the termination of the Council of Ireland. Merlyn Rees, the British Labour Party Secretary of State for Northern Ireland, refused to negotiate with strike leaders. Within a few days, Northern Ireland experienced a severe economic crisis involving shortages of food, electrical power, and other basic needs. Responding to strike coercion and the urgent requests of its moderate Unionist ally in the Coalition, the Social Democratic and Labour Party reluctantly agreed to the suspension of the Council of Ireland for four years. Sensing complete victory, Protestant extremists escalated their demands, insisting on the resignation of the Executive Committee and the Assembly and a call for new elections, obviously expecting the restoration of Protestant Ascendancy.

The SDLP demanded that the British government take action to sustain power sharing. On Friday, May 24, after insisting that he would preserve law, order, and the constitution in Northern Ireland, Harold Wilson, the British Prime Minister, sent 500 more soldiers into the Six Counties, bringing troop strength there up to 16,500. In the early morning hours of Sunday, May 26, the military occupied electrical power plants and some petrol service stations, but the Labour government had moved too late. Soldiers lacked the competence to operate the power plants, and the British show of strength only solidified Protestant opinion—urban and rural—against the Faulknerite, SDLP, Alliance Coalition. Finally Faulkner and his moderate Unionist colleagues resigned from the Executive Committee, destroying the power-sharing experiment. Britain then suspended the Executive Committee and the Assembly for a period of four years and returned Northern Ireland to the jurisdiction of Westminster.

In July, 1974, the British government offered another White Paper solution to the Northern Ireland problem. It called for a Convention to meet for the purpose of producing a consensus constitution based on the principle of power sharing. Elections for the Convention gave the ultra-Unionist factions forty out of seventy-eight seats. During the summer of 1975, the Convention prepared recommendations for presentation to the British government. Although there was a split in the ultra camp between Paisley and

Craig—the latter was willing to make some concessions to power sharing, in November the Convention submitted a report which insisted on a return to majority rule, and that the British government cease interfering with the right of Protestant unionists to control the destiny of Northern Ireland. Britain rejected Protestant Ascendancy and Northern Ireland remained under the authority of Westminster with the violence continuing as before.

Notwithstanding the collapse of the power-sharing experiment, civil-rights agitation, political confrontation, and finally violence did overcome institutional apartheid in Northern Ireland. The British government is committed to equal justice, and has gradually phased out internment as a policy.[8] Political changes have given Catholics predominate influence in local government in areas where they are the majority. And Catholics are playing a more significant role in the cultural, intellectual, and economic life of the Six Counties. Unless Britain would tolerate the restoration of Protestant Ascendancy, which would trigger massive minority resistance, Catholics will never again retreat to a position of group inferiority and political impotence.

Despite these Catholic advances, Northern Ireland faces a grim future. Protestants are unwilling to share power with Catholics or accept a United Ireland, and Britains seems reluctant to integrate Northern Ireland fully into the United Kingdom on a permanent or long-time arrangement. The IRA continues to insist on one Ireland. In effect, there is no prospect for any kind of solution that will satisfy a working majority of the population. Agitation and violence have polarized Catholic nationalists and Protestant unionists far beyond the 1968 level. A genocidal civil war is a distinct possibility if Britain succumbs either to temptation or pressure and withdraws her soldiers from Ulster.

Some American experts on Northern Ireland have suggested repartition and repatriation as the only practical escape from the Northern Ireland dilemma. They advise that Britain should transfer the Catholic majority counties of Fermanagh and Tyrone and Catholic pockets of strength in West Derry, South Armagh, and South Down to the Irish Republic. They further recommend that the British and Irish governments with perhaps Common Market and American help should finance the repatriation of those Catholics and Protestants who could not accept allegiance to either a diminished Northern Ireland or an expanded Republic.[9]

No significant portion of opinion in the South or the North has indi-

[8]The Special Powers Act has been repealed.

[9]For an articulate defense of repartition and repatriation see Joseph M. Curran, "Ulster Repartition: A Possible Answer?" *America*, Vol. 134, no. 4 (January 31, 1976), pp. 66–68. Curran intelligently argues that despite its problems and unpopularity in Ireland, at the present time repartition and repatriation is the only plausible alternative to an unacceptable level of violence in Northern Ireland and the implications of that violence for the United Kingdom and the Irish Republic.

cated any support for repartition or repatriation. It would be difficult for the Irish Republic with a 1976 unemployment figure of 117,038 to absorb the most depressed areas of Ulster and their impoverished people. Neither Ireland nor Britain have particularly healthy economies, and it is doubtful if either could stand the financial burden of repatriation without some assistance. Repartition would incite bursts of violence from the IRA because it would defeat the goal of Irish unity and from Protestant terrorists because they would consider it a Catholic nationalist victory over Northern Ireland Protestantism and unionism.

conclusion

In 1966, citizens of the Irish Republic commemorated the fiftieth anniversary of Easter Week. Amidst the festivities, politicians paid homage to Pearse, Connolly, and their comrades in the Volunteer and Citizen Armies; professional and amateur historians wrote about their brave deeds; towns and villages erected memorials to the heroes who died to free Ireland; bands played and singers sang patriotic tunes; and someone, probably a member of the IRA, blew up Nelson's Pillar in O'Connell Street. A prominent politician who participated in the 1916 freedom effort allegedly described the last event in newspaper headline style: "Noted British Admiral Leaves Dublin By Air." This anniversary celebration was more than a hymn to the past; it was also a tribute to the values and successes of physical-force nationalism. In 1966, Ireland appeared to be a model of productive revolution: a stable liberal democracy with an expanding economy, an example to other countries recently liberated from the fetters of imperialism and colonialism.

Now the logic of 1916 no longer seems infallible. The current Northern troubles have forced a reappraisal of the contributions of revolutionary versus constitutional nationalism. Scholars and politicians are reevaluating with praise the roles of O'Connell and Redmond in shaping modern Ireland. Turbulence and violence in the Six Counties have telescoped centuries of Irish history into a few short years: Protestant bigotry, Catholic desperation, the irresponsibility and insensitivity of British politicians, British

189

soldiers shooting Irishmen, Irish revolutionaries sniping at and ambushing British soldiers, coercion acts, curfews, and internment. Moderate nationalists are almost as appalled by IRA Provisionals exploding bombs that kill and maim innocent bystanders as they are by Tommies gunning down Catholic civilians or Protestant murder gangs using assassination for vengeance or as a terror weapon. Supporters of the IRA insist that violence has succeeded where reason has failed, by forcing Britain to concern herself with and make concessions to minority grievances. But they refuse to acknowledge the fact that it has also strengthened the physical and psychological walls of partition by intensifying sectarian bitterness.

Since the civil-rights demonstrations of 1968, television and newspaper journalism has made Northern Ireland one of the most reported crisis zones in a troubled world. But the more they present the views of Official and Provisional IRA leaders, of Paisleyite para-military and Faulkner unionists, and of representatives of the British government and military, plus their own editorial perspectives, the more journalists confuse the Six County situation for perplexed people attempting to understand the sources of violence in Ulster.

According to the Official IRA, tensions between Catholics and Protestants in Northern Ireland originated in a capitalist strategy to distract the poor from investigating and responding to the economic sources of their suffering and exploitation. Provisional IRA apologists insist that Ulster sectarianism is rooted in British divide and conquer tactics, and that once the Sassenach goes home, Catholics and Protestants will eventually compromise their differences in a united Ireland. Unionist champions claim that they are defending British Protestant political and cultural allegiances against the intrigues of Irish nationalists scheming to disrupt the United Kingdom and to create a 32-county Irish Catholic state. British politicians say that they are innocent peacemakers caught in the middle of a centuries-old civil war. Most American journalists seem to accept the British version of the Northern Ireland situation, presenting the crisis as an ancient Irish sectarian feud, and sympathizing with the poor British forced to confront the irrational passions of Irish bigotry.

All of these interpretations of the sources of violence in Northern Ireland are partially true. All are also largely false. Conflict in Northern Ireland is far more than a case study in capitalist manipulation of the emotions of the poor to prevent proletarian solidarity. And it is something beyond the fruits of British imperialism in Ireland. If the British army should leave the Six Counties in the immediate future, Catholics and Protestants would not embrace and become friends. Instead, they would probably start murdering each other, and blood would flow in the streets of Belfast, Derry, Newry, Omagh, Enniskillen, Dungannon, and other cities and towns in Northern

Ireland. And, no doubt, violence also would engulf the Irish Republic because the shadow of the gunman lies heavy over the whole island.

Unionists, too, are wrong when they argue that their opponents are trying to create a united Catholic Ireland. Nationalists have renounced Catholic power, and while the Protestant minority in the Republic has some legitimate complaints concerning the Catholic confessional tone of Irish society, they have enjoyed civil rights, power, and influence denied to the Catholic minority in Northern Ireland. And when British politicians, echoed by journalists from all over the world, describe the violence in Northern Ireland as the renewal of an ancient religious blood feud, they are oversimplifying a complex situation. The current Ulster crisis is not the latest manifestation of an Irish political ghost that periodically emerges from the Celtic mist to confound and confuse the Anglo-Saxon mind. Northern Ireland in the 1970's is not the seventeenth century revisited. It is a modern conflict.

Despite the sectarian labels, the struggle between Ulster Protestants and Catholics is a cultural rather than a religious war. Although Irish nationalist ideology has sincerely rejected any connection between religion and nationality, and has projected a liberal-democratic, nonsectarian Irish nation-state as a final representation of the Irish freedom effort, the Irish historical experience has contradicted nationalist theory by linking the Irish and Catholic, British and Protestant identities.

During the sixteenth and seventeenth centuries, Britain employed Protestantism as an emotional cause and a moral justification for the conquest and settlement of Ireland. In the eighteenth century, the British colony in Ireland evolved into an Anglo-Irish Protestant nation but refused to permit the Catholic majority to participate in the rights and privileges of citizenship. Despite the ecumenical mythology of Irish nationalism, Anglo-Irish Protestant patriotism was far more Protestant than Irish.

Nineteenth century Irish history strengthened the associations between religious and cultural identities. Protestants refused the invitations of nationalist leaders to join in a common effort to liberate Ireland from Britain. They constantly pledged their fidelity to British nationality and cultural identity, and loyalty to a British government that guarded their Ascendancy from the power and property appetites of the Catholic democracy. Throughout the nineteenth and into the twentieth century, the Protestants of industrial, northeast Ulster have been the most stubborn of British loyalists in Ireland. They have managed to prevent a complete victory for Irish nationalism by keeping their territory as part of the United Kingdom.

Ulster, once the most Gaelic and then the most British province in Ireland, is at present a kind of distillation of the Irish historical process. Northern Ireland Protestants are the progeny of Scots and English planters who came to Ireland as the agents of British colonialism to secure a frontier against restless natives. For centuries, they flaunted their religion as a badge of British allegiance. Six County Catholics are the descendents of native Irish victims of British conquest. They see themselves as the enemies of British political and cultural imperialisms holding out in their last Irish enclave, northeast Ulster.

British innocence is the most dangerous misrepresentation of the Northern Ireland situation, dangerous because it could lead to a premature withdrawal of the British army followed by a blood bath. Northern Ireland is a gory testimonial to centuries of British policy in Ireland. In the seventeenth century, the English government confiscated the lands of The O'Neill, The O'Donnell, and The Maguire and planted them with English and Scots Protestants, mostly Nonconformists. Throughout the seventeenth and eighteenth centuries, the Ulster colony was a source of British strength in Ireland, the main outpost of empire.

During the nineteenth century, Conservative British politicians encouraged, incited, and exploited anti-Irish-Catholic British nativism all over the United Kingdom as a strategy to frustrate Irish nationalism and to preserve the Union which they considered essential to maintaining the Empire. From 1912 to 1914, leaders of the Conservative opposition at Westminster conspired with Ulster Protestant Unionist fanatics to defeat the Third Home Rule Bill, defying the principles and spirit of the British constitution and leading the United Kingdom to the precipice of civil war. Contemporary violence in Northern Ireland is the direct harvest of British Conservatives playing the "Orange Card," promising that "Ulster will fight and Ulster will be right."

Some readers might ask: despite their sorry record in Ireland, have not the British dealt with the Irish in a more humane fashion than other imperial powers with their subject peoples? They might wonder if contemporary Britons should have to pay in pounds, lives, injuries, and terror for the sins of their ancestors? Of course, the British are more civilized imperialists than their competitors. They leave behind them a much richer cultural and institutional legacy. The liberal-democratic values of Irish nationalism came by transfusion from English and Anglo-Irish Whig and Radical veins. And the Irish were able to build from these values and their experience as reluctant participants in the British constitutional process a viable and successful twentieth century nation state.

If people in underdeveloped countries had to be conquered by someone, better the British than the Germans, Russians, French, Spaniards, Portugese, Japanese or Americans. But comparisons are relative. British conquest and occupation damaged the Irish and reparation is appropriate. History takes it tolls. Just as present-day white Americans must pay for the atrocities inflicted on blacks in the past, so should the British suffer the consequences of their nation's Irish policy.

The questions just posed and answered are part of the Northern Ireland debate. Yet they both distort and diminish the reality of British involvement, which is recent as well as ancient. If British politicians sincerely felt that they had to partition Ireland, why did they arrange and maintain such a ridiculous border? When the British Parliament was considering the Third Home Rule Bill, British M.P.'s insisted on guarantees to protect the Protestant minority in the proposed Irish state. In constructing Northern Ireland, why did they not insist on the same kind of securities for an even larger Catholic minority? And why for over fifty years did British governments and the Parliament at Westminster tolerate discrimination and violence against Catholics in Northern Ireland, a part of the United Kingdom? For all of those years, Britain, a self-proclaimed champion of liberal democracy, a foe of totalitarianism in other countries, gave tacit approval to apartheid and non-democratic programs in Northern Ireland, part of the national territory. Even more recently, when Britain did intervene, why did her officials show more energy in disarming and interning Catholic than Protestant extremists and allow soldiers in British uniforms to torture Irish nationalist internees and shoot protesters?

Considering her contributions to violence in Northern Ireland, Britain cannot in good conscience leave the Irish scene. Withdrawal would be a totally immoral act, the ultimate foul deed in a long list of atrocities against the Irish people. Britain would be responsible for the massacre that would inevitably follow from the retreat of her army. In Dante's inferno, the inmates of hell are sentenced to pursue hopelessly the pleasures of their vices through an eternity of boredom and frustration. Perhaps Northern Ireland is Britain's inferno, where contemporary politicians and their successors must try to disentangle the threads of centuries of ill-conceived and selfish Irish policies, always to be hopelessly thwarted by the duplicity of their ancestors.

recommended reading[1]

GENERAL STUDIES AND INTERPRETATIONS

BECKETT, J. C., *A Short History of Ireland* (3rd ed.). New York: Hutchinson's University Library, 1966.

———, *The Anglo-Irish Tradition*. Ithaca: Cornell University Press, 1976.

———, *The Making of Modern Ireland, 1603–1923*. New York: Alfred A. Knopf, Inc., 1966.

COSTIGAN, GIOVANNI, *A History of Modern Ireland*. New York: Pegasus, 1969.

CULLEN, L. M., *An Economic History of Ireland Since 1660*. London: B. T. Batsford, Ltd., 1972.

EDWARDS, RUTH DUDLEY, *An Atlas of Irish History*. London: Methuen and Co., 1973.

EVANS, E. ESTYN, *The Personality of Ireland: Habitat, Heritage, and History*. Cambridge, England: Cambridge University Press, 1973.

FREEMAN, T. W., *Ireland: A General and Regional Geography*. London: Methuen and Co., 1960.

LYONS, F. S. L., *Ireland Since the Famine*. New York: Charles Scribner's Sons, 1971.

McCAFFREY, LAWRENCE J., *The Irish Question, 1800–1922*. Lexington, Ky.: University of Kentucky Press, 1968.

---

[1]The vast majority of books and articles cited in this section have been published since 1955.

MACDONAGH, OLIVER, *The Irish Question, 1840–1920* (rev. ed.). Toronto: University of Toronto Press, 1964.

MOODY, T. W. and F. X. MARTIN, *The Course of Irish History*. New York: Keybright and Talley, Inc., 1967.

O'FAOLAIN, SEAN, *The Irish*. Harmondsworth, Middlesex, England: Pelican Books, 1969.

O'FARRELL, PATRICK, *England and Ireland Since 1800*. New York: Oxford University Press, 1975.

———, *Ireland's English Question*. New York: Schocken Books, Inc., 1972.

O'HEGARTY, PATRICK S., *A History of Ireland Under the Union, 1801–1922*. London: Methuen and Co., 1952.

OREL, HAROLD, editor, *Irish History and Culture: Aspects of a People's Heritage*. Lawrence, Kansas: University of Kansas Press, 1976.

STRAUSS, ERIC, *Irish Nationalism and British Democracy*. New York: Columbia University Press, 1961.

PRE-UNION IRELAND

BOLTON, G. C., *The Passing of the Act of Union*. London: Oxford University Press, 1966.

CONNELL, KENNETH, *The Population of Ireland, 1750–1845*. London: Oxford University Press, 1950.

DOLLEY, MICHAEL, *Anglo-Norman Ireland*. The Gill History of Ireland, Vol. 3, general editors, James Lydon and Margaret MacCurtain. Dublin: Gill and MacMillan, 1972.

EDWARDS, R. DUDLEY, *Ireland in the Age of the Tudors: The Destruction of Hiberno-Norman Civilization*. London: Croom Helm, 1977.

FERGUSON, O., *Jonathan Swift and Ireland*. Urbana: University of Illinois Press, 1962.

JAMES, FRANCIS GODWIN, *Ireland in the Empire, 1688–1770*. Cambridge, Mass.: Harvard University Press, 1973.

JOHNSTON, EDITH MARY, *Ireland in the Eighteenth Century*. The Gill History of Ireland, Vol. 8. Dublin: Gill and MacMillan, 1974.

LECKY, W. E. H., *A History of Ireland in the Eighteenth Century*. Abridged by L. P. Curtis, Jr.. Chicago: University of Chicago Press, 1972.

———, *The Leaders of Public Opinion in Ireland*. London: Longmans Greene, 1871, 1883, 1903.

LYDON, JAMES, *Ireland in the Later Middle Ages*. The Gill History of Ireland, Vol. 6. Dublin: Gill and Macmillan, 1972.

MACCURTAIN, MARGARET, *Tudor and Stuart Ireland*. The Gill History of Ireland, Vol. 7. Dublin: Gill and MacMillan, 1972.

MCDOWELL, R. B., *Irish Public Opinion, 1750–1800*. London: Faber and Faber, Ltd., 1944.

MACNIOCAILL, GEARÓID. *Ireland Before the Vikings*. The Gill History of Ireland, Vol. 1. Dublin: Gill and MacMillan, 1972.

NICHOLLS, KENNETH, *Gaelic and Gaelicized Ireland in the Middle Ages*. The Gill History of Ireland, Vol. 4. Dublin: Gill and MacMillan, 1972.

O'CONNELL, MAURICE R., *Irish Politics and Social Conflict in the Age of the American Revolution*. Philadelphia: University of Pennsylvania Press, 1965.

O'CORRÁIN, DONNCHA, *Ireland Before the Normans*. The Gill History of Ireland, Vol. 2. Dublin: Gill and MacMillan, 1972.

PAKENHAM, THOMAS, *The Year of Liberty: The Great Irish Rebellion of 1798*. London: Hodden and Stoughton, Ltd., 1969.

SENIOR, HEREWARD, *Orangeism in Ireland and Britain, 1795–1836*. New York: Hilary House Distribution Ltd., 1966.

WALL, MAUREEN, *The Penal Laws, 1691–1760*. Irish History Series, No. 1. Dundalk: Dundalgen Press, Ltd. for the Dublin Historical Association, 1961.

————, "The Rise of a Catholic Middle Class in Eighteenth Century Ireland," *Irish Historical Studies*, XI (September, 1958), 91–115.

WATT, JAMES, *The Church in Medieval Ireland*. The Gill History of Ireland, Vol. 5. Dublin: Gill and MacMillan, 1972.

FROM THE UNION THROUGH THE FAMINE

AKENSON, DONALD H., *The Irish Educational Experiment*. Toronto: University of Toronto Press, 1970.

BLACK, R. D. COLLISON, *Economic Thought and the Irish Question, 1817–1870*. Cambridge: Cambridge University Press, 1960.

BRODERICK, JOHN F., S. J., *The Holy See and the Irish Movement for the Repeal of the Union with England, 1829–1847*. Rome: Universitatis Gregorianne Press, 1951.

BROEKER, GALEN, *Rural Disorder and Police Reform in Ireland, 1812–1836*. Toronto: University of Toronto Press, 1970.

BROWN, THOMAS N., *Nationalism and the Irish Peasant 1800–1848*. American Committee for Irish Studies Reprint Series, Emmet Larkin and Lawrence J. McCaffrey, editors. Chicago: University of Chicago Press, 1971. (This essay was originally published in *The Review of Politics*, XV, No. 4 (October, 1953), 403–445; and has been republished in Lawrence J. McCaffrey, editor, *Irish Nationalism and the American Contribution*. New York: Arno Press, 1976).

CAHILL, GILBERT, "Irish Catholicism and English Toryism," *The Review of Politics*, XIX (January, 1957), 62–76.

————, Irish Popery and British Nativism: 1800–1848," *Cithara*, XIII (May, 1974), pp. 3–18.

————, "The Protestant Association and the Anti-Maynooth Agitation of 1845," *The Catholic Historical Review*, XLIII (October, 1957), 273–308.

DUFFY, CHARLES GAVAN, *Young Ireland*. London: T. Fisher Unwin, 1896.

EDWARDS, R. DUDLEY and T. DESMOND WILLIAMS, editors, *The Great Famine: Studies in Irish History, 1845–1852*. Dublin: Published for the Irish Committee for Historical Sciences by Browne and Nolan, 1956.

GASH, NORMAN, *Mr. Secretary Peel*. Cambridge, Mass.: Harvard University Press, 1961.

GRAHAM, A. H., "The Lichfield House Compact, 1835," *Irish Historical Studies*, XII (March, 1961), 209–225.

GWYNN, DENIS, *Daniel O'Connell: The Irish Liberator*. Cork: Cork University Press, 1947.

———, *O'Connell, Davis, and the Colleges Bill*. Cork: Cork University Press, 1948.

———, *Young Ireland and 1848*. Cork: Cork University Press, 1949.

LARGE, DAVID, "The House of Lords and Ireland in the Age of Peel, 1832–1850," *Irish Historical Studies*, IX (September, 1955), 357–369.

LARKIN, EMMET, "Church and State in Ireland in the Nineteenth Century," *Church History* XXI (September, 1962), 294–306.

———, "The Quarrel Among the Roman Catholic Hierarchy over the National System of Education in Ireland, 1838–1841," *The Celtic Cross*, Ray B. Browne, William Roscelli, and Richard J. Loftus, editors. Lafayette, Indiana: Purdue University Press, 1964.

LECKY, W. E. H., "Daniel O'Connell," *The Leaders of Public Opinion in Ireland*. London: Longmans Greene, 1871, 1883, 1903.

McCAFFREY, LAWRENCE J., *Daniel O'Connell and the Repeal Year*. Lexington: University of Kentucky Press, 1966.

McDOWELL, R. B., *Public Opinion and Government Policy in Ireland, 1801–1846*. London: Faber and Faber, Ltd., 1952.

———, *The Irish Administration, 1801–1914*. Toronto: University of Toronto Press, 1964.

MACHIN, G. I. T., *The Catholic Question in English Politics, 1820–1830*. London: Oxford University Press, 1964.

MACINTYRE, ANGUS, *The Liberator: Daniel O'Connell and the Irish Party, 1830–1847*. London: Hamish Hamilton, 1965.

MACLOCHLAINN, AILFRID, "The Racism of Thomas Davis: Root and Branch," *The Journal of Irish Literature*, V (May, 1976), 112–122.

MILLER, DAVID W. "Irish Catholicism and the Great Famine," *The Journal of Social History*, 9:1 (September, 1975) pp. 81–98.

NOWLAN, KEVIN, *The Politics of Repeal*. Toronto: University of Toronto Press, 1965.

O'CONNELL, MAURICE R., editor, *The Correspondence of Daniel O'Connell*, Vol. 1: 1792–1814; Vol. 2: 1815–1823; Vol. 3: 1824–1828. New York: Barnes and Noble Books, 1973, 1973, 1974.

O'FAOLAIN, SEAN, *King of the Beggars: A Life of Daniel O'Connell*. Dublin: Allen Figgis, Ltd., 1970.

O'NEILL, THOMAS P., "The Economic and Political Ideas of James Fintan Lalor," *Irish Ecclesiastical Record*, LXXIV (November, 1950), 398–409.

Ó TUATHAIGH, GEARÓID, *Ireland Before the Famine, 1798–1848*. Gill History of Ireland, Vol. 9. Dublin: Gill and MacMillan, 1972.

REYNOLDS, JAMES A., *The Catholic Emancipation Crisis in Ireland, 1823–1829*. New Haven, Conn: Yale University Press, 1954.

SALAMAN, R. N., *The History and Social Influence of the Potato*. Cambridge, Mass.: Harvard University Press, 1949.

TIERNEY, MICHAEL, editor, *Daniel O'Connell*. Dublin: Browne and Nolan, 1949.

WHYTE, JOHN H., "Daniel O'Connell and the Repeal Party," *Irish Historical Studies*, XI (September, 1959), 297–316.

————, "The Appointment of Catholic Bishops in Nineteenth Century Ireland," *The Catholic Historical Review*, XLVIII (April, 1962), 12–32.

————, "The Influence of the Catholic Clergy on Elections in Nineteenth Century Ireland," *The English Historical Review*, LXXV (April, 1960), 239–259.

WOODHAM-SMITH, CECIL, *The Great Hunger, Ireland, 1845–1849*. New York: Harper and Row Publishers, Inc., 1962.

FROM THE FAMINE TO THE FALL OF PARNELL

ARNSTEIN, W. L., "Parnell and the Bradlaugh Case," *Irish Historical Studies*, XIII (March, 1963), 215–235.

CLARK, SAM, "The Social Composition of the Land League," *Irish Historical Studies*, XVII (September, 1971), 447–469.

CORFE, THOMAS, *The Phoenix Park Murders, Conflict, Compromise and Tragedy in Ireland, 1879–1882*. London: Hodder and Stoughton, 1968.

CORISH, PATRICK J. "Political Problems, 1860–1878," *A History of Irish Catholicism*, Vol. 5, Patrick J. Corish, general editor. Dublin: H. M. Gill and Sons, Ltd., 1967.

CURTIS, L. P., JR., *Coercion and Conciliation in Ireland, 1880–1892*. Princeton, N.J.: Princeton University Press, 1963.

DAVITT, MICHAEL, *The Fall of Feudalism in Ireland*. New York: Harper and Brothers, 1904.

DUFFY, CHARLES GAVAN, *League of the North and South*. London: Chapman and Hall, 1886.

FEINGOLD, WILLIAM, "The Tenant's Movement to Capture the Irish Poor Law Board, 1879–1885," *Albion*, 7 (December, 1975), 216–231.

GLASER, JOHN A., "Parnell's Fall and the Nonconformist Conscience," *Irish Historical Studies*, XII (September, 1960), 119–138.

HAMMOND, J. L., *Gladstone and the Irish Nation* (2nd ed.). Hamden, Conn.: Shoe String Press, 1964.

HARMON, MAURICE, editor, *Fenians and Fenianism*. Seattle: University of Washington Press, 1970.

HEYCK, THOMAS WILLIAM, *The Dimensions of British Radicalism: The Case of Ireland, 1874–1895*. Urbana: University of Illinois Press, 1974.

HURST, MICHAEL, *Parnell and Irish Nationalism*. Toronto: University of Toronto Press, 1968.

LARKIN, EMMET, *The Roman Catholic Church and the Creation of the Modern Irish State, 1876–1886*. Philadelphia: The American Philosophical Society, 1975.

————, "The Roman Catholic Hierarchy and the Fall of Parnell," *Victorian Studies*, IV (June, 1961), 315–336.

————, "Mounting the Counter Attack: The Roman Catholic Church and the Destruction of Parnellism," *The Review of Politics*, XXV (April, 1963), 157–182.

LEE, JOSEPH, *The Modernization of Irish Society, 1848–1918*. The Gill History of Ireland, Vol. 10. Dublin: Gill and MacMillan, 1973.

LYND, HELEN MERRELL, *England in the 1880's: Toward a Social Basis for Freedom*. London: Oxford University Press, 1945.

LYONS, F. S. L., *Charles Stewart Parnell*. London: Oxford University Press, 1977.

——, *The Fall of Parnell, 1890–1891*. Toronto: University of Toronto Press, 1960.

MCCAFFREY, LAWRENCE J., *Irish Federalism in the 1870's: A Study in Conservative Nationalism*. Philadelphia: The American Philosophical Society, 1962.

MCCREADY, H. W., "Home Rule and the Liberal Party, 1880–1901," *Irish Historical Studies*, XIII (September, 1963), 316–348.

MAGNUS, PHILIP, *Gladstone*. New York: E. P. Dutton & Co., Inc., 1964.

MARLOW, JOYCE, *Captain Boycott and the Irish*. New York: E. P. Dutton & Co., Inc. 1973.

MOODY, T. W., editor, *The Fenian Movement*. Cork: Mercier Press, 1968.

——, "The New Departure in Irish Politics, 1878–1879," *Essays in British and Irish History in Honour of James Eadie Todd*. London: Muller, 1949.

NORMAN, E. R., *The Catholic Church and Ireland in the Age of Rebellion, 1859–1873*. Ithaca, New York: Cornell University Press, 1965.

O'BRIEN, CONOR CRUISE, *Parnell and His Party, 1880–1890*. Oxford: The Clarendon Press, 1960.

O'BRIEN, WILLIAM and DESMOND RYAN, editors, *Devoy's Post Bag, 1871–1928*, 2 Vols. Dublin: C. J. Fallon, Ltd., 1948, 1953.

Ó BROIN, LEON, *Fenian Fever: An Anglo-American Dilemma*. New York: New York University Press, 1971.

PALMER, NORMAN, *The Irish Land League Crisis*. New Haven: Yale University Press, 1940.

RYAN, DESMOND, *The Fenian Chief* (a biography of James Stephens). Dublin: Gill and MacMillan, 1967.

SKEFFINGTON, F. SHEEHY, *Michael Davitt Revolutionary Agitator and Labour Leader*. London: MacGibbon and Kee, 1967.

STEELE, E. D., *Irish Land and British Politics: Tenant Right and Nationality, 1865–1870*. Cambridge, England: Cambridge University Press, 1974.

THORNLEY, DAVID, *Isaac Butt and Home Rule*. London: Ambassador Press, 1964.

WHITE, TERENCE deVERE, *The Road of Excess* (a biography of Isaac Butt). Dublin: Browne and Nolan, 1946.

WHYTE, JOHN, *The Independent Irish Party, 1850–1859*. London: Oxford University Press, 1958.

——, "Political Problems, 1850–1860," *A History of Irish Catholicism*, Vol. 5, Patrick J. Corish, editor. Dublin: H. M. Gill and Sons, 1967.

FROM THE FALL OF PARNELL TO THE TREATY

BEASLAI, P., *Michael Collins Soldier and Statesman*. Dublin: Talbot Press, 1937.

BENNETT, RICHARD, *The Black and Tans*. Boston: Houghton Mifflin Co., 1959.

BOYCE, D. G., *Englishmen and Irish Troubles: British Public Opinion and the Making of Irish Policy, 1918–1922*. Cambridge, Mass.: M.I.T. Press, 1972.

BOYLE, JOHN, "Irish Labour and the Rising," *Eire-Ireland*, II (Autumn, 1967), 122–131.

BROMAGE, MARY, *DeValera and the March of a Nation*. New York: Noonday Press, Inc., 1956.

BUCKLAND, PATRICK, Irish Unionism Vol. I: The Anglo-Irish and the New Ireland, *1885–1922*. Dublin: Gill and MacMillan, 1972.

———, *Irish Unionism Vol. II: Ulster Unionism and the Origins of Northern Ireland, 1886–1922*. Dublin: Gill and MacMillan, 1973.

CLARKSON, J. DUNSMORE, *Labour and Nationalism in Ireland*. New York: Columbia University Press, 1925.

COFFEY, THOMAS, *Agony at Easter*. Baltimore: Penguin Books, Inc., 1969.

COSTIGAN, GIOVANNI, "The Anglo-Irish Conflict, 1919–1922: A War of Independence or Systematized Murder?," *University Review*, V (Spring, 1968).

CURTIS, L. P., JR. *Anglo-Saxons and Celts: A Study in Anti-Irish Prejudice in Victorian England*. Bridgeport, Conn.: Conference on British Studies, 1968.

———, *Apes and Angels: The Irishman in Victorian Caricature*. Newton Abbot, England: David and Charles, 1971.

DANGERFIELD, GEORGE, *The Strange Death of Liberal England*. New York: Capricorn Books, 1961.

———, *The Damnable Question*. Boston: Atlantic, Little, Brown & Co., Inc., 1976.

DAVIS, RICHARD, *Arthur Griffith and Non-Violent Sinn Fein*. Dublin: Anvil Books, 1974.

DUNLEAVY, GARETH, *Douglas Hyde*. Irish Writers Series. Lewisburg, Pa.: Bucknell University Press, 1974.

ELLIS, P. BERESFORD, *A History of the Irish Working Class*. New York: George Braziller, 1973.

FARRELL, BRIAN, *The Founding of Dáil Éireann*. Dublin: Gill and MacMillan, 1971.

FERGUSON, SIR. JAMES, *The Curragh Incident*. London: Faber and Faber Ltd., 1964.

GWYNN, DENIS, *The Life of John Redmond*. London: Harrap, 1932.

HOLT, EDGAR, *Protest in Arms: The Irish Troubles, 1916–1923*. London: McClelland, 1960.

HYDE, H. MONTGOMERY, *Carson*. London: Heinemann, 1953.

JENKINS, ROY, *Asquith*. London: Collins, 1965.

LARKIN, EMMET, *James Larkin, Irish Labour Leader, 1876–1947*. Cambridge, Mass.: M.I.T. Press, 1965.

LYONS, F. S. L., *The Irish Parliamentary Party, 1890–1910*. London: Faber and Faber Ltd., 1951.

———, *John Dillon*. Chicago: University of Chicago Press, 1968.

MACARDLE, DOROTHY, *The Irish Republic*. London: Farrar, Straus, 1965.

McDOWELL, ROBERT, *The Irish Convention, 1917–1918*. Toronto: University of Toronto Press, 1970.

McHUGH, ROGER, editor, *Dublin, 1916*. London: Arlington Books, 1966.

MARTIN, F. X. and F. J. BYRNE, editors, *The Scholar Revolutionary: Eoin MacNeill, 1867–1945 and the Making of the New Ireland*. New York: Barnes and Noble Books, 1973.

MILLER, DAVID W., *Church, State, and Nation in Ireland, 1898–1921*. Pittsburgh: University of Pittsburgh Press, 1973.

MITCHEL, ARTHUR, *Labour in Irish Politics, 1890-1930.* Shannon, Ireland: Irish University Press, 1974.

NOWLAN, KEVIN B., editor, *The Making of 1916.* Dublin: The Stationery Office, 1969.

O'BRIEN, CONOR CRUISE, editor, *The Shaping of Modern Ireland.* Toronto: University of Toronto Press, 1960.

O'BRIEN, JOSEPH V., *William O'Brien and the Course of Irish Politics, 1881-1918* Berkeley: University of California Press, 1976.

Ó BROIN, LEON, *Dublin Castle and the 1916 Rising.* New York: New York University Press, 1971.

————, *The Chief Secretary: Augustin Birrell in Ireland.* London: Chatto & Windus, 1969.

O'CONNOR, FRANK, *The Big Fellow: A Life of Michael Collins.* London: Corgi Books, 1961.

O'FAOLAIN, SEAN, *DeValera.* Harmondsworth, Middlesex, England: Penguin Books, 1939.

PAKENHAM, FRANK (Earl of Longford) and THOMAS P. O'NEILL, *Eamon De Valera* Boston: Houghton Mifflin Co., 1971.

PAKENHAM, FRANK, *Peace by Ordeal.* London: Mentor, 1967.

RYAN, A. P., *Mutiny at the Curragh.* New York: St. Martin's Press, 1956.

SAVAGE, D. C., "The Origins of the Ulster Unionist Party, 1885-1886," *Irish Historical Studies,* XII (March, 1961), 185-208.

STEWART, A. T. Q., *The Ulster Crisis.* London: Faber and Faber Ltd., 1967.

TAYLOR, R., *Michael Collins.* London: Four Square Books, 1958.

THOMPSON, WILLIAM IRWIN, *The Imagination of an Insurrection: Dublin, Easter 1916.* New York: Harper & Row, 1967.

WARD, ALAN J., *Ireland and Anglo-American Relations, 1899-1921.* London: Weidenfeld and Nicolson, 1969.

POST-TREATY IRELAND

AKENSON, DONALD, *Education and Enmity.* London: David and Charles, 1973.

BARRITT, DENIS P. and CHARLES F. CARTER, *The Northern Ireland Problem: A Study in Group Relations,* Oxford: Oxford University Press, 1962.

BELL, BOWYER, *The Secret Army: A History of the IRA, 1916-1970.* London: Sphere Books, 1972.

BELL, GEOFFREY, *The Protestants of Ulster.* London: Pluto Press Ltd., 1976.

BLAKE, JOHN W., *Northern Ireland in the Second World War.* Belfast: H. M. S. O., 1966.

CARROLL, JOSEPH T., *Ireland in the War Years, 1939-1945.* Dublin: Gill and MacMillan, 1976.

CASEY, WILLIAM VAN ETTEN, editor, *The Irish Issue* of *The Holy Cross Quarterly* (a volume of essays on the current crisis in Northern Ireland). Worcester, Mass: Spring, 1974.

CHUBB, BASIL, *The Government and Politics of Ireland*. Stanford: Stanford University Press.

COHAN, AL, *The Irish Political Elite*. Dublin: Gill and MacMillan, 1972.

COOGAN, TIMOTHY PATRICK, *Ireland Since the Rising*. New York: Praeger Publishers, Inc., 1966.

————, *The IRA*. London: Pall Mall Press, 1970.

CURRAN, JOSEPH M., "Ireland Since 1916," *Eire-Ireland*, Vol. I, No. 3 (1966), 14–28.

————, "The Irish Free State," *University Review*, V (Spring, 1968).

————, "The Decline and Fall of the IRB," *Eire-Ireland*, X (Earrach, 1975), 14–23.

————, "Ulster Repartition: A Possible Answer?", *America*, 134:4 January 31, 1976, 66–68.

DARBY, JOHN, *Conflict in Northern Ireland: The Development of a Polarized Community*. New York: Barnes and Noble Books, 1976.

DE PAOR, LIAM, *Divided Ulster*. Harmondsworth, Middlesex, England: Penguin Books, 1970.

EDWARDS, OWEN DUDLEY, *The Sins of Our Fathers: Roots of Conflict in Northern Ireland*. Dublin: Gill and MacMillan, 1970.

FARRELL, BRIAN, *Chairman or Chief? The Role of the Taoiseach in Irish Government*. Dublin: Gill and MacMillan, 1971.

HACHEY, THOMAS E., "The Partition of Ireland and the Ulster Dilemma," *The Problem of Partition: Peril to World Peace*, Thomas E. Hachey, editor. Chicago: Rand McNally & Co., 1972, 3–42.

HARKNESS, D. W., *The Restless Dominion: The Irish Free State and the British Commonwealth of Nations, 1921–1931*. Dublin: Gill and MacMillan, 1969.

HARRIS, ROSEMARY, *Prejudice and Tolerance in Ulster: A Study of Neighbors and Strangers in a Border Community*. Manchester: Manchester University Press, 1972.

HESLINGA, M. W., *The Irish Border as a Cultural Divide*. New York: Humanities Press, 1962.

London Sunday Times Insight Team, *Northern Ireland: A Report on the Conflict*. New York: Vintage Books, 1972.

McCAFFREY, LAWRENCE J., "The Roots of the Irish Troubles," *America*, 134:4 (January 31, 1976), 69–70.

McCRACKEN, J. L., *Representative Government in Ireland*. London: Oxford University Press, 1958.

MACMANUS, FRANCIS, editor, *The Years of the Great Test, 1926–1939*. Cork: Mercier Press, 1967.

MANNING, MAURICE, *The Blueshirts*. Dublin: Gill and MacMillan, 1971.

————, *Irish Political Parties*. Dublin: Gill and MacMillan, 1972.

MOODY, T. W. and J. C. BECKETT, editors, *Ulster Since 1800: A Social Survey*. London: British Broadcasting Company, 1957.

————, *Ulster Since 1800: A Political and Economic Survey*. London: B. B. C., 1955.

MURPHY, JOHN A., *Ireland in the Twentieth Century*. The Gill History of Ireland, Vol. 11. Dublin: Gill and MacMillan, 1975.

————, "The New IRA, 1925–1962," *Secret Societies in Ireland*, T. Desmond Williams, editor. New York: Barnes and Noble Books, 1973, 150–165.

————, "Identity in the Republic of Ireland Now," *Varieties of Ireland, Varieties of*

Irish-America, Blanche Touhill, editor. St. Louis: University of Missouri-St. Louis, 1977.

NOWLAN, KEVIN B. and T. DESMOND WILLIAMS, editors, *Ireland in the War Years and After, 1939–1951*. Dublin: Gill and MacMillan, 1969.

O'BRIEN, CONOR CRUISE, *States of Ireland*. New York: Vintage Books, 1973.

O'SULLIVAN, DONAL, *The Irish Free State and Its Senate*. London: Faber and Faber Ltd., 1940.

ROSE, RICHARD, *Governing Without Concensus: An Irish Perspective*. Boston: The Beacon Press, 1971.

———, *Northern Ireland: A Time of Choice*. New York: The MacMillan Co., 1976.

SCHMITT, DAVID E., *The Irony of Irish Democracy*. Lexington, Mass.: D.C. Heath and Co., 1973.

———, *Violence in Northern Ireland: Ethnic Conflict and Radicalization in an International Setting*. Morristown, N.J.: General Learning Press, 1974.

VALIULIS, MARYANN, "The Irish Army Mutiny of 1924," *Varieties of Ireland, Varieties of Irish-America*. Blanche Touhill, editor, St. Louis: University of Missouri, St. Louis, 1977.

WHITE, TERENCE DE VERE, *Kevin O'Higgins*. Tralee: Anvil Books, 1966.

WHYTE, JOHN, *Church and State in Modern Ireland*. New York: Barnes and Noble Books, 1971.

WILLIAMS, T. DESMOND, editor, *The Irish Struggle, 1916–1926*. Toronto: University of Toronto Press, 1966.

YOUNGER, CARLTON, *Ireland's Civil War*. London: Fontana Books, 1968.

SPECIAL TOPICS

Irish Nationalism

EDWARDS, OWEN DUDLEY, "Ireland," *Celtic Nationalism*, Owen Dudley Edwards, editor. New York: Barnes and Noble Books, 1968.

HACHEY, THOMAS, *Britain and Irish Separatism: From the Fenians to the Free State, 1867–1922*. Chicago: Rand McNally & Co., 1977.

RUMPF, E. and A. C. HEPBURN, *Nationalism and Socialism in Twentieth Century Ireland*. New York: Barnes and Noble Books, 1977.

KEE, ROBERT, *The Green Flag*. New York: The Delacorte Press, 1972.

Ó BROIN, LEON, *Revolutionary Underground: The Story of the Irish Republican Brotherhood, 1858–1924*. Totowa, N.J.: Rowman and Littlefield, 1976.

WILLIAMS, T. DESMOND, editor, *Secret Societies in Ireland*. New York: Barnes and Noble Books, 1973.

Literature and Irish Nationalism

BROWN, MALCOLM, *The Politics of Irish Literature from Thomas Davis to W. B. Yeats*. Seattle: University of Washington Press, 1972.

FLANAGAN, THOMAS, *The Irish Novelists, 1800–1850*. New York: Columbia University Press, 1959.

HARMON, MAURICE, *Sean O'Faolain: A Critical Introduction*. Notre Dame, Ind.: University of Notre Dame Press, 1966.

————, editor, *Sean O'Faolain Special Issue, Irish University Review* 6; (Spring, 1976).

————, "By Memory Inspired: Themes and Forces in Recent Irish Writing," *Eire-Ireland*, 8: 2 (Summer, 1973), 3–19.

HOWARTH, HERBERT, *The Irish Writers: Literature and Nationalism, 1880–1940*. New York: Hill and Wang, 1959.

KELLEHER, JOHN, "Irish Literature Today," *Atlantic*, 175: 3 (March, 1945), 70–76.

KIELY, BENEDICT, *Modern Irish Fiction*. Dublin: Golden Eagle Books, 1950.

LARKIN, EMMET, "A Reconsideration: Daniel Corkery and His Ideas on Irish Cultural Nationalism," *Eire Ireland*, VIII (Spring, 1973), 42–51.

LOFTUS, RICHARD, J., *Nationalism in Modern Anglo-Irish Poetry*. Madison: University of Wisconsin Press, 1964.

McCAFFREY, LAWRENCE J., "Trends in Post-Revolutionary Irish Literature," *College English*, 18 (October, 1956), 26–30.

————, "Daniel Corkery and Irish Cultural Nationalism," *Eire-Ireland*, VIII (Spring, 1973), 35–41.

MARTIN, AUGUSTINE, "Literature and Society," *Ireland in the War Years and After, 1939–1951*, Kevin B. Nowlan and T. Desmond Williams, editors. Dublin: Gill and MacMillan, 1969.

O'CONNOR, FRANK, *An Only Child*. London: MacMillan and Co., 1961.

————, *My Father's Son*. London: MacMillan and Co., 1968.

O'FAOLAIN, SEAN, *Vive Moi*. Boston: Atlantic-Little, Brown, and Co., 1963.

The Land Question

CROTTY, R. D., *Irish Agricultural Production: Its Volume and Structure*. Cork: Cork University Press, 1966.

DONNELLY, JAMES S., Jr., *The Land and the People of Nineteenth Century Cork* London: Routledge & Kegan Paul, 1975.

————, *Landlord and Tenant in Nineteenth Century Ireland*. Dublin: Gill and Mac-Millan, 1973.

POMFRET, JOHN, *The Struggle for Land in Ireland*. Princeton: Princeton University Press, 1930.

SOLOW, Barbara Lewis, *The Land Question and the Irish Economy, 1870–1903*. Cambridge, Mass.: Harvard University Press, 1971.

Irish Catholicism[2]

FENNELL, DESMOND, editor, *The Changing Face of Catholic Ireland*. London: Geoffrey Chapman, 1968.

---

[2]The multi-volume *A History of Irish Catholicism*, general editor Patrick J. Corish, published in Dublin by Gill and MacMillan over the last few years is useful. Akenson, Donald, *The Church of Ireland: Ecclesiastical Reform and Revolution, 1800–1885*. New Haven: Yale University Press, 1971, provides an interesting look at the Church of Ireland.

LARKIN, EMMET, *The Historical Dimensions of Irish Catholicism.* New York: Arno Press, 1976. [In addition to an Introduction, this volume contains essays that Larkin has previously published in *The American Historical Review:* "Economic Growth, Capital Investment, and the Roman Catholic Church in Nineteenth Century Ireland," *LXXII; 3 (April, 1967); "The Devotional Revolution in Ireland, 1850–1875," LXXVII: 3 (June, 1972); "Church, State, and Nation in Modern Ireland," LXXX: 5 (December, 1975).*

The American Dimension to Irish History

ADAMS, WILLIAM FORBES, *Ireland and Irish Emigration to the New World From 1815 to the Famine.* New York: Russell and Russell, 1967.

AKENSON, DONALD, *The United States and Ireland.* Cambridge, Mass.: Harvard University Press, 1973.

BROWN, THOMAS N., *Irish-American Nationalism.* Philadelphia: J. B. Lippincott Co., 1966.

COLEMAN, TERRY, *Going to America.* New York: Pantheon, 1972.

D'ARCY, WILLIAM, *The Fenian Movement in the United States, 1858–1886.* Washington, D.C.: Catholic University Press, 1947.

DOYLE, DAVID, *Irish-Americans, Native Rights, and National Empires: The Structure, Divisions, and Attitudes of the Catholic Minority in the Age of Expansion, 1890–1901.* New York: Arno Press, 1976.

FUNCHION, MICHAEL, *Chicago's Irish Nationalists, 1881–1890.* New York: Arno Press, 1976.

GREELEY, ANDREW M., *That Most Distressful Nation.* Chicago: Quadrangle Books, 1973.

HANDLIN, OSCAR, *Boston Immigrants.* New York: Athanaeum, 1968.

HERNON, JOSEPH M., JR., *Celts, Catholics and Copperheads.* Columbus: Ohio State University Press, 1968.

JENKINS, BRIAN, *Fenians and Anglo-American Relations During Reconstruction.* Ithaca, N.Y.: Cornell University Press, 1969.

MCCAFFREY, LAWRENCE J., *The Irish Diaspora in America.* Bloomington: University of Indiana Press, 1976.

―――, editor, *Irish Nationalism and the American Contribution.* New York: Arno Press, 1976. [This volume contains the following essays: Lawrence J. McCaffrey, "The American and Catholic Dimensions of Irish Nationalism," and "Irish Nationalism and Irish Catholicism: A Study in Cultural Identity," reprinted from *Church History,* XLII (December, 1973); Thomas N. Brown, "Nationalism and the Irish Peasant, 1800–1848, reprinted from *The Review of Politics,* XV (October, 1953); and "The Origins and Character of Irish-American Nationalism," reprinted from *The Review of Politics* XVIII (July, 1956); and Alan J. Ward, "America and the Irish Problem, 1899–1921," reprinted from *Irish Historical Studies,* XVI (March, 1968).]

MCMANAMIN, FRANCIS G., *The American Years of John Boyle O'Reilly, 1870–1890.* New York: Arno Press, 1976.

O'GRADY, JOSEPH PATRICK, *Irish-Americans and Anglo-American Relations, 1880–1888.* New York: Arno Press, 1976.

POTTER, GEORGE W., *To The Golden Door,* Westport, Conn.: The Greenwood Press, 1974.

RODCHECHKO, JAMES PAUL, *Patrick Ford and His Search for America: A Case Study of Irish-American Journalism, 1870–1913.* New York: Arno Press, 1976.

SCHRIER, ARNOLD, *Ireland and the American Emigration, 1850–1900.* Minneapolis: University of Minnesota Press, 1958.

SHANNON, WILLIAM V., *The American Irish.* New York: The MacMillan Co., 1963.

TARPEY, MARIE VERONICA, *The Role of Joseph McGarrity in the Struggle for Irish Independence.* New York: Arno Press, 1976.

WITTKE, CARL, *The Irish in America.* New York: Russell and Russell, 1970.

index